RECONSTRUCTING WOMAN

ROMANCE STUDIES

TITLES IN PRINT

Career Stories:
Belle Epoque Novels of Professional Development
JULIETTE M. ROGERS

Reconstructing Woman: From Fiction to
Reality in the Nineteenth-Century French Novel
DOROTHY KELLY

Territories of History: Humanism, Rhetoric, and the Historical
Imagination in the Early Chronicles of Spanish America
SARAH H. BECKJORD

RECONSTRUCTING WOMAN

From Fiction to Reality in the Nineteenth-Century Novel

DOROTHY KELLY

THE PENNSYLVANIA STATE UNIVERSITY PRESS
UNIVERSITY PARK, PENNSYLVANIA

LIBRARY OF CONGRESS
CATALOGING-IN-PUBLICATION DATA

Kelly, Dorothy, 1952–
Reconstructing woman : From fiction to
reality in the nineteenth-century novel / Dorothy Kelly.
p. cm. — (Penn State Romance Studies series)
Includes bibliographical references and index.
ISBN 978-0-271-03266-5 (cloth : alk. paper)
ISBN 978-0-271-03267-2 (pbk. : alk. paper)
1. French fiction—19th century—History and criticism. 2. Women in literature.
3. Sex role in literature. I. Title.

PQ653.K43 2007
843'.70935222–dc22
2007019589

Printed in the United States of America
Published by The Pennsylvania State University Press,
University Park, PA 16802-1003

The Pennsylvania State University Press
is a member of the
Association of American University Presses.

It is the policy of The Pennsylvania State University Press
to use acid-free paper. Publications on uncoated stock satisfy the
minimum requirements of American National Standard for
Information Sciences—Permanence of Paper for
Printed Library Material, ANSI Z39.48–1992.

This book can be viewed at
http://publications.libraries.psu.edu/eresources/978-0-271-03266-5

CONTENTS

ACKNOWLEDGMENTS

I would like to thank my Boston University colleagues Odile Cazenave and Aline Livni for their assistance with certain thorny translations from the French. My gratitude also goes to Mary Donaldson-Evans and Doris Kadish, who gave me useful suggestions for improvement and revision, and to Lesley Yoder for her help in proofreading. As always, the annual Nineteenth-Century French Studies Colloquium provided the opportunity to present nascent ideas and receive valuable suggestions from colleagues. I send many thanks to all those who have given their time to organize these colloquia, and to the many colleagues who have contributed to this work through their comments.

I also thank my family, Paul, Eric, and Beth, who have been living with this book as long as Beth has been alive.

I appreciate the following permissions to reprint previously published material.

Chapter 1 contains some material from my essay "Rewriting Reproduction: Balzac's Fantasy of Creation," in *Peripheries of Nineteenth-Century French Studies: Views from the Edge,* edited by Timothy Raser (Newark: University of Delaware Press, 2002; London: Associated University Presses, 2002), reprinted with permission from Associated University Presses.

An early version of a section of Chapter 2 appeared as "Singes, mères, et langage dans les textes de Flaubert," in *Langues du XIXe siècle,* edited by Graham Falconer, Andrew Oliver, and Dorothy Speirs, À la recherche du XIXe siècle 3 (Toronto, Canada: Centre d'Études Romantiques Joseph Sablé, St. Michael's College, 1998), reprinted with permission from the series editor.

A portion of Chapter 3 appeared in my "Experimenting on Women: Zola's Theory and Practice of the Experimental Novel," in *Spectacles of Realism: Gender, Body, Genre,* edited by Margaret Cohen and Christopher Prendergast, Cultural Politics 10 (Minneapolis: University of Minnesota Press, 1995), reprinted with permission from the University of Minnesota Press.

INTRODUCTION: THE SCIENCE OF CONTROL

Mais la civilisation, dans sa tendance à diviser le travail, a toujours abouti à créer une femme artificielle, c'est-à-dire à développer certaines aptitudes en vue d'assurer la supériorité de l'office spécial, au détriment de la valeur d'ensemble. [But civilization, in its tendency to divide labor, has always led to creation of an artificial woman, that is to say, to development of certain abilities that guarantee the superiority of a particular function, to the detriment of the quality of the whole.]

—"FEMMES," DICTIONNAIRE ENCYCLOPÉDIQUE DES SCIENCES MÉDICALES, 1877

Honoré de Balzac's Raphaël de Valentin describes himself as a new Pygmalion who transforms a lovely flesh-and-blood woman into his imaginary creation. Gustave Flaubert's Frédéric Moreau ultimately prefers his ideal reveries about Madame Arnoux to a real relationship with her. Émile Zola's Claude Lantier neglects his wife and desires instead to give life to the women he has painted on his canvas and for whom his wife has sometimes posed. Villiers de l'Isle-Adam's Thomas Edison replaces Alicia Clary with a perfect android woman. In all these cases, in various ways, the real woman is replaced by man's artificial re-creation of her.

This book looks in depth at the fantasy of a male being able to create a woman in the works of these four French novelists. My premise is that this shared representation stems in part from what Mark Seltzer describes as the discovery in the nineteenth century "that bodies and persons are things that can be made."[1] One of the major factors contributing to this discovery is the science of the time, and throughout the readings, we will look at selected scientific trends that attracted one or more of the authors: mesmerism, dissection, transformism and evolution, new understandings of human reproduction, spontaneous generation, *puériculture,* and the experimental method. These ideas and practices provided the novelists with a scientific context in which controlling, changing, and creating human bodies became imaginable. In the second part of this introduction,

1. Mark Seltzer, *Bodies and Machines* (New York: Routledge, 1992), 3.

I pull out from this science a number of themes and structures that will inform the specific readings of the literary texts that follow in the main chapters.

The four authors studied here pursue this fantasy in different ways, but each depicts the basic scenario of creating an artificial, man-made woman who would replace a real, natural woman. In Chapter 1 a study of that new Pygmalion, Raphaël, along with five other artists, authors, or scientists with mesmeric powers (Balthazar Claës, Sarrasine, Frenhofer, Louis Lambert, and, in a more limited way, Vautrin), reveals how the literal and material power of thought and language creates, writes, human identity, and particularly woman's identity.

In Chapter 2 the crisis of the distinction between man and animal and between man and machine in Flaubert's texts emerges as a nodal point of conflict. Analyses of his minor and major works, which include *Madame Bovary, Salammbô, L'éducation sentimentale,* and his correspondence, bring out a thematic subtext that locates the origin of this crisis of distinction in woman, natural reproduction, and the mechanics of social construction. The potential of science and language to control the reshaping or creation of humans (particularly women) promises the possibility of resolving this crisis. However, Flaubert's texts show as well the dangers involved in the attempt.

In Chapter 3 the reproductive function of woman in Zola's *Rougon-Macquart* series is shown to be a mechanical transmission of deleterious traits passed on through heredity. This mechanical process is expressed metaphorically in Zola's equation of woman with the troubling aspects of an increasingly mechanized society and is embodied in the symbols of giant modern constructions described as mechanical wombs. Thus the "natural" woman figures a degenerate, tainted process of mechanical reproduction that may be cured by the work of a group of heroes (Étienne Lantier, Serge Mouret, Claude Lantier, and Pascal) who at various times shy away from natural reproduction and attempt to give birth to a new woman or a new humanity.

Chapter 4 presents a reading of *L'Ève future,* the science-fiction tale about Thomas Edison's invention of a female android, together with a discussion of the ideas of a French scientist who was well known during Villiers's time: Étienne-Jules Marey. A comparison of the experiments represented and imagined in *L'Ève future* with those carried out by Marey (and described in *La nature,* a scientific journal most likely consulted by Villiers) shows how both novelist and scientist envision the body as a kind of writing that can be recorded and thus replicated and improved.

In the Conclusion, I answer the following questions: Why did these authors imagine re-creating humans? Why re-create woman in particular? To provide these answers, I draw out common aspects of this scenario in the texts of these authors and draw on current-day analyses of nineteenth-century mechanization and attempts to control nature. I end with a theoretical look at the crucial performative function of language represented by these writers.

My critical approach is thematic in its analysis of this recurring image of man's construction or reconstruction of an artificial woman. It also draws on several types of critical theory. First, its point of view is feminist in that it questions the reasons for and the results of this male usurpation of the reproductive power of woman. Current feminist critiques of the practice of the science of the time, as well as specific feminist readings of the texts of these authors, can enrich our understanding of this collective fantasy.

Second, Pierre Bourdieu's theories of social construction, particularly his concept of the habitus, provide a vocabulary and structure that give access to an understanding of the construction of persons represented by these authors. For Bourdieu, habitus is a structured set of dispositions and propensities that society instills in individuals, a kind of cultural programming, a "diffuse and continuous socialization."[2] Bourdieu emphasizes the somatic nature of the habitus because for him it is not only social but also bodily "identity" that is formed. In particular, Bourdieu's discussion of gender construction brings out the fusion of the physical and the social: "Femininity is imposed for the most part through an unremitting discipline that concerns every part of the body and is continuously recalled through the constraints of clothing or hairstyle. The antagonistic principles of male and female identity are thus laid down in the form of permanent stances, gaits and postures which are the realization, or rather, the naturalization of an ethic" (Bourdieu, *Masculine Domination,* 27). Our nineteenth-century authors represent both this social and this physical construction of identity.

What is most important in Bourdieu's conception of social construction, however, is his use of the idea of the performative, which originates in J. L. Austin's *How to Do Things with Words.*[3] The act of promising illustrates Austin's concept of performative language: when I say "I promise," I complete the act of promising, and I can do this only through language.

2. Pierre Bourdieu, *Masculine Domination,* trans. Richard Nice (Stanford, Calif.: Stanford University Press, 2001), 23.

3. J. L. Austin, *How to Do Things with Words* (Cambridge: Harvard University Press, 1962).

Thus language acts in the social world, and Austin reviews the necessary social conditions that permit the performative to function. Bourdieu's basic use of the concept of the performative moves out from this definition to a broader view of the power of language to create representations in the social world, to bring them into existence, and thus essentially to change the world, particularly in the political sphere:

> Heretical subversion exploits the possibility of changing the social world by changing the representation of this world which contributes to its reality or, more precisely, by counterposing a *paradoxical pre-vision,* a utopia, a project or programme, to the ordinary vision which apprehends the social world as a natural world; the *performative* utterance, the political pre-vision, is in itself a pre-diction which aims to bring about what it utters. It contributes practically to the reality of what it announces by the fact of uttering it, of pre-dicting it and making it pre-dicted, of making it conceivable and above all credible and thus creating the collective representation and will which contribute to its production [...] Many "intellectual debates" are less unrealistic than they seem if one is aware of the degree to which one can modify social reality by modifying the agents' representation of it.[4]

It is here that Bourdieu's representation of the performative power of language parallels that of our authors. They envision their very texts as performing this function of changing the world, of manipulating the linguistic and social construction of identities and bodies. The symbol of the construction of woman stands for the fantasy shared by these authors that the power of their very texts can act performatively to create or transform the real.

In the investigation of this fantasy of the artificial construction of woman, I ask the following questions: Why is the artificial being a woman? How does this theme relate to the writing, the creation, of the fiction itself? What are the contexts of this representation of creation? Foremost in the area of contexts is that of nineteenth-century science, which pursues questions relating to the ways in which human beings are

4. Pierre Bourdieu, *Language and Symbolic Power* (translation of *Ce que parler veut dire*), ed. John B. Thompson, trans. Gino Raymond and Matthew Adamson (Cambridge: Harvard University Press, 1991), 128.

made, questions homologous to this novelistic fantasy of creation. Science figures as a subject in its own right in these texts, but it also serves as a form of material representation and figuration for certain contemporary social problems for the authors, a way of metaphorically embodying intangible questions of identity and difference. This scientific context is, on the one hand, the familiar one of transformism, evolution, and heredity that informed the works of these authors and that has often been explored in relation to their texts. On the other hand, it is the scientific context of stranger ideas that can be fascinating, bizarre, and sometimes outrageous to our contemporary sensibilities. From the mesmeric, magnetic "fluids" sent out by Balzacian characters, to the zany experiments of Félix-Archimède Pouchet, who thought he was creating new life from ancient bones and who attracted Flaubert's interest, these "scientific" contexts for the novelists revolve around issues of the manipulation and control of human beings and the creation and origin of life.

Science is not simply a context for literature, however; the two interact with each other in nineteenth-century France in different ways. Obviously, in the area of content, the very substance of science and its developments entered into the matter of the novel: mesmerism, hysteria, hypnotism, evolution, artificial insemination, heredity, steam engines. All four of the novelists studied here were familiar with the science of the day, and all four expressed particular interest in, often fascination with, certain issues raised there. Indeed, literary texts were themselves viewed by authors and readers as "scientific"—most obviously in the case of Zola's self-proclaimed experimental novel. This is not to say that science dictated the interests of the novelists, but rather that some of the main scientific ideas of the day either paralleled interests of novelists or resonated with issues of importance to them. Science and literature in the nineteenth century were not entirely distinct but existed more as overlapping fields of cultural production in the general intellectual context of the time.[5]

5. Michel Serres reflects profoundly on this in his *Feux et signaux de brume, Zola* (Paris: B. Grasset, 1975). A concrete example of this permeation of science into a more general intellectual culture can be found in Schivelbusch's discussion of the way in which the "medical" metaphor of the healthy physical body appeared in many different guises: circulation of traffic, blood, and consumer goods. Wolfgang Schivelbusch, *The Railway Journey: The Industrialization and Perception of Time and Space* (Berkeley and Los Angeles: University of California Press, 1986), 194–95. Allen Thiher provides a sustained reflection on the relationship of literature and science in nineteenth-century France in his *Fiction Rivals Science: The French Novel from Balzac to Proust* (Columbia: University of Missouri Press, 2001), which focuses on the realists' attempt to rival science and presents findings that complement my work.

In the case of these authors, the overlapping of the two fields shows clearly in the personal and professional connections that they shared with the scientific world: all of them knew important scientists of their time. Balzac corresponded with Geoffroy Saint-Hilaire, who read and admired Balzac's works; Flaubert read the works of his respected friend, the elder Pouchet, and stayed in the home of Pouchet's son, watching him admiringly as he dissected fish. Zola corresponded with scientists as he meticulously researched the backgrounds of his novels; he was even the object of a medico-psychological work by a doctor, Édouard Toulouse.[6] Villiers was friends with Charles Cros, who was both a scientist and a poet and who invented plans for the phonograph at the same time as Edison. Thus this link between science and literature should be viewed less as a one-way direction of influence and more as a mutual nourishment of ideas and congruence of interests in social and intellectual issues.[7]

More than this literal presence of science in the texts and lives of these authors, however, it is the development and influence at this time of what Michel Foucault has analyzed as a change in the concept of visibility in science, which had been taking place just before and during this time and which generated a new way of looking at the world and of envisaging and speaking the truth.[8] For Foucault, the scientific gaze seemed to have the power to look into the body, read it, and discover its hidden truth, and many have noted the parallelism between this clinical gaze and realist observation. To be more specific, in these authors one particular manifestation of the clinical gaze, dissection, by its physical penetration of the body, renders possible the clinical goal of observing and analyzing the hidden and of penetrating the mystery of life in order to understand its workings.[9] Ludmilla Jordanova summarizes the importance of dissection in

6. Édouard Toulouse, *Émile Zola,* vol. 1: *Enquête médico-psychologique sur les rapports de la supériorité intellectuelle avec la névropathie* (Paris: Société d'Éditions Scientifiques, 1896).

7. See David Bell's eloquent analysis of this question in his *Circumstances: Chance in the Literary Text* (Lincoln: University of Nebraska Press, 1993), 9–12. See also Mary Donaldson-Evans's fine study of the presence of the discourses of medicine in nineteenth-century texts: *Medical Examinations: Dissecting the Doctor in French Narrative Prose, 1857–1894* (Lincoln: University of Nebraska Press, 2000).

8. Michel Foucault, *The Birth of the Clinic: An Archaeology of Medical Perception,* trans. A. M. Sheridan Smith (New York: Vintage Books, 1994), 195–96.

9. Foucault speaks of the need experienced at that time to go deeper into the invisible world of the inner body, in his *Order of Things: An Archaeology of the Human Sciences* (New York: Vintage Books, 1973), 229.

nineteenth-century medicine: "Through the dominance of Paris hospital medicine, this field [pathological anatomy] endowed the act of dissection with a special status in nineteenth-century medicine. Dissection became the symbolic core of scientific medicine—the place where signs of pathology were revealed to the medical gaze."[10]

Practitioners of dissection had a known influence on the writers studied here. Balzac mentions several times the work of Bichat, who had a "passionate engagement with dissection" (Jordanova, *Sexual Visions,* 57).[11] As a child, Flaubert watched his father dissect cadavers, and again, he enjoyed watching Pouchet dissect fish. The work of Zola's scientific mentor, Claude Bernard, can be viewed generally as one that is "surgical" in its philosophical bent, as John E. Lesch states: "Bernard's experimental work, like Magendie's, displayed a strikingly surgical character" (Magendie is also mentioned by Balzac).[12]

As is well known, this metaphor of dissection appears in descriptions of realist style by writers of the time. The careful observation of reality, which is carved and laid out bit by bit by the realist description and which claims objectivity and seeks truth, seemed to be a cutting up of reality and a penetration of it by the author's gaze. Critics frequently claimed that Balzac's descriptions tended to "dissect like an anatomist."[13] This metaphor also occurs in the works of the novelists themselves. Observation cuts to the heart of life in order to arrive at the truth in its depths, as Flaubert states: "Le relief vient d'une vue profonde, d'une *pénétration, de l'objectif.*"[14] [Depth comes from a deep gaze, from a *penetration, of the lens.*] Indeed, this penetrating gaze of Flaubert's writer connects metonymically with literal dissection, because a mere eight sentences before this analysis of penetrating observation Flaubert describes his memory of watching his father dissect cadavers: "Je vois encore mon père levant la tête de dessus sa dissection

10. Ludmilla Jordanova, *Sexual Visions: Images of Gender in Science and Medicine Between the Eighteenth and Twentieth Centuries* (Madison: University of Wisconsin Press, 1989), 100.

11. Bichat believed that the only way to understand tissue structure was to "decompose" it. See William Coleman, *Biology in the Nineteenth Century: Problems of Form, Function, and Transformation* (New York: Wiley, 1971), 20–21.

12. John E. Lesch, *Science and Medicine in France: The Emergence of Experimental Physiology, 1790–1855* (Cambridge: Harvard University Press, 1984), 208.

13. Bernard Weinberg, *French Realism: The Critical Reaction, 1830–1870* (New York: Modern Language Association of America; London: Oxford University Press, 1937), 42.

14. Letter to Louise Colet, 7 July 1853. Gustave Flaubert, *Correspondance,* ed. Jean Bruneau (Paris: Gallimard, 1980), 2:377. All further references to Flaubert's correspondence are to this edition. Translations from the French are my own unless otherwise specified; I have translated as literally as possible to aid readers who may benefit from assistance with the original.

et nous disant de nous en aller" (*Correspondance*, 2:376).[15] [I still see my father raising his head from his dissection and telling us to go away.] Thus the tools of the anatomist and the novelist are the knife and the eye,[16] and one could add that, for writers, the pen was like the knife, as Sainte-Beuve claimed of Flaubert: "Son and brother of distinguished doctors, Mr. Gustave Flaubert holds his pen the way others hold the scalpel."[17]

In Zola, dissection becomes a metaphor for his very text, the study of the life of a family, when Doctor Pascal's investigation of his family's heredity (which is a figure of the *Rougon-Macquart* series itself) begins with the dissection of corpses and moves on to a metaphoric dissection of living subjects: "Il ne s'en tenait pas aux cadavres, il élargissait ses dissections sur l'humanité vivante, frappé de certains faits constants parmi sa clientèle, mettant surtout en observation sa propre famille, qui était devenue son principal champ d'expérience, tellement les cas s'y présentaient précis et complets."[18] [He did not limit himself to cadavers, he expanded his dissections to living humanity, because he was struck by certain constants among his clientele, and he observed above all his own family, which had become his principal experimental domain, because so many precise and concise cases came up there.] Villiers titles a chapter of his work "Dissection," and both the theme and the method of the chapter are described by that word.

Dissection, then, has always been linked to the works of these authors, but what is most significant about the common interest in dissection on the part of scientists and novelists is its philosophic aim. Jordanova provides an intriguing interpretation of this aim in the realm of science:

15. Flaubert discusses his fascination with the act of dissection in a letter to Ernest Feydeau, 29 November 1859: "C'est une chose étrange, comme je suis attiré par les études médicales (le vent est à cela dans les esprits). J'ai envie de disséquer" (*Correspondance*, 3 [1991]: 59). [It is a strange thing, how I am attracted to medical studies (this is the intellectual trend now). I long to dissect.] If Flaubert had watched his surgeon father dissect human cadavers, he believed that he himself knew how to dissect the human soul, particularly his own: "Je me suis moi-même franchement disséqué au vif en des moments peu drôles" (*Correspondance*, 2:346). [I have frankly dissected myself alive in certain unhappy moments.] In literary circles, a rumor even circulated that Flaubert himself had attended medical school; see René Descharmes and René Dumesnil, *Autour de Flaubert: Études historiques et documentaires, suivies d'une biographie chronologique, d'un essai bibliographique des ouvrages et articles relatifs à Flaubert et d'un index des noms cités* (Paris: Mercure de France, 1912), 99–100.

16. It is Coleman, *Biology in the Nineteenth Century*, 22, who states that the tools of the pathological anatomist are the eye and the knife.

17. Charles-Augustin Sainte-Beuve, *Causeries du lundi*, vol. 13 (Paris: Garnier Frères, 18??), 363.

18. Émile Zola, *Les Rougon-Macquart, histoire naturelle et sociale d'une famille sous le Second Empire*, ed. Armand Lanoux and Henri Mitterand (Paris: Gallimard, 1967), 5:945. All further references to the *Rougon-Macquart* are to this edition unless otherwise noted.

"Penetrating inside organisms was a way of approaching the origins of life" (Jordanova, *Sexual Visions*, 57). This interest in life's origin took place in science on the one hand at the microscopic level, because improvements in the microscope over the course of the nineteenth century enabled scientists to view reproduction, to see life forming and developing (Coleman, *Biology in the Nineteenth Century*, 22-23). The demystification of the process of reproduction, and the possibility of understanding generation, took the origin of life out of religious speculation and placed it in the physical world. Thus the origin of individual human life could be viewed, understood, and possibly controlled. Flaubert, Zola, and Villiers explicitly depict scientific aspects of the origin of life in their works.

On the macroscopic level, on the other hand, interest in origins is the interest in the origin of the human species, and here the familiar contexts of transformism, evolution, and heredity appear. Lamarck, with his theory of the transformation of organic forms developed at the turn of the nineteenth century, depicted man as a part of nature and subject to its transformist laws. Jordanova summarizes Lamarck's understanding of transformism as follows: "Nothing in nature is constant; organic forms develop gradually from each other and were not created all at once in their present form; all the natural sciences must recognize that nature has a history; and the laws governing living things have produced increasingly complex forms over immense periods of time."[19] There developed, then, a new understanding of nature and man as having been made, formed, over time.

This transformist concept helped to shape Balzac's fictional project, as exemplified in the well-known description of Madame Vauquer and her *pension*, where her nature both is explained by and explains the environment in which she lives. Later, Darwinian evolution entered into the notes, letters, and texts of Flaubert and Zola. For them, man seemed to be, in a sense, fabricated by heredity and environment. Our writers aim to understand that fabrication: Balzac through his idea of the influence of the environment, Flaubert in his study of the fatal textual formation of Emma Bovary, Zola in his view of man as a product of hereditary and environmental factors, and Villiers in his philosophical discussions of man as artificially created. For these authors, man's body and identity seemed, then, to be malleable, changeable, and not given once and for all at birth or at the point of origin of mankind.

19. Ludmilla Jordanova, *Lamarck* (New York: Oxford University Press, 1984), 71.

As the scientific gaze began to penetrate the mystery of man's origins, it also uprooted traditional understandings of man's place in the world and emphasized his physical, animal nature by placing him closer to the animal kingdom. Lamarck, for example, placed man with other animals in a new, less important place in the structure of things and "refused to draw an absolute distinction between man and animal" (Jordanova, *Lamarck,* 90). The act of lessening the distance between man and the animal world problematizes the distinction of man from animal, a problem that, with many others, participates in a general crisis of distinction that follows the Revolution. Many critics have discussed the social crisis of distinction at the time, such as Christopher Prendergast, who succinctly describes the panic "in which the basic categories of social distinction go into a kind of vertiginous spin."[20] Ross Chambers delineates the attempt of post-1848 French writers to distinguish their discourse from the bourgeois "discourse of the tribe," to establish their difference from cliché, and in doing so they express what he calls "the anxiety of difference: 'difference' is simultaneously that which distinguishes one from the crowd and—because there can be no difference without similarity—that which integrates one into the crowd."[21] In another context, Naomi Schor links René Girard's idea of the literary structure of the sacrificial crisis to a crisis of the distinction between the sexes.[22]

Indeed, the panic and ambiguity created by the increasingly concrete idea of man the animal, formed over time by various forces, appears as an anxiety-producing element in the texts of our authors. This particular crisis of distinction, as we shall see, combines with social states in transformation: class and, most particularly for us here, gender. Bourdieu's analysis of the various strategies of distinction, among which he includes that of man from animal (Bourdieu, *Distinction,* 93, 196), will inform our readings of these representations of anxieties of distancing, particularly in terms of gender. In the texts studied here, ambiguities about man's identity, his

20. Christopher Prendergast, *The Order of Mimesis: Balzac, Stendhal, Nerval, Flaubert* (New York: Cambridge University Press, 1986), 93. The notion of distinction receives extended treatment in the work of Bourdieu, particularly in his *Distinction: A Social Critique of the Judgement of Taste,* trans. Richard Nice (Cambridge: Harvard University Press, 1984). In nineteenth-century France, the crisis of distinction is first and foremost one of social class; more generally, it describes the shifting boundaries between categories that resulted from the immense changes in France after the Revolution.

21. Ross Chambers, "Irony and Misogyny: Authority and the Homosocial in Baudelaire and Flaubert," *Australian Journal of French Studies* 26, no. 3 (1989), 274.

22. Naomi Schor, *Zola's Crowds* (Baltimore: Johns Hopkins University Press, 1978), 34.

distinction from all "others," play a large role in the fantasy of constructing and controlling that "other" in the figure of the artificial woman.

The newfound closeness of the connection between man and animal adds new intensity to the French tradition of thinking of man as an animal machine. The understanding of the human body as a machine, which established itself firmly with Descartes and La Mettrie, "forcefully reentered physiology toward 1840" (Coleman, *Biology in the Nineteenth Century,* 121). For all our authors, the way in which man is formed by various physiological and environmental processes makes it seem as if man is "programmed" mechanically by inner and outer material reality. This metaphor of mechanical man adds to the understanding of man's nature as having been "constructed" rather than created from nothing.[23]

This two-part crisis of distinguishing man from animal and man from machine also belongs to a more general system of cultural metaphors that seek to negotiate the changing understanding of the natural and the technological and its relationship to man, of what is produced by nature (man the animal) and what is made by man (man the maker of the artificial), that marks both scientific and literary texts of this time. Natural reproduction and artificial production, the organic and the mechanical, interact, overlap, and conflict with one another in scientific and literary attempts at understanding and defining man and his origin. The shifting boundaries of the organic and the artificial haunt the texts we shall be studying.

The programmed nature of man, the animal-machine, appears in all the literary texts studied here and serves to represent what one might call the "mechanics" of the reproduction of human beings as well as the more symbolic reproduction of such social forms as gender difference and class structure, the reproduction of culture itself. It is at the intersection of the natural and the artificial in the struggle to define the nature of man where woman comes in. Woman, the natural creator, is herself re-created artificially by man in these texts, and this creation in its various forms is one strategy employed in the attempt to negotiate the crisis of distinction.

23. The newfound vigor of this idea of the man/machine was in part generated by an intensification of the industrialization of France at the time, which prompted changes and disruptions in many aspects of culture, including literature (one need think only of the progress in mechanized printing). Industrialization, accelerated by scientific and engineering discoveries, both figures in and structures the literary texts we shall study. Three authors who have produced excellent studies of this effect are Schivelbusch, *Railway Journey;* Anson Rabinbach, *The Human Motor: Energy, Fatigue, and the Origins of Modernity* (Berkeley and Los Angeles: University of California Press, 1992); and Seltzer, *Bodies and Machines.*

In order to create woman, man must understand how creation itself works. Here, once again, the rich metaphor of dissection provides a clue. If, as we saw Jordanova claim, dissection allowed access to the place of man's origin, what better way of approaching these origins than by cutting open the woman's body to see the place in which human life originates? Jordanova links the aim of looking deeply into the female body with the quest to understand origins and to master and control them:

> By the end of the eighteenth century, then, there were a number of ways in which the idea of organic depth manifested itself, through changing practices, ideas and metaphors. This interest in depth was especially significant for the construction of femininity in two distinct although related ways. The first was by promoting the actual unveiling of women's bodies to render visible the emblematic core of their sex in the organs of generation. The second was by giving expression to a model of knowledge, based on looking deeply into and thereby intellectually mastering nature–a model infused with assumptions about gender.[24] (Jordanova, *Sexual Visions*, 57-58)

Thus the dissection of women's bodies was linked specifically to learning how the organs of generation worked, how life originated, and to the continued aim of dominating nature (and woman).[25] Mark Seltzer claims that realism itself is a kind of gaze at the inside of the body that is obstetric in nature: "The requirement of embodiment, of turning the body inside out for inspection, takes on a virtually *obstetrical* form in realist discourse" (Seltzer, *Bodies and Machines*, 96).

24. It is significant that Flaubert, in the above quotation, in which he expresses his fascination with dissection, goes on to speak about a medical course on female illnesses, strangely linking dissection with mad women. In the same letter, in which he states "I long to dissect," he goes on to say: "Si j'étais plus jeune de dix ans, je m'y mettrais. Il y a à Rouen un homme très fort, le médecin en chef d'un hôpital de fous, qui fait pour des intimes un petit cours très curieux sur l'hystérie, la nymphomanie, etc." (To Ernest Feydeau, 29 November 1859 in *Correspondance*, 3:59). [If I were ten years younger, I'd try it. There is a great man in Rouen, the chief physician in a mental hospital, who gives to a select few a curious little course on hysteria, nymphomania, etc.]

25. See my "Experimenting on Women: Zola's Theory and Practice of the Experimental Novel," in *Spectacles of Realism: Body, Gender, Genre*, ed. Margaret Cohen and Christopher Prendergast, 231–46 (Minneapolis: University of Minnesota Press, 1995), for an extended analysis of these ideas in Zola. Jordanova's *Sexual Visions* provides a fascinating analysis of the tie between the dissection of woman and the aim of unveiling origins.

This relationship of medicine and surgery to the fantasy of penetrating to the core of woman is one we find in each of our four authors. In Balzac's *La peau de chagrin,* Raphaël believes that Foedora is "un sujet précieux pour l'observation médicale"[26] [a valuable subject for medical observation], and she in turn feels that she has been placed on display (referring to dissection) "sur un amphithéâtre" (Balzac, *La peau de chagrin,* 10:158) [in an amphitheater]. In the 1831 version of this text, Émile's mocking questioning of Raphaël makes the following link between mothers (the origin of life) and dissection: "As-tu, comme cet étudiant de Padoue, disséqué, sans le savoir, une mère que tu adorais?" (10:1272 note b). [Have you, like the student from Padua, dissected, without knowing it, a mother you adored?] The inventory of Emma Bovary's things seems to be an autopsy: "Ils examinèrent ses robes, le linge, le cabinet de toilette; et son existence, jusque dans ses recoins les plus intimes, fut, comme un cadavre que l'on autopsie, étalée tout du long aux regards de ces trois hommes." [They examined her dresses, the linen, the dressing room; and her existence, into its most intimate recesses, was, like a cadaver being autopsied, spread out under the gaze of these three men.][27] Pascal, in Zola's text, gains knowledge about human reproduction by dissecting the corpses of dead pregnant women. And finally, Villiers's Edison shows us the internal workings of his female android, Hadaly, who is compared to a corpse being autopsied. Indeed, Villiers makes mention there of the famous engraving by Vesalius in which a woman's body is opened up before a number of male onlookers.

The aim of dissection, the understanding of origins, participates in a final theme that is shared by these literary texts and the science of the time: experimentation. It is generally accepted that scientific research at the end of the eighteenth century and through the nineteenth century shifted emphasis from speculation toward observation, and later in the century toward experimentation and practice. Indeed, the development of science and medicine over the course of the nineteenth century, in the change from a science of observation to a science of experiment and intervention, has been viewed by some as a move from passivity to a stance of active

26. Honoré de Balzac, *La peau de chagrin,* vol. 10 of *La comédie humaine,* ed. Pierre-Georges Castex et al. (Paris: Gallimard, 1976–81), 158. All references to *La comédie humaine* are to the edition cited here.

27. Gustave Flaubert, *Madame Bovary,* in *Oeuvres complètes,* ed. Bernard Masson (Paris: Éditions du Seuil, 1964), 1:674. All references to Flaubert's literary texts are to this edition of the *Oeuvres.*

involvement. As François Jacob describes it, the goal is to reproduce what nature brings about (through disease).[28]

Balzac's fantastic if mocking representation of animal hybridization, Flaubert's enthusiastic description of Pouchet's experiments in spontaneous generation, Zola's activist promotion of Bernard's experimental method, and Villiers's representations of Edison's experiments and inventions demonstrate on the thematic level their attention to scientific experimental possibilities.[29] Realist and naturalist texts were themselves viewed, as we have seen, as a kind of experiment in the dissection of the real.

However, it is the aim of experimentation that is of philosophical importance to both literary authors and scientists:

> Experiment, whatever else it may mean or be, must guarantee *control* over the appearance and variability of the phenomena under investigation. Whether one proceeds as vivisectionist, relying on surgical intervention in the affairs of the organism, or exploits narrowly the concepts and instruments of the physical sciences, physiologists could agree that *mastery* of vital phenomena was their achievable goal. These convictions were at the heart of both the experimentalists' practice and Bernard's well-considered reflections on the methods of his science. They depend on a firm belief in the regularity of natural processes and derive as well from an inverse reading of the time-honored conviction that knowledge is power—to control is to know. (Coleman, *Biology in the Nineteenth Century,* 159; emphasis added)

If dissection reveals the origins of human life to be mechanistic processes of the body, if the human body is a machine that follows predictable natural laws, the possibility of our being able to control this machine arises.

In Paris hospitals, a discovery of another role of dissection was its usefulness in determining the source of illness in patients, and illness will play a significant role in our texts: "Toward 1800 physicians in the Paris hospitals effected a revolution in medicine. Their essential contribution was to combine postmortem physical examination of the cadaver with a clinical

28. François Jacob, *The Logic of Life: A History of Heredity,* trans. Betty E. Spillmann (New York: Pantheon Books, 1974), 184.

29. Jacques Noiray discusses the insistence with which theorists of the novel from Taine to Zola link the realist aesthetic to experimental science; see Noiray's indispensable *Le romancier et la machine: L'image de la machine dans le roman français, 1850–1900* (Paris: José Corti, 1981), 1:40.

description of the patient's affliction" (Coleman, *Biology in the Nineteenth Century,* 20). As numerous recent studies show, the nineteenth century tended generally to pathologize woman,[30] and thus the link among dissection, malady, and women seems well motivated in the culture of the time and is a prime motivating factor in the literary texts. Our nineteenth-century authors take on the role of pathological anatomists who fantasize a cure for the illness of their contemporary society in the rewriting of woman.

As the century progressed, this lure of controlling the human machine became the lure of the possibility of improving on nature itself and of engineering a new nature: "A new kind of interest in control of life arose in the late nineteenth century [. . .] A number of biologists began to think of themselves and their work within the framework of engineering. They argued that the fundamental purpose of their science ought to be the control of organisms. They envisioned *manipulation, transformation, and creation* of all the phenomena subsumed under the word 'life.'"[31] Jordanova, in fact, specifically links the interest in the dissection of the human body not simply with the quest for knowledge but also with the desire to create life: "Once you think about pulling the body apart in order to build up skeletons for study or to examine its constituent parts, you are close to the enormous transgression of Frankenstein" (Jordanova, *Sexual Visions,* 108). The understanding that life was not given in its final form but was transformable; that the living body was a kind of machine that could be manipulated, engineered; that life might be created artificially, without sexual reproduction, in the laboratory; that the inheritance of acquired characteristics could allow us to improve man's lot; that man could make creations superior to those of nature—all these ideas, which developed at different times in the nineteenth century, provided for the novelists that scientific context in which creating ideal human beings entered the realm of possibility. And replacing natural reproduction with man's superior creation is there symbolized by man's artificially creating the natural reproducer, woman. We shall see how, for our nineteenth-century authors, their dissecting writing practices, which aimed at the

30. For two excellent analyses of this pathologization, see Ruth Harris, *Murders and Madness: Medicine, Law, and Society in the Fin de Siècle* (New York: Oxford University Press, 1989); and Yvonne Knibiehler and Catherine Fouquet, *La femme et les médecins: Analyse historique* (Paris: Hachette Littérature Générale, 1983).

31. Philip J. Pauly, *Controlling Life: Jacques Loeb and the Engineering Ideal in Biology* (New York: Oxford University Press, 1987), 4. Emphasis added.

understanding of the maladies of nature and woman, led them to fantasize and posit a new, improved model of woman and creation.

The final guiding principle in our examination of the new, scientific twist to the myth of Pygmalion is the legibility of the human body. In the scientific realm, during the eighteenth and nineteenth centuries (and beyond) the human body was viewed as a sign that could be decoded, "read": "During the eighteenth and nineteenth centuries it was taken for granted that the human body was legible, even if there was not consensus on exactly how it could and should be 'read' [. . .] The principle of legibility was [. . .] important because it sanctioned a particular form of inferential thinking, that moved from visible indicators on a surface (either the body itself or clothes) to invisible traits inside the body" (Jordanova, *Sexual Visions,* 51–52). As Foucault describes it, this legibility seemed to exist already in the world itself, a world that is always already a kind of language: "The gaze implies an open field, and its essential activity is of the successive order of reading; it records and totalizes; it gradually reconstitutes immanent organizations; it spreads out over a world that is already the world of language, and that is why it is spontaneously related to hearing and speech" (Foucault, *The Birth of the Clinic,* 121). Our nineteenth-century novelists clearly represented such a possibility of reading the real and the "writing" on the body in their texts: one need think only of Balzac and phrenology, Flaubert's more abstract level of the social inscription of codes, Zola's legible traces of hereditary *tares,* and Villiers's reinscription or rerecording of the body's language in such inventions as the phonograph.[32] The body seemed to be a kind of code that one could crack, a text to be read, and novelists explored this obvious relay between their writing and the decoding of the world around them. Here Bourdieu's understanding of the materialization of social signs on the body and their inscription on an individual's dispositions, signs that are also related to gender, will help us to understand the social construction explored by these authors.

What becomes ever more crucial to these authors, however, is the specific importance of human language in the definition—indeed, construction—of human identity. In the scientific realm, with the understanding of evolutionary forces, language was the main factor that distinguished man from animals; it was what defined human nature. Thus in a general sense it is

32. Christopher Rivers, *Face Value: Physiognomical Thought and the Legible Body in Marivaux, Lavater, Balzac, Gautier, and Zola* (Madison: University of Wisconsin Press, 1994), is an excellent study of the legible body in French literature and its scientific contexts.

the technical tool of language that makes man what he is—a kind of product of his own tools and technology—and the line between nature and artifice grows ever more tenuous.

But as we shall see, our authors take this understanding of the role of language in human identity one step further when each of them explores the literal ways in which the social codes lodged in language define and construct human identity.[33] The most obvious case is that of Flaubert and the *bêtise* of our imprisonment in cliché. Customs, codes, clichés, and myths shape the way man acts, the way he thinks, the way he views the world; they mold him and his choices. Social codes, embodied in language, make man, write him, embody themselves in him, as Bourdieu would say. If language inscribes identity on the human being, language takes on a performative function and acts. Thus in our conclusions we shall explore the way in which these authors fantasize that their own texts, the novels and stories that we read, will be the linguistic code that will create, performatively, the new woman.

33. See Seltzer, *Bodies and Machines,* 107, for the way in which "narration, personality, and characterization are everywhere threatened by their exposure as merely effects of certain practices of writing."

1

TRANSFORMATION, CREATION, AND INSCRIPTION: BALZAC

Le poète [. . .] change, comme le sublime chevalier de la Manche, une fille des champs en princesse. [The poet (. . .) transforms, like the sublime knight of La Mancha, a peasant girl into a princess.]

—BALZAC, SPLENDEURS ET MISÈRES DES COURTISANES

"La parole est devenue une puissance." [Words have become a power.]

—ÉTUDES ANALYTIQUES, PRÈFACE

Transforming Humans

Raphaël de Valentin, the main character of Balzac's *La peau de chagrin,* lives in an apartment rented from a kind, poor woman and her pure, beautiful daughter, Pauline. The situation is ripe for romance, but Balzac does not meet our expectations in the way we imagine he will, because Raphaël is not interested in this impoverished Pauline, who cannot afford the feminine trappings he desires. He would like to turn the real Pauline into the dream woman he forms in his imagination; he would like to transform this real human being into his own, new creation, a transformation linked, as we shall see, to the early evolutionary ideas of transformism. He would like to construct, literally, his perfect woman by remolding an existing body and soul.[1] He does this in part through education, as he takes on the role of both parent and artist: "Enfin, c'était mon enfant, ma statue" (*La peau de chagrin,* 10:141). [In short, she was my child, my statue.] Unlike a

1. The poet Lucien appears to do this as well by means of his love for Esther: "Ces passions, inexplicables pour la foule, sont parfaitement expliquées par cette soif du beau idéal qui distingue les êtres créateurs. N'est-ce pas ressembler un peu aux anges chargés de ramener les coupables à des sentiments meilleurs, n'est-ce pas créer que de purifier un pareil être?" Honoré de Balzac, *Splendeurs et misères des courtisanes,* vol. 6 of *La comédie humaine,* 459. [These passions, inexplicable for the masses, are perfectly explained by that thirst for ideal beauty that distinguishes those beings who create. Is it not the case that they resemble the angels charged with bringing the guilty back to better sentiments; is it not the case that to purify such a being is to create her?]

lover who might want to undress Pauline, Raphaël, more like the parent he envisions, dresses and "fashions" Pauline in his imagination and transforms her in his thoughts into his ideal woman: "Combien de fois n'ai-je pas vêtu de satin les pieds mignons de Pauline, emprisonné sa taille svelte comme un jeune peuplier dans une robe de gaze, jeté sur son sein une légère écharpe en lui faisant fouler les tapis de son hôtel et la conduisant à une voiture élégante" (10:143).[2] [How many times did I put satin shoes on Pauline's darling feet; imprison her figure, slim as a young poplar, in a gauze dress; throw a light scarf over her breast, while having her tread on the carpets of her mansion and leading her to an elegant carriage.]

The woman he desires is thus artificial; he longs for the social trappings that define femininity: "Certes, je me suis cent fois trouvé ridicule d'aimer quelques aunes de blonde, du velours, de fines batistes, les tours de force d'un coiffeur, des bougies, un carrosse, un titre, d'héraldiques couronnes peintes par des vitriers ou fabriquées par un orfèvre, enfin tout ce qu'il y a de factice et de moins femme dans la femme; je me suis moqué de moi, je me suis raisonné, tout a été vain" (*La peau de chagrin,* 10:143). [Of course, I often found myself ridiculous in my love for a few yards of lace, velvet, and fine batiste, for the *tours de force* of a hairdresser, candles, a carriage, a title, heraldic crowns painted by glaziers or crafted by a goldsmith; in short for everything that is most artificial and least womanly in woman; I mocked myself, I reasoned with myself, all was in vain.] Like an artist, he would turn this beautiful, young Pauline into his imaginary and thus lifeless statue: "Pygmalion nouveau, je voulais faire d'une vierge vivante et colorée, sensible et parlante, un marbre" (10:141). [A new Pygmalion, I wanted to turn a maiden who was alive and rosy-cheeked, who felt and spoke, into marble.] What is most remarkable is that this new Pauline imagined by Raphaël later becomes real, comes to life, in the course of the text. From the poor "Pauline de l'hôtel Saint-Quentin" she becomes "cette maîtresse accomplie, si souvent rêvée, jeune fille spirituelle, aimante, artiste, comprenant les poètes, comprenant la poésie et vivant au sein du luxe" (10:227) [that accomplished mistress, so often imagined, a spiritual, loving, artistic young woman, who understands the poets, who understands poetry, and who lives in the lap of luxury].

2. If Raphaël seems to want to turn real people into dolls, as he would like to do with Pauline "pour en faire la poupée fantasque de nos salons" (*La peau de chagrin,* 10:143) [to make her into the fanciful doll of our salons], he appears to succeed in his task in the case of the *antiquaire* who is described as "cette espèce de poupée pleine de vie" (10:222) [this doll full of life].

What might lie behind this odd rewriting of the myth of Pygmalion, in which it is not an artist who creates a statue that later comes to life, but rather a writer who takes a real woman and attempts to turn her into his perfect living "statue," his artificial but living re-creation? How does this new myth, which will function in various forms in the texts of Flaubert, Zola, and Villiers, relate to Balzac's fiction and to its purpose, as we might interpret it? How extensive is this fantasy in his texts, and what are its contexts? In order to answer these questions, we will rely on *La peau de chagrin* as our primary text, while enlarging our perspective with other Balzac works, in order to delve into the world of his understanding of the physical and social construction and encoding of the human being.

As we saw in the Introduction, Mark Seltzer (*Bodies and Machines,* 3) claims that the nineteenth century in general "discovers" that human beings are made in a very physical sense. For Balzac, this discovery is linked to his knowledge of and admiration for the work of Geoffroy Saint-Hilaire concerning the formation and differentiation of animal species (ideas that had been circulating ever more widely since the turn of the nineteenth century and that came to the fore in a heated public debate in the landmark year of 1830).[3] Balzac took from these theories the idea of the original similarity in form of animal bodies as well as the understanding that differences in that basic form were subsequently generated. Balzac famously articulates in the "Avant-propos" Geoffroy Saint-Hilaire's claim that the animal body varies from the basic form because of the environment in which it must live: "Il n'y a qu'un animal. Le créateur ne s'est servi que d'un seul et même patron pour tous les êtres organisés. L'animal est un principe qui prend sa forme extérieure, ou, pour parler plus exactement, les différences de sa forme, dans les milieux où il est appelé à se développer. Les Espèces Zoologiques résultent de ces différences."[4] [There is only one animal. The creator used one and the same pattern for all organized beings. The animal is a principle that takes its exterior form, or, to speak more exactly, the differences of its form, from

3. The debate was waged between Cuvier and Geoffroy Saint-Hilaire: "The excitement generated by the clash of the titans in a single meeting of the Academy of Sciences electrified the French and sent powerful shock waves far beyond the French borders." Robert E. Stebbins, "France," in *The Comparative Reception of Darwinism,* ed. Thomas E. Glick, 117 (Austin: University of Texas Press, 1972).

4. Balzac, "Avant-propos" to the *Comédie humaine,* in vol. 1 of *La comédie humaine,* 8. Foucault sees Cuvier as the more "radical" thinker, closer to the spirit of evolution; Balzac took ideas from both but seems closer here in philosophy to Saint-Hilaire. Foucault, *The Order of Things,* 274–75.

the environment in which it has been called to develop. Zoological species result from these differences.] Thus there is an important relationship between the formation of the animal body, which includes the human body, and the physical world around it. This then makes possible the thought that human form may change.

Because man himself is one variation of the basic animal, the idea that he is an animal like another partakes of the general nineteenth-century crisis of distinction we shall follow in our authors. How much of an animal is man? Balzac, of course, frequently draws together humans and animals—for instance, in his use of metaphors that describe people as having the appearance of a particular animal.[5] Balzac takes note specifically of man's link with apes: "Les naturalistes ne considèrent en l'homme qu'un genre unique de cet ordre de Bimanes, établi par Duméril, dans sa Zoologie analytique, page 16, et auquel Bory-Saint-Vincent a cru devoir ajouter le genre Orang, sous prétexte de le compléter."[6] [Naturalists consider man to be only a unique genus of the order of bimana, established by Duméril in his *Analytic Zoology,* page 16, and to which Bory-Saint-Vincent believed should be added the genus Orangutan, in order to complete it.] This recognition of man's animal nature destroys the comfortable divisions that separate and distinguish man from beast; difference becomes not one of quality but one of quantity, more difficult to evaluate. And Balzac explicitly although perhaps belatedly ties the origin of his *Comédie humaine* to this link between man and animal: "Cette idée (l'idée première de *La comédie humaine*) vint d'une comparaison entre l'Humanité et l'Animalité" ("Avant-propos," 1:7). [This idea (the first idea for the *Comédie humaine*) came from a comparison between Humanity and Animality.]

The belief that man is related to animals and that he is transformable opposes the concept of human identity as fixed and innate; man's body has now become something that is constructed in time, and thus man's identity results from the environment and from changes to the body brought about by time, by history. To cite once again the best-known example of one aspect of Balzacian transformism, Madame Vauquer has been "penetrated" and shaped by the milieu of the pension in which she lives: "L'embonpoint blafard de cette petite femme est le produit de cette vie, comme le typhus est

5. "Les ressemblances animales inscrites sur les figures humaines, et si curieusement démontrées par les physiologistes, reparaissaient vaguement dans les gestes, dans les habitudes du corps" (*La peau de chagrin,* 10:107). [The animal resemblances inscribed on human faces, and so curiously revealed by physiologists, vaguely reappeared in the gestures, in the habits of the body.]

6. Balzac, *Physiologie du mariage,* vol. 11 of *La comédie humaine,* 922.

la conséquence des exhalaisons d'un hôpital."[7] [The pallid corpulence of this little woman is the product of this life, just as typhus is the consequence of hospital emanations.] That Balzac should describe the influence of the milieu in the metaphoric terms of illness shows the "malady" of the real (and of woman, for that matter, in this case), which the authors we shall be reading aim to cure, as well as a certain anxiety provoked by the idea that human bodies are penetrable by this dangerous outer world. The limits of the body are put in question, and the crisis of distinction, in addition to that between animal and man, here becomes the crisis of distinguishing between the human body and what lies outside it.

For Balzac, when the environment performs these transformations on human bodies, it leaves traces behind in a kind of writing that can be deciphered by knowledgeable eyes. When Raphaël at the beginning of *La peau de chagrin* enters a gaming casino, his body is described as a kind of text imprinted with signs that the other gamblers can read: "Au premier coup d'oeil les joueurs *lurent* sur le visage du novice quelque horrible mystère, ses jeunes traits étaient *empreints* d'une grâce nébuleuse, son regard attestait des efforts trahis, mille espérances trompées! La morne impassibilité du suicide donnait à ce front une pâleur mate et maladive, un sourire amer dessinait de légers plis dans les coins de la bouche, et la physionomie *exprimait* une résignation qui faisait mal à voir" (*La peau de chagrin,* 10:61; emphasis added). [At a glance the gamblers *read* on the novice's face some horrible mystery, his young features were *imprinted* with a nebulous grace, his expression bore witness to failed efforts, to a thousand hopes dashed! The dismal impassibility of suicide gave to this brow a dull and sickly pallor, a bitter smile traced faint wrinkles in the corners of his mouth, and his face *expressed* a resignation that was painful to see.] The text then goes on to speculate about the history, the "environment" that might have written this text, that might have been at the origin of this transformation of a promising young gentleman: "Était-ce la débauche qui *marquait* de son sale cachet cette noble figure jadis pure et brûlante, maintenant dégradée? Les médecins auraient sans doute attribué à des lésions au coeur ou à la poitrine le cercle jaune qui encadrait les paupières, et la rougeur qui *marquait* les joues, tandis que les poètes eussent voulu reconnaître à ces *signes* les ravages de la science, les *traces* de nuits passées à la lueur d'une lampe studieuse" (10:61–62; emphasis added). [Was it debauchery that *marked* with its vile seal that noble face, so pure and ardent in the past, now so degraded? Doctors

7. Balzac, *Le père Goriot,* vol. 3 of *La comédie humaine,* 55.

would doubtless have attributed to some malady of the heart or lungs those yellow circles that surrounded his eyelids, and the red that *marked* his cheeks; whereas poets would have wanted to recognize in these *signs* the ravages of science, the *traces* of nights passed under the light of a study lamp.] The section of the novel in which Raphaël recounts his past explains the events that caused this transformation and their outcome, as it retraces or rewrites the formation of the text that is Raphaël. In the beginning pages of the novel, the as yet uninterpreted text of Raphaël's body is figured by his missing name; he is "[l]'inconnu" (10:58) [the stranger] and his name appears very late in the novel, thirty or so pages after the beginning. Here, then, the representation of the text is a re-presentation of the writing that is slowly inscribed on Raphaël's body.

It is significant that the two specialists who might decipher this body/text are doctors and poets, scientists and writers, titles that Balzac might well like to apply to himself as well as to Raphaël, who is "un homme de science et de poésie" (*La peau de chagrin,* 10:80) [a man of science and poetry] in Balzac's transformist point of view and literary aims and methods. Thus this novel pursues an explanation of present form through a study of the past situations that shaped it, in a variation of the method of Georges Cuvier, who is described in the text as one of the century's greatest *poets* in his ability to read and rewrite the past from the fragmentary relics of the present: "Cuvier n'est-il pas le plus grand poète de notre siècle? Lord Byron a bien reproduit par des mots quelques agitations morales; mais notre immortel naturaliste a reconstruit des mondes avec des os blanchis, a rebâti comme Cadmus des cités avec des dents, a repeuplé mille forêts de tous les mystères de la zoologie avec quelques fragments de houille, a retrouvé des populations de géants dans le pied d'un mammouth" (10:75). [Is not Cuvier the greatest poet of our century? Lord Byron certainly reproduced in words certain moral agitations; but our immortal naturalist reconstructed worlds by means of bleached bones, rebuilt cities, like Cadmus, with teeth, repopulated a thousand forests with all the mysteries of zoology using a few fragments of coal, found populations of giants in the foot of a mammoth.] For Balzac, the human body is legible like the world is for Cuvier, the environment has written its history on it, and one can decipher external signs to reach the inner depths of identity or the distant past history of the individual or the world.[8]

8. Rivers, in his *Face Value,* examines in detail this textual world and its scientific origins and includes an important section on Balzac.

Balzac famously extended the idea of the physical formation of the body of man to that of the cultural formation of man by society, and he used this idea of man's malleable nature in his explanation of the various types and characters of the *Comédie humaine:* "La Société ne fait-elle pas de l'homme, suivant les milieux où son action se déploie, autant d'hommes différents qu'il y a de variétés en zoologie?" ("Avant-propos," 1:8).[9] [Does not society make from man, depending on the environments in which his actions unfold, as many different men as there are varieties in zoology?] Humans are thus, for Balzac, the product not only of physical transformism but also of a kind of construction by society, by the social itself. What is most important in this social aspect of construction in Balzac's representations is not just the general sense that social codes make up our beings, but more specifically that language itself plays a determining role in the establishment of the identity of the individual. At a very banal level this importance of a name, of the social role of language, is everywhere clear in nineteenth-century prose. In a humorous vein, Rastignac in *La peau de chagrin* (10:165) describes a publisher by saying, "Ce n'est pas un homme, c'est un nom" [He's not a man, he's a name]. More seriously, Raphaël later (199), when imagining his future humiliation at being in debt and having his name circulated, says: "Notre nom, c'est nous-mêmes" [One's name is oneself]. It is one's name as it is viewed by society—and certainly an aristocratic one, in this case—that determines just who one is. Bourdieu's analysis of the celebrity of an artist applies to the reputation of the aristocrat in Balzac because one's name actually "makes" something that has a certain value in society, a certain symbolic capital: "Words, names of schools or groups, proper names—they only have such importance because they make things into something: distinctive signs, they produce existence in a universe where to exist is to be different, 'to make oneself a name,' a proper name or a name in common (that of a group)."[10] To lose the social value of his name would be not simply a loss of "capital" but also a kind of death for the aristocratic Raphaël.

However, language acts on a more subtle and powerful level because it is language that inscribes, creates, and transforms human social identity. Balzac's *Le colonel Chabert* most clearly shows that language has the power

9. Lamarck, before Balzac, "applied his biological ideas to ethics and politics" (Jordanova, *Lamarck,* 92).

10. Pierre Bourdieu, *The Rules of Art: Genesis and Structure of the Literary Field,* trans. Susan Emanuel (Stanford, Calif.: Stanford University Press, 1996), 157.

to determine man. Chabert, who fought with Napoleon's army and suffered a horrific head injury that left him with amnesia for a number of years, regains his memory and comes back to Paris to reclaim his wife, fortune, position, and identity. However, he finds that he has been officially declared dead, and so he goes to the lawyer Derville to attempt to reclaim his life. In this text, it is not just his identity that is at stake but his very existence. Is he alive or dead? Words keep him "dead"; as he says, his death has been written down as history: "Malheureusement pour moi, ma mort est un fait historique consigné dans les *Victoires et conquêtes,* où elle est rapportée en détail" (*Le colonel Chabert,* 3:323). [Unfortunately for me, my death is a fact of history recorded in the *Victoires et conquêtes,* where it is recounted in detail.] It is this written document that counts most.

The text sets up two different kinds of burial for this undead Chabert. The first is the more literal burial of the two, that of his body: after he was wounded, he was assumed dead and put in a mass grave with other dead soldiers. Chabert was able to escape from this more literal burial of his body but then, ironically, is confronted with his second, symbolic one, his burial by the social proclamation of his death. As he says, first he was buried under dead people, now he is buried under words, under social documents: "J'ai été enterré sous des morts, mais maintenant je suis enterré sous des vivants, sous des actes, sous des faits, sous la société tout entière, qui veut me faire rentrer sous terre!" (*Le colonel Chabert,* 3:328). [I was buried under the dead, but now I am buried under the living, under documents, under facts, under all of society, which wants to make me go back underground!] If human corpses were weighing down his body in the first instance, now society inters his identity, weighs down on his chest like earth in a grave: "Le monde social et judiciaire lui pesait sur la poitrine comme un cauchemar" (3:343). [The social world and the judicial world weighed on his chest like a nightmare.]

Chabert rightly realizes that only words, documents, can restore him to "life": "Depuis le jour où je fus chassé de cette ville par les événements de la guerre, j'ai constamment erré comme un vagabond, mendiant mon pain, traité de fou lorsque je racontais mon aventure, et sans avoir ni trouvé, ni gagné un sou pour me procurer les actes qui pouvaient prouver mes dires, et me rendre à la vie sociale" (*Le colonel Chabert,* 3:327). [Since the day I was driven away from that town by the events of the war, I have constantly wandered like a vagabond, begging for my bread, being treated like a madman when I told my adventure, and not having found or earned even a sou with which to obtain the documents that could prove my statements and return me to life in society.] The textual representation of his identity becomes more important than the actual presence of his nondead body—indeed, it effaces whatever a "natural" or physical identity could be for him. If he escaped the physical death of his body, he cannot escape the social death brought about by words. It is remarkable that when this text confronts the literal meaning of corporeal life and death with the social definition of life and death, the social definition prevails and Chabert, who is alive and whose bodily presence imposes itself on his lawyer and his wife, in the end gives up and becomes a mere number, a material, nonhuman object without an identity: "Je ne suis plus un homme, je suis le numéro 164" (3:372). [I am no longer a man, I am number 164.]

In his dealings with Derville, Chabert has a difficult time understanding why he should have to compromise in any agreement about his existence. As he asks, is he alive or is he dead? Life and death seem to be two oppositions between which no negotiation should be possible. He is there in body, but this literal presence cannot outweigh society's proclamations. Balzac's text shows in this case that the literal world comes second after our linguistic definition of it; language, the social proclamation of Chabert's identity, supersedes reality.[11] Chabert's reappearance and its resulting contradictions—he is alive and he is dead—reveal the primacy of the social, yet this revelation is not enough to bring about a change in the course of his destiny of social death.

The ascendancy of the social over the "natural" is figured as well by the circumstances of the youth and old age of Chabert, both of which he spent in societal institutions; an orphan raised by the state, in old age he is a "madman" looked after by the state, as Derville, one of those Balzacian characters who understands society, says: "Quelle destinée! [. . .] Sorti de l'hospice des *Enfants trouvés,* il revient mourir à l'hospice de la *Vieillesse*"

11. Bourdieu explains this by saying that the social defines or produces reality and thus seems to be natural. Pierre Bourdieu, *The Logic of Practice*, trans. Richard Nice (Stanford, Calif.: Stanford University Press, 1990), 71. Sandy Petrey provides a fascinating analysis of the construction of Chabert's identity in his *In the Court of the Pear King: French Culture and the Rise of Realism* (Ithaca: Cornell University Press, 2005). Petrey interprets this construction not as the linguistic, performative construction of identity but rather as the representation of political and social processes that occurred in and just after 1830. His earlier article on Chabert, "The Reality of Representation: Between Marx and Balzac," *Critical Inquiry* 14, no. 3 (1988), looks at the linguistic nature of Chabert's identity from the poststructuralist view of the disconnect between sign and signifier, and he again interprets the construction of identity in relation to the political context of the text.

(*Le colonel Chabert,* 3:373). [What a fate! (...) Having started out from the *Enfants trouvés* (an institution for abandoned children), he comes back to die in the *Hospice de la vieillesse* (an institution for the elderly).] It is significant that Chabert thinks of Napoleon as his father; he is a child of the state: "Je me trompe! j'avais un père, l'Empereur!" (3:331). [I'm wrong! I had a father, the Emperor!] Symbolically, then, one's identity comes not from one's biological parents but from the social constructions that define our place. We are the children of language and society more than we are children of our parents, Balzac seems to be saying. Human identity is not a given; it is constructed by social rules and conventions, it is defined by text. Because identity is so constructed, one could imagine that it would be possible to control and rewrite that construction.

Indeed, one of the crucial bridges between the idea of body language and social construction in Balzac is that of the *social* writing on the physical body of man. As a metaphor of this power of imprinting, one might think of the symbolism of Vautrin's socially embodied, literally written criminal identity represented by the letters "T.F."[12] Balzac pursues this idea of social writing in his various treatises on the way the body is used and perceived in culture. Once again, bodies are legible, coded; they send out signs that can be read: "L'inclination plus ou moins vive d'un de nos membres; la forme télégraphique dont il a contracté, malgré nous, l'habitude; l'angle ou le contour que nous lui faisons décrire, sont empreints de notre vouloir, et sont d'une effrayante signification."[13] [The way we bend a limb more or less energetically; the telegraphic form that limb has acquired through habit without our knowledge; the angle or contour that we make it trace—all are imprinted with our will and have frightening significance.] Such a thing as nobility, for example, which is both physical identity that comes from the body of one's noble parents and a social identity of class, is something that the body expresses physically: a newly named *pair de France* will still be a commoner when he is seen walking, whereas Lamartine reveals himself immediately as a noble by his aristocratic gait (*La théorie de la démarche,* 12:279).

Balzac, however, adds an important nuance that once again gives precedence to the social. He claims that this distinction of aristocratic

12. I touch on this body writing and the making of meaning in a psychoanalytical context in my "Between Bodies and Texts: A Psychoanalytic Reading of *Le père Goriot,*" in *Approaches to Teaching "Old Goriot,"* ed. Michal Ginsburg (New York: Modern Language Association of America, 2000), 109–17.

13. Balzac, *La théorie de la démarche,* vol. 12 of *La comédie humaine,* 280.

elegance does not have its origin in the physical nature of the parents' bodies, but rather is learned, is a product of habit: "Tous les enfants de l'aristocratie ne naissent pas avec le sentiment de l'élégance, avec le goût qui sert à donner à la vie une poétique empreinte; et cependant, l'aristocratie de chaque pays s'y distingue par ses manières et par une remarquable entente de l'existence!—Quel est donc son privilège? . . . L'éducation, l'habitude [. . .] Or, l'élégance, n'étant que la perfection des objets sensibles, doit être accessible à tous par l'habitude" (*Le traité de la vie élégante,* 12:231–32).[14] [Not all the children of the aristocracy are born with the sense of elegance, with good taste that gives life a poetic stamp: yet the aristocracy of each country distinguishes itself there by its manners and by a remarkable shared understanding of existence! What, then, is its privilege? . . . Education, habit. (. . .) Thus elegance, being only the perfection of tangible things, must be accessible to all by means of habit.] In a conversation in *La peau de chagrin* (at 10:103), this metaphor of inscription by habit is couched in the terms of a kind of monetary minting process that presses identities onto human coins, a practice that, in democracy, causes a leveling-out of distinctions of any kind: "'Votre enseignement mutuel fabrique des pièces de cent sous en chair humaine,' dit un absolutiste en interrompant. 'Les individualités disparaissent chez un peuple nivelé par l'instruction.'" ["Your mutual instruction forges hundred-sous coins out of human flesh," interrupted an absolutist. "Individualities disappear in a people leveled out by instruction."] This metaphor of imprinting culture on the "coin" of the body creates what one might (tongue-in-cheek) call social "capital" in Bourdieu's sense—and indeed, this notion of the socially conditioned "habits" of the body, rather than the "naturalness" of physically inherited class, is close to Bourdieu's idea of the "habitus":

> The body is the most indisputable materialization of class taste, which it manifests in several ways. (Bourdieu, *Distinction,* 190)

> The schemes of the habitus [. . .] embed what some would mistakenly call *values* in the most automatic gestures or the apparently most insignificant techniques of the body—ways of walking or blowing one's nose, ways of eating or talking—and engage the most fundamental

14. Prendergast, *The Order of Mimesis,* has an excellent section (92–95) on Balzac's recognition of the possibility of playing with the "traditional markers of class difference" (93) and the anxiety this crisis of distinction brings with it.

> principles of construction and evaluation of the social world, those which most directly express the division of labour (between the classes, the age groups and the sexes) [. . .] as if to give them the appearances of naturalness. (Bourdieu, *Distinction,* 466)

Thus for Balzac as for Bourdieu, the human body is a text that has been inscribed not only by physical forces, such as one's physical milieu but also physically changed and inscribed by social forces: it has been constructed by these combined forces. The symbolic, social world thus invades and rewrites the physical world of the body, and their very distinction becomes problematic. This blurring of the social, cultural, and linguistic realms with the bodily, material world is an important element in Balzac's fantasy of creation: the symbolic world, be it of culture, art, or science, can indeed transform and "create" the body.

The materiality of this social influence on the body acts in conjunction with another element of Balzac's world: the "science" of mesmerism, or animal magnetism, and his theories of human will. In mesmerism Balzac finds the possibility of controlling another human being by thought, or more precisely by the power of the will.[15] He describes the will as a strange kind of unseen force that can act on the real world, and mesmerism as a science that taps into that power and can manipulate it. In the world of the early nineteenth century, mesmerism seemed to be a manifestation of the fact that man was "surrounded by wonderful, invisible forces; Newton's gravity, made intelligible by Voltaire; Franklin's electricity, popularized by a fad for lightning rods and by demonstrations in the fashionable lyceums and museums of Paris; and the miraculous gases of the Chalières and Montgolfières that astonished Europe by lifting man into the air for the first time in 1783. Mesmer's invisible fluid seemed no more miraculous" (Darnton, *Mesmerism,* 11). The power of steam and of invisible mesmerist streams were united in Balzac's imagination, where the will seems to have the power of steam: [L]a volonté humaine était une force matérielle semblable à la vapeur" (*La peau de chagrin,* 10:149) [Human will was a

15. Mesmerism was definitely in the public view at the time and was all the rage in the late 1700s and early 1800s in Europe. Darnton claims that he would restore Mesmer to "his rightful place, somewhere near Turgot, Franklin, and Cagliostro in the pantheon of that age's most-talked-about men." Robert Darnton, *Mesmerism and the End of the Enlightenment in France* (Cambridge: Harvard University Press, 1968), viii. A useful analysis of mesmerism in Balzac's works can be found in K. Melissa Marcus, *The Representation of Mesmerism in Honoré de Balzac's "La comédie humaine"* (New York: Peter Lang, 1995).

material force similar to steam], claims Raphaël to Foedora. In addition to its relation to spiritism and to fascinating powerful fluids, the will's link to mesmerism, and thus to the possibility of the direct, physical influence of one human being on another, makes it a concentration of force and energy that has, for Balzac, the potential to bring about great change in the life of the targeted person.

Today in hindsight, mesmerism is viewed as, in part, the discovery of hypnotism and suggestion. At that time, the hypnotic trances induced in Mesmer's patients were thought to be manifestations of artificial somnambulism; Mesmer considered them a secondary phenomenon, less important than his discoveries of magnetic fluids and influences. But by means of his "animal magnetism," he appeared able to cure patients who were probably suffering from hysterical illnesses, such as Maria Paradis, who was partially cured of her blindness by Mesmer's magnetic therapies. Others, such as Puységur, "hypnotized" many patients and transcribed descriptions of his ability to cure illness and relieve pain.[16]

Yet what we think of today as a psychological phenomenon was seen in Balzac's time as a physical, material process. It was the magnetic fluid that passed from magnetizer to patient and restored proper circulation. Indeed, it would certainly seem easier to imagine that a physical ailment was being cured by a material process than to imagine that it was merely the suggestion of the magnetizer that accomplished the cure.

This power of the magnetizer fascinated Balzac, who frequented magnetizers with his mother and devoured their writings.[17] In the "Avant-propos" (1:16), speaking of his work *Séraphîta* and of mesmerism, Gall, and Lavater, he describes a fantastic ability, an electric power "qui se métamorphose chez l'homme en une puissance incalculée" [that metamorphoses in man into an incalculable power]. The mesmerist dream was a dream of control, as Starobinski states: "The mesmerist dream is a volontarist dream [relating to the will, *volonté*]; even more, it is a dream of domination [. . .] Magnetic theory, in its beginnings, valorizes to the extreme the activity and powers of the magnetizer."[18]

Preevolutionary ideas, a vision of the workings of the social construction of identities and bodies, and mesmerist powers combine in Balzac's

16. Alan Gauld, *A History of Hypnotism* (New York: Cambridge University Press, 1992), 39–50.

17. Notes to the "Avant-propos," 1:1114 n. 1, 1136 n. 1.

18. Jean Starobinski, *La relation critique* (Paris: Gallimard, 1970), 203.

works, therefore, to reveal not only that the human being was transformable, the product of a kind of inscription and construction, but also that one human being could control another, could perhaps "inscribe" another human being. And it is significant that, in terms of mesmerism, this controlling and changing happened for the most part to women.[19] As we shall see, this manipulated change of a human being takes the form of a fantasy of a new kind of creation, the creation and control of another's identity and person, specifically a woman's, which we shall now investigate in a rich tapestry of interconnected themes and images in the Balzacian text, taking *La peau de chagrin* as a base from which to expand to other works.

The Will and Creation

Raphaël is an apt representative of a small, select group of characters in *La comédie humaine* who in various ways appear to possess the power to control people and reality by means of thought, will, and language. Like Raphaël and Cuvier, two powerful intellects of *La peau de chagrin,* these characters tend to be scientists (in the very broad sense of the word, which includes alchemists and mesmerists), artists (writers, sculptors, painters), or some combination of the two (as Balzac may have imagined himself). In this group of characters, the artist's power to create is linked to the scientist's power to invent and manipulate. Six characters will lead us deeper into this fantasy of creation, and all six are described by Balzac as being some form of mesmerist, either with knowledge of mesmeric theory and/or with magnetic powers. Even though these characters may have deep flaws, may fail in their attempts, or may be portrayed ironically, what is important for us is not their success or failure but rather that Balzac imagines that they envision the creation of reality, even of life.

Our Raphaël de Valentin in *La peau de chagrin* is an "artist," a literary author who writes a "scientific" treatise on the human will (his *Théorie de la volonté*) [*Theory of the Will*], which completes Mesmer's work (*La peau de*

19. Suspicions of the erotic nature of the relationship between the magnetizer and the patient surfaced when magnetizers touched women's bodies and secluded them in mattress-lined rooms (this perhaps links it even more closely to the psychiatric treatment of hysteria at the end of the nineteenth century and beyond, to Freud) (Darnton, *Mesmerism*, 4–5). A secret report on mesmerism by the Franklin commission in 1786 was sent to the king of France; this report warned that mesmerism might be linked to women's sexuality. Adam Crabtree, *From Mesmer to Freud: Magnetic Sleep and the Roots of Psychological Healing* (New Haven: Yale University Press, 1993), 92–94.

chagrin, 10:138). Raphaël himself has a kind of telepathic power that Balzac equates with certain skilled observers. Raphaël describes his first attempt at gambling as a manifestation of this power of telepathic perception, which, even though he is separated from the gambling table and the fate of his money by a crowd of chattering people, allows him to hear their conversation: "malgré tous ces obstacles, par un privilège accordé aux passions et qui leur donne le pouvoir d'anéantir l'espace et le temps, j'entendais distinctement les paroles des deux joueurs" (10:124) [despite all these obstacles, by a privilege granted to the passions that gives them the power to annihilate space and time, I distinctly heard the words of the two gamblers]. He claims as well to be able to use his magnetic powers to dominate (significantly) a woman: "Je vainquis alors la comtesse par la puissance d'une fascination magnétique" (10:187). [I then conquered the countess with the power of magnetic fascination.] Another artist, Sarrasine, manifests several of the telltale signs of the magnetic personality, specifically in his influence over Zambinella (who is a kind of artificial woman in the text): "Son regard flamboyant eut une sorte d'influence magnétique sur Zambinella, car le *musico* finit par détourner subitement la vue vers Sarrasine, et alors sa voix céleste s'altéra" (*Sarrasine,* 6:1072). [His burning gaze had a kind of magnetic influence on Zambinella, because the *musico* suddenly turned to look toward Sarrasine, and then his celestial voice faltered.] A third artist, Frenhofer, in "Le chef d'oeuvre inconnu," has green eyes "ternis en apparence par l'âge, mais qui, par le contraste du blanc nacré dans lequel flottait la prunelle, devaient parfois jeter des regards magnétiques au fort de la colère ou de l'enthousiasme" ("Le chef d'oeuvre inconnu," 10:415) [dulled in appearance by age, but which, in contrast to the pearly white in which they floated, would at times cast magnetic glances in the midst of anger or enthusiasm].

Vautrin represents a special case in this group. He has significant mesmerist powers, as when he makes Mademoiselle Michonneau collapse merely with a glance: "son regard magnétique tomba comme un rayon de soleil sur Mlle Michonneau, à laquelle ce jet de volonté cassa les jarrets" (*Le père Goriot,* 3:217) [his magnetic gaze fell like a ray of sunlight on Mademoiselle Michonneau, whose knees buckled from that strong burst of will]. Although he is not literally a writer or an artist, he calls himself one: "Je suis un grand poète. Mes poésies, je ne les écris pas: elles consistent en actions et en sentiments" (3:141). [I am a great poet. As for my poems, I don't write them: they consist in actions and feelings.] He uses his magnetic power to control men also, as we see in his power over Lucien: "[I]l arrêta sur Lucien un de ces regards fixes et pénétrants qui font entrer la volonté des gens forts dans l'âme des gens faibles. Ce regard fascinateur [. . .] eut pour effet de détendre toute résistance" (*Splendeurs et misères des courtisanes,* 6:502).[20] [He fixed on Lucien one of those steady and penetrating gazes that infuses the will of the strong into the soul of the weak. This fascinating gaze (. . .) had the effect of dissolving all resistance.]

Two "scientists" join this group of magnetizers. The first, Louis Lambert, although ignorant of Mesmer's works, manages to come to the same discoveries in his own lost *Traité de la volonté* [*Treatise on the Will*]: "La découverte de Mesmer, si importante et si mal appréciée encore, se trouvait tout entière dans un seul développement de ce Traité, quoique Louis ne connût pas les oeuvres, d'ailleurs assez laconiques, du célèbre docteur suisse" (*Louis Lambert,* 11:631). [Mesmer's discovery, so important and still so poorly appreciated, could be found in totality in just one argument of this treatise, even though Louis did not know the rather laconic works of the famous Swiss doctor.] The second scientist, Balthazar Claës, whose practice lies somewhere between that of a chemist and an alchemist, has the magnetic fluid of the mesmerist in his gaze, which he also uses on women: "Séduisant comme le serpent, sa parole, ses regards épanchaient un fluide magnétique, et il prodigua cette puissance de génie, ce doux esprit qui fascinait Joséphine, et il mit pour ainsi dire ses filles dans son coeur" (*La recherche de l'absolu,* 10:788). [As seductive as a serpent, his words, his glances poured forth a magnetic fluid; and he lavishly dispensed this power of genius, this gentle spirit that fascinated Joséphine, and he lodged, so to speak, his daughters in his heart.]

These six mesmerists can impose their will on another person, can make their thoughts act to change that person, and because this thought-transfer is a physical process of magnetism, the material, invisible fluid manipulated by mesmerists suggests that thought itself is a material substance: "Louis avait été conduit invinciblement à reconnaître la matérialité de la pensée" (*Louis Lambert,* 11:637). [Louis had been led inevitably to recognize the materiality of thought.] Mesmerism seemed to show that this material thought could be transported from one person to another, as magnetic charges could. In this way, the material world and the world of thought originate in the same element: "les principes constituants de la Matière et

20. Both Vautrin and Sarrasine use their powers to control the men they desire, although Sarrasine does not know that the object of his desire is a man.

ceux de la Pensée [...] procèdent de la même source" (11:630) [the constituent elements of Matter and those of Thought (...) come from the same source]. As we saw earlier, cultural codes, which belong more to the symbolic world than to the material world, have the power to write bodies in Balzac's example of aristocratic elegance, although the mechanism of this writing remains, in those texts, habit and education. Here, however, thought, which is normally considered, like culture, to be intangible, is integrated into the material world in Balzac's imagination and is able to have a physical influence on the real.

Balzac does indeed suggest in *Louis Lambert* that thought has power not only over other people's wills but also over the material world itself: "Une logique et simple déduction de ses principes lui avait fait reconnaître que la Volonté pouvait, par un mouvement tout contractile de l'être intérieur, s'amasser; puis, par un autre mouvement, être projetée au dehors, et même être confiée à des objets matériels" (*Louis Lambert,* 11:631). [A logical and simple deduction from these principles led him to see that the Will could be accumulated by means of a contractile movement of one's inner being, then, by another movement, could be projected and even be imparted to material objects.] This raises the possibility that one might control material reality in very real ways by means of this power of thought and will, either literally in the way thought can act materially on the world, or more symbolically in the enormous power that thinking man has over nature. Raphaël claims that a man can "tout modifier relativement à l'humanité, même les lois absolues de la nature" (*La peau de chagrin,* 10:150) [modify everything concerning mankind, even the absolute laws of nature]. This real, material influence of thought is symbolized by Balthazar Claës's scientific ability to use the power of his intelligence to create reality, to create material objects. In this way his thoughts, translated into scientific experiments, not only alter the real world but actually create a new, real thing when he succeeds in creating a diamond: "'Je fais les métaux, je fais les diamants, je répète la nature,' s'écria-t-il" (*La recherche de l'absolu,* 10:720).[21] ["I make metals, I make diamonds, I repeat nature," he cried.]

This power of the will, particularly of mesmerist artists, then becomes the fantasy of their power to create, reshape, in a very real way, a human being by means of their art. This begins as the simple metaphor of a

21. Don Juan and his father in Balzac's "L'élixir de longue vie" also use alchemy, or magic, in their case to re-create life from death.

painting that seems to become real, where the real would be a secondary product derived from art. Chabert is "un portrait de Rembrandt, sans cadre" (*Le colonel Chabert,* 3:321) [a portrait by Rembrandt without a frame], as is Frenhofer "une toile de Rembrandt marchant silencieusement et sans cadre" ("Le chef d'oeuvre inconnu," 10:415) [a painting by Rembrandt walking silently and without a frame]. The *antiquaire* in *La peau de chagrin* (10:78) ressembles the "*Peseur d'or* de Gérard Dow [. . .] sorti de son cadre" [*Money Changer* by Gérard Dow (. . .) out of its frame]. But, to be more specific, through the concept of willpower the Balzacian myth of Pygmalion receives a new, "scientific" force: three mesmerist artists, Sarrasine, Frenhofer, and, as we have seen, Raphaël, are all identified with Pygmalion. Sarrasine "dévorait des yeux la statue de Pygmalion, pour lui descendue de son piédestal" (*Sarrasine,* 6:1061) [devoured with his eyes Pygmalion's statue, which had come down from its pedestal for him].[22] Frenhofer, in discussing the substantial length of time it takes for him to complete his painting, brings up the example of Pygmalion for comparison: "Nous ignorons le temps qu'employa le seigneur Pygmalion pour faire la seule statue qui ait marché!" ("Le chef d'oeuvre inconnu," 10:425). [We don't know how much time it took Pygmalion to make the only statue that ever walked!] And, once again, Raphaël, in *La peau de chagrin,* calls himself a new Pygmalion.[23]

The clearest representation of the idea of an artist creating a woman appears in "Le chef d'oeuvre inconnu" in the case of Frenhofer and the woman he has painted. Frenhofer states that the goal of his art is, in fact, to actually create a living, breathing woman, and he criticizes his colleague, Porbus, whose paintings do not succeed in this task: "[M]algré de si louables efforts, je ne saurais croire que ce beau corps soit animé par le tiède souffle de la vie [. . .] [I]ci c'est une femme, là une statue, plus loin un cadavre" ("Le chef d'oeuvre inconnu," 10:417). [Despite such laudable efforts, I could not believe that this beautiful body was animated by the

22. Lambert and Claës, "scientists" who are not artists, do not attempt to create women. However, they plunge into the life of the mind and abandon the real women in their lives for their creations; the dreamer Lambert goes mad on the day before his marriage, seemingly because of his intense musings; and Claës, obsessed with his work, neglects his wife. Thus, although they do not create new women they become immersed in the life of the mind, which in a sense replaces the women in their lives.

23. Alexandra Wettlaufer's richly argued book, *Pen vs. Paintbrush: Girodet, Balzac, and the Myth of Pygmalion in Postrevolutionary France* (New York: Palgrave, 2001), studies three Balzacian Pygmalions (Frenhofer, Sarrasine, and Sommervieux) as she explores Balzac's uses of the myth to dominate in art and in gender struggles.

warm breath of life (. . .) Here it is a woman, there a statue, over there a corpse.] Frenhofer would seem to believe that he, however, has succeeded in creating a real woman in his painting: "[C]e n'est pas une toile, c'est une femme! une femme avec laquelle je pleure, je ris, je cause et pense" ("Le chef d'oeuvre inconnu," 10:431). [This is not a painting, it is a woman! A woman with whom I cry, I laugh, I talk and think.] When the two other artists look at his work and see almost nothing, Frenhofer says: "Vous êtes devant une femme et vous cherchez un tableau" (10:435). [You are standing before a woman and you are looking for a painting.] Frenhofer, the painter with magnetic eyes, represents the fantasy of the artist who, through his own creative powers, through his thoughts, his will, and the artistic material translation of them, might make a woman. Even though he fails, this fantasy is itself important.

The Pygmalion theme finds multiple expression in *La peau de chagrin.* Raphaël, that self-proclaimed new Pygmalion who dreams of re-creating Pauline, begins by admitting that he prefers his own thoughts and dreams to the real woman: "En présence de mes romanesques fantaisies, qu'était Pauline?" (*La peau de chagrin,* 10:143). [Compared with my romantic fantasies, what was Pauline?] His thoughts are better than the real world around him, so he attempts to refashion reality from those thoughts, not just in the case of Pauline but also in the case of Foedora. Before he even meets Foedora, he creates his own idea of her in his thoughts: "Je me créai une femme, je la dessinai dans ma pensée, je la rêvai" (10:146). [I created a woman for myself, I drew her in my thoughts, I dreamed her.] What he must have later, as he says, is not the real Foedora but rather his imaginary construction of her: "'Il ne s'agit plus de la Foedora vivante, de la Foedora du faubourg Saint-Honoré, mais de ma Foedora, de celle qui est là,' dis-je en me frappant le front" (10:191). ["It is no longer about the living Foedora, the Foedora of the Faubourg Saint-Honoré, but about my Foedora, the one who is here!" I said tapping my forehead.] What he would like is to have the Foedora who is his work of art, the Foedora who was "plus qu'une femme, c'était un roman" (10:151) [more than a woman, she was a novel], his "novel" that he has written and that would come to life.[24] Finally, the self-proclaimed action-poet, Vautrin, nearly succeeds in transforming the prostitute Esther into a cultured Catholic lady: "J'en ai

24. Zambinella too is described with nearly the identical words: "C'était plus qu'une femme, c'était un chef-d'oeuvre!" (*Sarrasine,* vol. 6 of *La comédie humaine,* 1061). [She was more than a woman, she was a work of art!]

fait une femme chaste, pure, bien élevée, religieuse, une femme comme il faut" (*Splendeurs et misères des courtisanes,* 6:478).[25] [I made of her a chaste woman, pure, well brought up, religious, a proper lady.]

The myth of Pygmalion, however, shares its place in Balzac's texts with another traditional image of artistic creation that will also appear in the other authors we shall study. The materiality of thought in Balzac's world, and its ability to create physical things, join up with the fantasy that, through thought, the artist or scientist can "give birth" to a child. This metaphor is not unusual or surprising; artists create, and the symbol of childbirth is apt. However, in Balzac a network of birth and creation metaphors combines with the "scientific" theme of the power of thought and language to grow into a more literal fantasy of gestation and procreation, into the fantasy of the male artist or scientist creating life, creating a real person by means of thought.

First, in many of Balzac's works the male scientist or artist metaphorically gestates works—such as Frenhofer, who describes "le long enfantement d'une grande oeuvre" ("Le chef d'oeuvre inconnu," 10:432) [the lengthy birth of a great work], or Louis Lambert, who claims: "[J]'enfante ici dans un grenier des idées sans qu'elles soient saisies" (*Louis Lambert,* 11:652). [I give birth here in an attic to ideas that are not grasped.] Vautrin calls himself Lucien's mother: "Enfant, tu as dans le vieil Herrera une mère dont le dévouement est absolu" (*Splendeurs et misères des courtisanes,* 6:477). [Child, you have in old Herrera a mother whose devotion is absolute.] Balzac links his own writing with gestating, in a metaphor that equates the detailed, preparatory work of his literary descriptions (here of a house) with the carrying of a child to term: "[M]ais avant de la décrire, peut-être faut-il établir dans l'intérêt des écrivains la nécessité de ces préparations didactiques contre lesquelles protestent certaines personnes ignorantes et voraces qui voudraient des émotions sans en subir les principes générateurs, la fleur sans la graine, l'enfant sans la gestation" (*La recherche de l'absolu,* 10:657) [But before describing it, in the interest of writers, I should perhaps prove the necessity of these didactic preparations, against which protest certain ignorant and voracious people who would like to have emotions without having been exposed to their generating principles, the flower without the seed, the child without gestation.] These "principes générateurs" are, in fact, the descriptions of the milieu and history that inscribe human bodies and identities, thus we

25. Vautrin also attempts to change a man, Lucien, and again nearly succeeds.

have birth as inscription. In this way, Balzac's very text, the techniques of which he is in the process of defending, is representative of this type of symbolic procreation.[26]

Yet beyond this familiar metaphor, the weight of the scientific context makes this fantasy seem possible. Louis Lambert speaks of thoughts as children who flourish or who die for lack of enough "substance génératrice" (*Louis Lambert,* 11:632) [generative substance]. Again, given Lambert's theories of the materiality of thought, this generative substance seems quite physical, as if a thought and, more important, language, were a real, physical child. Lambert writes that "*la* PAROLE [. . .] *engendre incessamment la* SUBSTANCE" (11:686) [*the* WORD . . . *incessantly engenders* SUBSTANCE]. Although Claës does not create a child, he does create a diamond.[27] And Balzac represents quite mundane ways in which a scientist could create a new being. One of the scientists consulted by Raphaël actually creates a new form of life in his scientific work, and this creation of life involves indirect procreation. The scientist, Monsieur Lavrille, has organized a mating between two different kinds of ducks, and he hopes that the offspring will comprise a thirty-eighth species, which will bear his name. Here, through the work of scientific thought, he aims to create a new living being, indeed, a creature that, like his own child, will be named after him. Science thus provides the real, tangible opportunity for the creation of new forms of life through thought.

Transformist theories give an added twist to this metaphor of thought generating new beings. In a rather curious and little-known short story

26. At times, the method used to create is one that relies on machines, an idea that will become much more important later in this study. The mechanical represents artificial creation as opposed to natural procreation. Louis Lambert claims that in order to create anew, to re-create the world, which is a machine in this case, one must first be a cog in that machine: "Il faudrait embrasser tout ce monde, l'étreindre pour le refaire; mais ceux qui l'ont ainsi étreint et refondu n'ont-ils pas commencé par être un rouage de la machine?" (*Louis Lambert,* 11:655). [One must embrace this whole world, grasp it in order to remake it; but those who have thus grasped and remade, did they not begin as a cog in the machine?] Balthazar Claës seems to become one with his own machine when he works to create nature, the diamond. He, in a kind of automatism of concentration, stares fixedly at the machines that will help him to create nature: "Ses yeux horriblement fixes ne quittèrent pas une machine pneumatique" (*La recherche de l'absolu,* 10:779). [His eyes, horribly fixed, did not leave a pneumatic machine.] It is in fact the apparatus he sets up that does allow him to create a diamond, even though he does not understand at the time how this happened.

27. In *La recherche de l'absolu,* 11:690, we find the common theme of rivalry between woman and work when the scientist's desire to create conflicts symbolically with the natural method of procreation, when the scientist's love for science conflicts with his love for his wife. Joséphine understands this well when she "se découvrit une rivale dans la Science qui lui enlevait son mari" [discovered a rival in Science, which took her husband from her]. The same rivalry between woman and art appears as well in "Le chef d'oeuvre inconnu."

entitled "Guide âne à l'usage des animaux qui veulent parvenir aux honneurs" [An Ass's Guide for the Use of Animals Who Want to Acquire Honors], Balzac presents the 1830 Cuvier/Geoffroy Saint-Hilaire battle in a humorous vein, but one that is significant for our purposes in many ways.[28] In this story, an ass tells the tale of how his master took him to Paris, how the ass underwent a strange operation (we return to the surgical context of our Introduction here) that included application of an unknown fluid, the results of which turned the ass into a hybrid that could walk like a giraffe, was similar to a yellow-and-black-striped zebra, and had a cow's tail. This tale is told in a sardonic tone, and the experiment is a kind of charlatanism. Even so, the mere idea of a kind of "scientific" grafting of one animal body part onto another (the cow's tail on the ass) expresses the idea of the human rewriting of nature and the creation of new animal forms, in a kind of takeover of nature's transformist role. Thus, in this satirical fantasy of the transformation of nature by man, one could see a representation of the fact that man might intervene and change nature and perhaps man himself.

A desire to experiment on humans, in the different, almost eugenic context of understanding their failings in order to cure them, appears in a remarkable letter in which Balzac speculates on an experiment that would actually remake a human brain: "Enfin, il y aurait une belle expérience à faire et à laquelle j'ai pensé depuis vingt ans: ce serait de refaire un cerveau à un crétin, de savoir si l'on peut créer un appareil à pensée, en en développant les rudiments. C'est en refaisant des cerveaux qu'on saura comment ils se défont."[29] [In short, there would be a good experiment to do, one that I have thought about for twenty years: this would be to remake the brain of a cretin, to know if one can create a thinking apparatus by developing its rudiments. It is by remaking brains that we will learn how they come undone.] This fantasy of the "rewriting" of nature, which we saw in Raphaël's artistic desire to refashion Pauline, is manifested in the scientific context of a kind of cure for human ills and can be seen more generally in the desire of Benassis, in *Le médecin de campagne,* to cure a village population.

28. Honoré de Balzac, "Guide âne à l'usage des animaux qui veulent parvenir aux honneurs," in *Vie privée et publique des animaux, vignettes par Grandville,* ed. P. J. Stahl [pseud.] (Paris: J. Hetzel & Paulin, 1880), 267–86. Gallica: http://gallica.bnf.fr/ark:/12148/bpt6k203884z/CadresFenetre?O=NUMM-203884&M=tdm.

29. To Doctor J. Moreau, December 1845. In Honoré de Balzac, *Correspondance de H. de Balzac, 1819–1850* (Paris: Calmann Lévy, 1876), 2:210.

Thus, through the various lenses of art, mesmerism, science, and procreation, Balzac expresses the possibility that one might "usurp God" (Notes to the "Avant-propos," 1:1123 n. 5), scientifically and/or artistically, and thus he articulates a kind of situation that would make actually creating a new woman possible. The literary example that best illustrates this combination of themes, the scientific Galatea, is La Zambinella, who pushes to the extreme the fantasy of creating an artificial woman through art, mesmerism, and science, and with this as well comes creation of anxieties about the dangers of this act.

First, although Zambinella has not been created by Sarrasine, she is for him (as we have seen) Pygmalion's statue come to life, the incarnation of Sarrasine's ideal beauty. If she has not been created by our mesmerist Sarrasine, she is nevertheless a woman who has been created, literally "sculpted," in the operation that altered her sex, and here our introductory concept of dissection becomes the interventionist act of castrative surgery. "Man," through medical "science," creates Sarrasine's perfect woman, who is, not surprisingly, equated (in later life) with a machine, with a man-made, technological product: "Un sentiment de profonde horreur pour l'homme saisissait le coeur quand une fatale attention vous dévoilait les marques imprimées par la décrépitude à cette casuelle machine" (*Sarrasine,* 6:1051). [A feeling of profound horror for man seized the heart when one's fateful observation revealed the marks that decrepitude imprinted on that accidental machine.] The first appearance of this artificial creature (somewhat of an "homme artificiel" or a "création artificielle" [6:1047, 1052] [artificial man, artificial creation]) seems to come about by means of a kind of theatrical machinery, perhaps even, a kind of birth from the machine, the technological, itself: "Il semblait être sorti de dessous terre, poussé par quelque mécanisme de théâtre" (6:1050). [He seemed to have emerged from underground, pushed by some theatrical mechanism.]

Second, this artificial, man-made "woman" appears in a text in which Balzac explicitly evokes the fantasy that our thoughts, our "chimeras," can become real, that Jupiter's head could give birth to a real woman: "Par un des plus rares caprices de la nature, la pensée en demi-deuil qui se roulait dans ma cervelle en était sortie, elle se trouvait devant moi, personnifiée, vivante, elle avait jailli comme Minerve de la tête de Jupiter, grande et forte, elle avait tout à la fois cent ans et vingt-deux ans, elle était vivante et morte" (*Sarrasine,* 6:1050). [By one of the rarest caprices of nature, the thought half-draped in mourning, which was turning round in my head, emerged; it was there before me, personified, alive; it had sprung forth like

Minerva from the head of Jupiter, tall and strong; it was at once a hundred years old and twenty-two; it was alive and dead.] The narrator's thought has sprung to life in this artificial creature, just as the surgeon's blade that intervened in nature to make Zambinella created the perfect artificial woman who would encounter the eager Sarrasine. Thus *Sarrasine* draws together all the elements of Balzac's fantasy—mesmerism, surgery and science, thought, and art-become-real—all in the service of artificially creating a new, perfect "woman."[30]

The surgeon's blade, this very material tool used to transform humans, ultimately becomes the writer's pen, the pen of Balzac himself. It is the literary author who would create the new woman by means of his very text, through the power of language, the technological tool that writes human identity in Balzac's world.[31] The Balzacian object that best figures this performative power of language to operate on the real world is the fantastical *peau de chagrin,* a wild ass's skin (nature, the real) that has been treated (whether by scientific, magical, or religious means is unclear, but most likely by the technological "art" of man) to become a magical, powerful tool with which to realize one's will in the world.[32] Furthermore, it is a natural object that, in this transformation, has been imbued with language (words are mysteriously inscribed on the *peau,* in a way similar to that in which the environment writes on the human body in Balzac's representation of transformism, or man writes on fellow man by branding on Vautrin the letters "T.F."). Ultimately, the *peau* could be viewed as a symbol for language itself, a special type of language whose material form

30. Indeed Balzac, in *Les secrets de la princesse de Cadignan,* 6:964, goes so far as to say that woman is actually already an artificial creation whose author is society: "L'une des gloires de la Société, c'est d'avoir créé *la femme* là où la Nature a fait une femelle." [One of Society's glories is to have created *woman* where nature made a female.] Flaubert writes later: "*Dieu a créé la femelle, et l'homme a fait la femme;* elle est le résultat de la civilisation, une oeuvre factice" (To Louise Colet, 27 March 1853, *Correspondance,* 2:284). [*God created the female, and man made woman;* she is the result of civilization, an artificial work.]

31. We recall that Balzac in his time was the surgeon, "an anatomist, who dissects with the aid of the microscope and the scalpel," and, in particular, a dissector of women (Weinberg, *French Realism,* 42).

32. It is significant that the type of ass from which this talisman was made has, as Balzac notes, a kind of mesmeric eye: "[S]on oeil est muni d'une espèce de tapis réflecteur auquel les Orientaux attribuent le pouvoir de la fascination" (*La peau de chagrin,* 10:240). [Its eye is endowed with a kind of reflective cover to which Orientals attribute the power of fascination.] See my article "Language as Knowledge or Language as Power: Performative and Constative Language in *La peau de chagrin,*" in *Linguistics in Literature* 5, no. 3 (Fall 1980), 35–58, for a very different, rhetorical analysis of the relationship of the performative and constative functions of language in this text to its rhetorical structures.

is a kind of signifier (its size) that coincides with its symbolic meaning, its signified (its decreasing size stands for the shortened length of the life of the owner). In this "sign," the concept, the idea, equals its physical form, the *peau;* language and the real coincide.

And the *peau* is the object that represents just what Raphaël's language does. The *peau* offers to its owner the power to change the real through the power of language, to carry out the will (desire and thought). It gives him the ability to make thought real. After Raphaël makes his pact with the *peau,* all he has to do is say "I wish" and his words become reality. He uses words to wish aloud for a dinner, and he gets one; he expresses the wish that the *antiquaire* will fall in love with a dancer, and that happens. Language itself, the *peau* as sign, appears to have the power to control the real. In fact, if Raphaël is not mad, language creates the real here in a very literal way.[33] And the *peau,* as language and as the title of this novel itself, represents Balzac's very text that would change the real, have the power to create.

Balzac plays with the idea of his own ability to manipulate and perhaps rewrite what he calls the "codes" of identity in the *Études analytiques.* As we saw in his analyses of artistocratic gait, elegance is a learned habit; it is a code that can be communicated: "Codifier, faire le code de la démarche. En d'autres termes, rédiger une suite d'axiomes pour le repos des intelligences faibles ou paresseuses [...] En étudiant ce code, les homme progressifs, et ceux qui tiennent au système de la perfectibilité, pourraient paraître aimables, gracieux, distingués, bien élevés, fashionables, aimés, instruits, ducs, marquis ou comtes; au lieu de sembler vulgaires, stupides, ennuyeux, pédants, ignobles, maçons du roi Philippe ou barons de l'Empire" (*La théorie de la démarche,* 12:278–79).

33. Louis Lambert similarly describes the power of words and actually theorizes about it (*Louis Lambert,* 11:592). In *La peau de chagrin,* this linguistic power of language and thought belongs in another example to science as well, thus again uniting the roles of writer and scientist. Cuvier, through his imaginative reconstruction of the past, is a kind of scientific poet who re-creates life by means of language and numbers and by means of his ability to decipher the inscriptions of the transformations of history: "Il est poète avec des chiffres, il est sublime en posant un zéro près d'un sept. *Il réveille le néant sans prononcer des paroles artificiellement magiques,* il fouille une parcelle de gypse, y aperçoit une *empreinte,* et vous crie: 'Voyez!' *Soudain les marbres s'animalisent,* la mort se vivifie, le monde se déroule!" (*La peau de chagrin,* 10:75; emphasis added). [He is a poet with numbers; he is sublime when putting a zero next to a seven. *He reawakens the void without speaking artificially magic words;* he scours a fragment of gypsum, sees an *imprint* in it, and cries out "Look!" *Suddenly marble turns into an animal,* death is given life again, the world unfolds!] Immediately after this description of Cuvier, the works of art in the *antiquaire*'s store seem to come to life before the eyes of Raphaël: "Les tableaux s'illuminèrent, les têtes de vierge lui sourirent, et les statues se colorèrent d'une vie trompeuse" (10:76). [The paintings were illuminated, virgin faces smiled at him, and statues became colored with a deceptive life.]

[To codify, to formulate the code of the human gait. In other words, to compose a set of axioms to help weak or lazy minds (. . .) By studying this code, progressive men, and those who hold to the system of perfectibility, could appear likeable, gracious, distinguished, well brought-up, fashionable, loved, educated, dukes, marquis, or counts, instead of appearing vulgar, stupid, boring, pedantic, ignoble, masons of King Philip or barons of the Empire.] Distinction, which is visible and legible in the body, is a code that can be learned and "plagiarized." Balzac thus, in this work, himself gives the code for rewriting human identity and provides the means to create new humans.

Does this power of codes, of language, in particular as represented by the *peau,* embody the fantasy of Balzac himself, who, speaking through Louis Lambert, would like to make his own thoughts and words into living flesh: "Le: *Et verbum caro factum est!* lui semblait une sublime parole destinée à exprimer la formule traditionnelle de la Volonté, du Verbe, de l'Action se faisant visibles" (*Louis Lambert,* 11:639)? [*Et verbum caro factum est!* seemed to him a sublime statement meant to express the traditional formula of the Will, of the Word, of Action becoming visible.] The following metaphor found in the "Avant-propos" would seem to provide an affirmative answer. Here, *La comédie humaine* was first Balzac's dream, significantly a dream of a woman, or rather of a chimera of ambiguous identity, who became real: "L'idée première de *La comédie humaine* fut d'abord chez moi comme *un rêve,* comme un de ces projets impossibles que l'on caresse et qu'on laisse s'envoler; une chimère qui sourit, qui montre *son visage de femme* et qui déploie aussitôt ses ailes en remontant dans un ciel fantastique. Mais la chimère, comme beaucoup de chimères, *se change en réalité,* elle a ses commandements et sa tyrannie auxquels il faut céder" ("Avant-propos," 1:7; emphasis added). [My first idea for *La comédie humaine* was in the beginning like *a dream,* like one of those impossible projects that one caresses and lets take wing, a chimera who smiles, who shows *her woman's face* and who spreads her wings, rising back again into a fantastic sky. But this chimera, like many chimeras, *becomes real;* she has her demands and her tyranny to which one must yield.] We might then rewrite the description of Foedora—she was "plus qu'une femme, c'était un roman" [more than a woman, she was a novel]—to "c'était plus qu'un roman, c'était une femme" [she was more than a novel, she was a woman]. Balzac, as Flaubert and Zola after him, metaphorically represents that his very works generate individuals, here a woman, through his thoughts and words. The path is clear now to see how Balzac's understanding of human codification (social convention and language that construct and transform human identity), together with the fantasy of controlling that construction, combine in his texts to lead to a specific fantasy involving the literary text itself; it is the writer, the new Pygmalion, who could create a new human being through the power of will and language, through the literary text itself.[34] Bourdieu's explanations of the real power of language and social codes indeed make Balzac's fantasy more "realistic."

From Balzac to Flaubert: Anxieties of Distinction

Raphaël has the power to realize wishes, but he does not want to use it. If he utters the words "I wish," even though he does not really want this wish to be granted, the words set in motion a kind of machine of fate that accomplishes the act. This happens when his former teacher pays him a visit in hopes of having Raphaël intervene in his problems at work. Raphaël uses the typical words that one might say when one has no power to intervene in the situation but still wants to be encouraging: "*Je souhaite bien vivement* que vous réussissiez" (*La peau de chagrin,* 10:219) [*I heartily wish* that you succeed]. Even though his intention was not to use the power of the *peau,* his words mechanically act, and the *peau* shrinks. This mechanical functioning of language points out that, once words are unleashed, they continue to generate meanings and act in the world, and intention has nothing to do with their workings. Language, our tool, what distinguishes us from the beast, in fact controls us, defines us, and we have no power over its action. Our powerlessness is perhaps figured in this text by the fact that Raphaël himself becomes a kind of machine, "une sorte d'automate" (10:217) [a kind of automaton]. This may signify that language's mechanical definitions of our identity force us into becoming mechanized, "programmed" beings. *La peau de chagrin,* in fact, takes up the theme of man's mechanical functioning, when Raphaël deliberately assumes a mechanical lifestyle as a defense against the *peau*'s perceived power. He "mena la vie d'une machine à vapeur" (10:217) [lived the life of a steam engine], and his

34. We should recall that in other contexts Balzac was, in fact, interested in "perfecting" the human condition. Education, for instance, could serve to augment the quantity of good in society, as he explains in the "Avant-Propos," 1:12–13. Education will be an important theme below.

body is a machine, as one doctor says: "[L]'étincelle divine, l'intelligence transitoire qui sert comme de lien à la machine et qui produit la volonté, la science de la vie, a cessé de régulariser les phénomènes journaliers du mécanisme et les fonctions de chaque organe" (10:260–61).[35] [The divine spark, that transitory intelligence that serves to connect the machine together and that produces will, the science of life, has ceased to regularize the daily phenomena of the mechanism and the functions of each organ.] Man, rather than controlling his technological productions, is controlled by his own tools, becomes a cog in the machine of language.

If, in Balzac's world, language is a machine that runs on its own, even more threateningly it generates ambiguities rather than certainties. This can be seen in *La peau de chagrin,* where the word "chagrin" takes on two meanings that stand for two opposing interpretations of the book. On the one hand, "chagrin" means unhappiness, and this would stand for the realist explanation for Raphaël's illness and death; he dies because he worries about his problems. On the other hand, "chagrin" means the type of wild ass's skin that magically transforms Raphaël's life; this represents the fantastic interpretation of the book. Language, the word "chagrin," which creates our world, churns out opposing meanings that cannot be resolved but that have crucial importance in determining the status of the real. If one links language, man's tool, with his technological creations, then this machine controls man, but in unpredictable and even uninterpretable ways.

Man as victim of the machine of language, man as machine—both these ideas express anxieties about the crisis of distinction common to all our authors. From the indefinite divide between man and machine, the ambiguity grows, and our six mesmeric characters manifest certain ambiguities of identity that express the crisis of distinction between inner and outer, the imaginary and the real, language and reality. For five of these characters, the ambiguous line between thought and reality becomes the line between madness and sanity. At first sight of Zambinella, Sarrasine has an attack of madness: "Il n'applaudit pas, il ne dit rien, il éprouvait un mouvement de folie, espèce de frénésie qui ne nous agite qu'à cet âge où le désir a je ne sais quoi de terrible et d'infernal" (*Sarrasine,* 6:1061). [He did not applaud, he said nothing, he experienced a mad impulse, a kind of frenzy that affects us only at that age when desire has something terrible and infernal about it.] Frenhofer, when he learns that he has painted a massive

35. Balzac was influenced by La Mettrie, "Avant-propos," 1:1118 n. 11.

confusion of colors on his canvas, says he is mad and then burns his paintings and kills himself. Louis Lambert's gifts put him in a dangerous state near insanity: "Déjà ses sensations intuitives avaient cette *acuité* qui doit appartenir aux perceptions intellectuelles des grands poètes, et les faire souvent approcher de la folie" (*Louis Lambert,* 11:615). [Already his intuitive sensations had that *acuity* that belongs to the intellectual perceptions of great poets, and that often brings them to the brink of madness.] He then becomes "mad" at the end of his life. Balthazar Claës's wife fears that he is going mad, and he becomes one of Balzac's monomaniacs (*La recherche de l'absoulu,* 10:674, 779–80). Finally, there always remains the possibility that Raphaël merely imagines that he gains powers from the *peau,* and thus that he is mad.[36] The blurring of borders between language/will and reality seems linked in Balzac's imagination with the blurring of the borders between madness and sanity, between what happens in the mind and in language and what happens in the real world.[37]

The second ambiguity shared by several of these characters is that of gender identity. Two of these men are described in various ways as having particularly feminine qualities, or as lacking male qualities. Lambert becomes "pâle et blanc comme une femme" [pale and white like a woman], has a "teint de femme" [a woman's complexion], is "vaporeux autant qu'une femme" (*Louis Lambert,* 11:605, 610, 612) [as diaphanous as a woman], and has to be prevented from castrating himself (11:679). Raphaël too is feminine and is associated with castration: "[I]l s'était fait chaste à la manière d'Origène, en châtrant son imagination" (*La peau de chagrin,* 10:217). [He had made himself chaste as did Origen, by castrating his imagination.] Sarrasine, of course, is associated with castration.[38] Thus the power of these men to use thought and language to control reality is associated with gender ambiguities and problems, possibly in a manifestation of anxiety about the extent to which gender identity, more specifically than identity alone, is constructed.[39] Indeed, one remarkable

36. Although Vautrin does not go mad, one might say that he loses his "self" in several ways. He is a kind of protean man who can play many roles and who is ultimately transformed at the end of *Splendeurs et misères des courtisanes* when he symbolically dies after Lucien commits suicide and is then reborn as the head of the police.

37. For Chabert, who embodies the socially constructed nature of identity, Charenton always lurks in the offing as a possibility for him, and indeed he becomes "mad" in the end.

38. I explore gender identity in *Sarrasine* and in *La peau de chagrin* in two previous books, *Fictional Genders* and *Telling Glances.*

39. See Bourdieu, *Distinction,* 474–75, for a description of the anxious, emotional reaction to this kind of ambiguity.

sentence in *Louis Lambert* (11:608) describes the manner in which a social construct can work in a kind of transformism to feminize a man (court etiquette feminizes the king's body): "[L]es lois de l'étiquette et des cours influent sur la moelle épinière au point de féminiser le bassin des rois, d'amollir leurs fibres cérébrales et d'abâtardir ainsi la race."[40] [The rules of etiquette and of royal courts affect spinal marrow to the point of feminizing the pelvis of kings, softening their cerebral fibers, and so degenerating their race.]

Thus in Balzac the idea that language and social codes create us grows in strength, and in fact gives rise in part to the crisis of distinction itself. The question becomes: What is real and what is mere illusion? If thought and language can erase boundaries between the imaginary and the real, between man and woman, between nature and artifice, are there any distinctions at all? Balzac's texts ask this question while at the same time suggesting that there is no difference because the social is the real, the symbolic and the fictional are our reality. It is the *illusio,* "the collective adhesion to the game" of participation in the coded social world, that determines the reality of man's identity and his world (Bourdieu, *Rules of Art,* 167). Even though this understanding brings with it anxieties, Balzac imagines that he himself, the poet/scientist, can intervene in that illusion; his own texts might participate in that construction of the social "reality" that will make the new Paulines.

40. This idea appears also in *La théorie de la démarche,* 12:299. Vautrin once again presents a different and interesting case. He does not have an ambiguous gender identity because he is a "manly" man in the descriptions that use the cultural tags that label gender identity in the context of his time (strength, fearlessness, hairiness, and so on) and also in his relationship to Lucien, whom he calls "[e]ffeminé par tes caprices" [effeminate in your caprices] (even though he says Lucien is also "viril par ton esprit" [virile in your mind]) (*Splendeurs et misères des courtisanes,* 6:477). However, in terms of his sexual orientation, he is not like the other characters in this group because he is homosexual, although that is not a term used at that time.

2

WOMEN, LANGUAGE, AND REALITY: FLAUBERT

L'art grec n'était pas un art, c'était la constitution radicale de tout un peuple, de toute une race, du pays même. [Greek art was not an art, it was the radical constitution of an entire people, of an entire race, of the country itself.]

—FLAUBERT TO LOUISE COLET, 24 APRIL 1852

Un jour j'accoucherais peut-être d'une oeuvre qui serait mienne, au moins. [Some day I might perhaps give birth to a work that would be my own, at least.]

—FLAUBERT TO DU CAMP, 21 OCTOBER 1851

IN GUSTAVE FLAUBERT'S TEXTS, man's animal and mechanical nature, and the surgical attempt to improve on that nature, appear together in one of the most famous operations in French literature, retold here with a deliberately exaggerated emphasis on those elements. A human being cheerfully gallops around like a deer on a malformed foot as wide as that of a horse: "Mais, avec cet équin, large en effet comme un pied de cheval, à peau rugueuse, à tendons secs, à gros orteils, et où les ongles noirs figuraient les clous d'un fer, le stréphopode, depuis le matin jusqu'à la nuit, galopait comme un cerf" (*Madame Bovary,* 1:634). [But, with this equinus, in fact as wide as a horse's hoof, with rough skin, dry tendons, and large toes, whose black toenails looked like the iron nails of a horse's shoe, the strephopode galloped like a deer from morning until night.] The type of foot even bears that horselike scientific name of an *équin,* and its owner's name, Hippolyte, conjures up images of mythological horsemanship. A medical practitioner's surgical intervention aims to improve on this imperfect, animal foot and to refashion it into the surgeon's created, "artificial" perfection.[1] As part of

1. One is reminded of Sarrasine in noting that in Freud the foot has phallic significance; here it could be an improvement of the masculine constitution, as Homais tells Hippolyte: "Alors Homais lui représentait combien il se sentirait ensuite plus gaillard et plus ingambe, et même lui donnait à entendre qu'il s'en trouverait mieux pour plaire aux femmes, et le valet d'écurie se prenait à sourire lourdement" (*Madame Bovary,* 1:633). [Then Homais made him see how much more vigorous and nimble he would feel afterward, and he even insinuated that Hippolyte would be in better shape to please women, and the stable boy began to smile awkwardly.]

the procedure, the surgeon constructs a strange contraption, a "moteur mécanique" (1:634) [mechanical motor], that takes over the healing process after the surgical operation and that will participate in the desired improvement. At the end of the entire operation (after an amputation), the patient becomes a kind of cyborg, part machine, when his deformed leg is replaced with a gleaming mechanical one, "une mécanique compliquée" (1:638) [a complicated mechanism].

This admittedly skewed retelling of Charles's surgical operation on Hippolyte's foot brings to the fore what are, after all, the decidedly strange details of this surgery and frames the questions we shall explore in Flaubert's works. What do this figural animality and this strange mechanics mean in this novel and in Flaubert's works in general? Does this desire to improve on animal nature manifest itself elsewhere in Flaubert's works, even if it is in a form deeply ironized by Flaubert, as it is here? Does this curative impulse figure in Flaubert's literary project itself? How does this desire for perfection relate to women in Flaubert's texts? An analysis of the animal and the mechanical in Flaubert will lead us to the origin of imperfect human nature in his world, and then to Flaubert's fantasized female perfections.

The Miming Animal

Flaubert's representations of our animal nature go hand in hand with transformist ideas (which influenced Balzac before him and develop into evolution in the second part of the century) and lead to some of the deepest and darkest elements of his understanding of our human condition and our relationship to language. His interest in our simian nature reveals itself from the earliest moments of his literary career. The year is 1837, and the newspapers have been filled with stories and articles about humanoid apes and their resemblance to humans.[2] The young Flaubert, still immersed in Romanticism, writes a story entitled "*Quidquid volueris,*" a bizarre tale of horror that begins as a young man, Paul, is about to wed his fiancée, Adèle. Paul is accompanied by a strange, silent companion named Djalioh. During the wedding celebration, Paul recounts to his friends that Djalioh is the product of his scientific "experiment," the coupling of a black slave woman with an orangutan. Time passes, and two years after the marriage, Djalioh, who is desperately in love with

2. Jean Bruneau, *Les débuts littéraires de Gustave Flaubert, 1831–1845* (Paris: Armand Colin, 1962), 129–31.

Adèle, takes her year-old child from its cradle and smashes its head on the ground. He then rapes Adèle, who dies, leaving Djalioh to dash his own head on the chimney. Paul remarries and continues his life of wealthy leisure.

Certainly, this tale written by the adolescent Flaubert must be taken for what it is: a literary experiment, an exaggerated melodrama by a young writer who was influenced by the stories and articles circulating at that time. But it is also important because the themes, and even the details in this story, reappear numerous times in Flaubert's later works, as if they express several core themes of Flaubert's imaginary world.[3] Our simian nature appears, for instance, in a comic form in Flaubert's post-Darwinian, unfinished *Bouvard et Pécuchet:* "'Non! Laissez-moi parler!' Et Bouvard, s'échauffant, alla jusqu'à dire que l'homme descendait du singe! Tous les fabriciens se regardèrent, fort ébahis et comme pour s'assurer qu'ils n'étaient pas des singes."[4] ["No! Let me speak!" And Bouvard, getting worked up, went so far as to say that man descended from the ape! All the vestrymen looked at each other, quite astounded, as if to assure themselves that they weren't monkeys.] And it appears in Flaubert's enthusiastic reception of the translation of Ernst Haeckel's work in 1874: "Je viens de lire *La création naturelle* de Haeckel. Joli bouquin, joli bouquin! Le Darwinisme m'y semble plus clairement exposé que dans les livres de Darwin, même" (To George Sand, 3 July 1874, *Correspondance,* 4 [1998]: 824). [I have just read Haeckel's *History of Creation*. Fine book, fine book! It seems to me that Darwinism is more clearly presented there than in Darwin's own books.] Two of the main topics of Haeckel's book (quite popular at that time) are man's relationship to apes and the new understanding that evolution provides about man's origin and place in nature: "The importance of man's place in nature and his relations to the entirety of things, this question of questions for humanity [. . .] is definitively answered by the knowledge of the animal origin of humans [. . .] The origin of man is linked first to that of mammalian simians."[5] Both these topics prove to have significance in Flaubert's works.

3. Leyla Perrone-Moisés discusses the various ways in which critics have dealt with this early work, in her "*Quidquid volueris:* The Scriptural Education," in *Flaubert and Postmodernism,* ed. Naomi Schor and Henry F. Majewski (Lincoln: University of Nebraska Press, 1984), 139–59. Sartre also sees obsessive and repetitive themes from early to later works, although he discusses different themes, such as aging, or discusses the image of the animal in a different way. Jean-Paul Sartre, *The Family Idiot: Gustave Flaubert, 1821–1857,* trans. Carol Cosman (Chicago: University of Chicago Press, 1981), 1:175.

4. Flaubert, *Bouvard et Pécuchet* in *Oeuvres complètes,* 2:231.

5. Ernst Haeckel, *Histoire de la création des êtres organisés d'après les lois naturelles* (Paris: C. Reinwald, 1874), 6. Even though many of Flaubert's texts could be said to criticize the positivism of his age, I believe that Thiher, *Fiction Rivals Science,* 99, is correct in saying that Flaubert's intellectual honesty forced him to respect the findings of science and to deal with them seriously in his works and thought.

It is in particular the following elements of "*Quidquid volueris*" that orient us as we begin an investigation of the importance of man's animal origin in Flaubert's texts. First is the problem of identity manifested in the hybrid nature of Djalioh, part man, part ape, and in man's relationship to other animals that appear in Flaubert's works, a hybridity that puts into question our distinctness from them (parrots, monkeys, and bears—literally our *bêtise* [stupidity, which in French has the word "beast" as its base]). This problematic identity of man's nature takes part in the more general crisis of distinction in Flaubert's works, the differentiation of man from animal,[6] but in Flaubert it is also the distinctness of humans from each other. Second, man "monkeys" with the natural process of childbirth as he takes control of it and generates an artificial, "unnatural" form of reproduction (Paul's manipulation of the animal/human coupling). Man, in a sense, experiments with new ways of making life, and this intervention in reproduction will take shape in other contexts as the fantasy of a male creating a woman. Finally, in this takeover, the woman is eliminated in a rewriting of the birth story; she dies literally in the story, and figuratively she is a kind of incubator for the experiment. Again, the tone of the story does not allow us to privilege this scientific experiment here and say that this is what Flaubert thinks should happen; rather, what matters for us is the idea that Flaubert imagines situations like these, and the analysis of their significance.

This crisis of the distinction of man from beast appears in different guises in Flaubert's texts, most notably in the oft-repeated image of the similarity between monkeys and men: "Je n'aime guère les singes, et pourtant j'ai tort, car ils me semblent une imitation parfaite de la nature humaine. Quand je vois un de ces animaux,—je ne parle pas ici des hommes,—il me semble me voir dans les miroirs grossissants: mêmes sentiments, mêmes appétits brutaux, un peu moins d'orgueil—et voilà tout" ("*Quidquid volueris*," 1:111) [I don't much like monkeys, yet I am wrong, because they seem to me to be a perfect imitation of human nature. When I see one of these animals—I'm not speaking here of men—it seems to me that I see myself in magnifying mirrors: the same feelings, the same brutal appetites, a bit less pride, and there you have it]; "Je ne sais jamais si c'est moi qui regarde le singe ou si

6. Mary Orr, *Flaubert: Writing the Masculine* (New York: Oxford University Press, 2000), 145, sees this same need for differentiation in the *Trois contes:* "I will argue for Flaubert's *conte* as a study of nature versus culture, of what it is that makes one human rather than animal or superhuman."

c'est le singe qui me regarde. Les singes sont nos aïeux" (*Notes de voyages,* 2:460).[7] [I don't ever know if it is I looking at the monkey or if it is the monkey looking at me. Monkeys are our ancestors.] Just after this scene of simian gazes, Flaubert recounts a dream he had about monkeys that would seem to be closely allied with the context of "*Quidquid volueris.*" The dream symbolism expresses, perhaps, Flaubert's anxiety about man's animal nature, as well as an aggressive need to eliminate that animality:

> J'ai rêvé, il y a environ trois semaines, que j'étais dans une grande forêt toute remplie de singes; ma mère se promenait avec moi. Plus nous avancions, plus il en venait: il y en avait dans les branches, qui riaient et sautaient; il en venait beaucoup dans notre chemin, et de plus en plus grands, de plus en plus nombreux. Ils me regardaient tous, j'ai fini par avoir peur. Ils nous entouraient comme dans un cercle; un a voulu me caresser et m'a pris la main, je lui ai tiré un coup de fusil à l'épaule et je l'ai fait saigner; il a poussé des hurlements affreux. Ma mère m'a dit alors: "Pourquoi le blesses-tu, ton ami? qu'est-ce qu'il t'a fait? ne vois-tu pas qu'il t'aime? comme il te ressemble!" Et le singe me regardait. Cela m'a déchiré l'âme et je me suis réveillé . . . me sentant de la même nature que les animaux et fraternisant avec eux d'une communion toute panthéistique et tendre (*Notes de voyages,* 2:460)[8]
>
> [I dreamt about three weeks ago that I was in a large forest completely filled with monkeys; my mother was walking with me. The farther we advanced, the more of them came out: there were some in the branches that were laughing and jumping; many of them came into our path, and then larger and larger ones, more and more numerous. They were all looking at me; I ended up being afraid. They surrounded us in a kind of circle; one tried to caress me and took my hand; I shot him in the shoulder with a gun and

7. Haeckel as well struggled with the articulation of the distinction between man and ape. For him, the beginnings of life, the germ cells, are alike in all vertebrates (Haeckel, *Histoire de la création,* 266–77); there is thus no distinction at the point of our origin. In the first month of development, the human continues to share the qualities of other species: it has a tail like a monkey (273). As the discussion of man's link to apes continues, the question inevitably becomes: How do we distinguish ourselves from them? Haeckel emphasizes that we can no longer hold on to the belief that we are somehow superior in the way that we were created: "You will certainly allow that I don't at all accept the widespread prejudice that assigns man a privileged place in creation" (262).

8. It is significant that in *La tentation de saint Antoine,* 1:536, we read: "[C]elui qui tue un animal deviendra cet animal." [He who kills an animal will become that animal.]

> I made him bleed. He let out horrible wails. My mother then said to me: "Why are you hurting it, your friend? What did it do to you? Don't you see that it loves you? How it resembles you!" And the monkey looked at me. That tore my heart out and I woke up . . . feeling that I was of the same nature as the animals and fraternizing with them in an entirely pantheistic and tender communion.]

His mother chides him for his violent attempt to break out of the circle of apes: her appearance here ties the image of the mother to the monkey theme, a strong tie that I investigate below.[9] His shooting of the monkey seems to be an attempt to escape his predicament; however, he too is the victim in the end when he recognizes that he and the monkey are one. He accepts his fraternal, simian heritage.

This dream taps into a kind of obsessive image in Flaubert's texts. It resembles the familiar scene in "Saint Julien l'Hospitalier" in which Julien is surrounded by animals (including monkeys) and is threatened by their gaze: "[Ç]à et là, parurent entre les branches quantité de larges étincelles, comme si le firmament eût fait pleuvoir dans la forêt toutes ses étoiles. C'étaient des yeux d'animaux [. . .] Et tous les animaux qu'il avait poursuivis se représentèrent, faisant autour de lui un cercle étroit" (*Trois contes,* 2:184).[10] [Here and there a number of large sparks appeared between the branches, as if the firmament had rained down all its stars on the forest. They were animal eyes (. . .) And all the animals he had pursued appeared again, making a tight circle around him.] In that story, Julien's actions clearly make him more beastly than the beasts that surround him.[11] The mother also appears there when Julien's explicitly bestial nature confronts her: "[I]l rentrait au milieu de la nuit, couvert de sang et de boue, avec des épines dans les cheveux et sentant l'odeur des bêtes farouches. Il devint comme elles. Quand sa mère l'embrassait, il acceptait froidement son étreinte" (2:180).[12] [He came back in the middle of the night, covered with blood and dirt, with thorns in his hair and smelling of wild beasts. He became like them. When his mother kissed him, he coldly accepted

9. One might interpret this scene as a representation of the "animal" and incestuous desire for the mother. In order to break out of the inner circle where he is with his mother and dominated by the animal, he must eliminate the animal.

10. Biasi notes the repetitive nature of this scene in his *Carnets de travail: Gustave Flaubert,* ed. Pierre-Marc de Biasi (Paris: Balland, 1988), 262–63.

11. In *Mémoires d'un fou,* 1:234, we find again the bestial nature of man: "Que sera l'homme alors, lui qui est déjà plus féroce que les bêtes fauves, et plus vil que les reptiles?" [What will man be then, he who is already more ferocious than wild animals, viler than reptiles?]

12. In "Passion et vertu," 1:117, Mazza's husband's kisses seem to her like those of an ape.

her embrace.] In both the dream and the short story, the "animal" nature of man has a contextual link to the son's relations with his mother.

In the scene in which the staring animals surround Julien, we find alongside the monkey another favorite animal in the Flaubert bestiary, the parrot: "C'étaient des yeux d'animaux, des chats sauvages, des écureuils, des hiboux, des perroquets, des singes" (*Trois contes,* 2:184). [They were animal eyes, of wildcats, squirrels, owls, parrots, monkeys.] Parrots, of course, resemble man in that they speak, and they resemble both man and monkey in that they mimic.[13] Flaubert himself made the connection between the two animal species: "Les perroquets sont des singes ailés" [Parrots are winged monkeys].[14]

It is in "Un coeur simple" that the parrot becomes important. Here the animal is linked to the sublime, whereas the human, Félicité, is "bête" in the more figural sense of the word meaning stupid. Indeed, in "Un coeur simple" the parrot ends up speaking much more understandably than does the human, Félicité, who in her old age answered her Loulou "par des mots sans plus de suite, mais où son coeur s'épanchait" (*Trois contes,* 2:175) [by disconnected words, but in which her heart poured itself out]. The monkey does not fail to appear in this story too, in the comical context of the "géographie en estampes" [a geography book with engravings], but its context is the same as that of "*Quidquid volueris,*" the monkey as the violent ravager of women, a scene reminiscent of *Candide:* "Elles [les estampes] représentaient différentes scènes du monde, des anthropophages coiffés de plumes, un singe enlevant une demoiselle" (*Trois contes,* 2:168).[15] [The engravings represented different scenes from around the world, cannibals with feather headdresses, a monkey kidnapping a damsel.]

13. Perron-Moisés, "*Quidquid volueris,*" 158 n. 25, notes the hominid nature of these two animals and points out that, because of the close historical link between Normandy and Brazil, there were representations of these animals linked with savages very close to Flaubert's home: "Up through the nineteenth century, there existed a house in Rouen called the Ile du Brésil; its wooden ornaments can still be found at the city's museum of antiquities. In these friezes one can see savages, parrots, and apes."

14. Gustave Flaubert, *Plans, notes et scénarios de "Un coeur simple,"* ed. François Fleury (Rouen: Lecerf, 1977), 30 (fol. 388r of the manuscript). All three species—monkey, communicating bird, and man—occur together in another work projected by Flaubert (*Carnets de travail,* 262–63).

15. The ambiguous and comical sense of "*bêtise*" has received wonderful treatment by Tony Tanner, Jonathan Culler, and Julian Barnes, especially the recurrent bovine detail in *Madame Bovary* and in Flaubert's vision of himself as a bear (bears would seem to resemble humans in form when they stand upright and, for Flaubert, in personality). Tony Tanner, *Adultery in the Novel: Contract and Transgression* (Baltimore: Johns Hopkins University Press, 1979), 236. Jonathan Culler, "The Uses of Madame Bovary," in *Flaubert and Postmodernism,* ed. Naomi Schor and Henry F. Majewski (Lincoln: University of Nebraska Press, 1984), 1–12. Julian Barnes, *Flaubert's Parrot* (New York: McGraw-Hill, 1985).

Mechanical Man

The animal aspect of man's nature converges in Flaubert's works, as it does in Balzac's, with the theme of man as a kind of machine. Flaubert singled out the mechanical nature of life as revealed by evolutionary theory in some notes that he took on Darwin's *Descendance de l'homme:* "On procède à l'analyse d'un corps organisé comme on procéderait à celui *d'une machine très compliquée.* Le mouvement ne procède plus de la force vitale, mais d'une quantité de chaleur fournie par la combustion" (*Carnets de travail,* 491–92; emphasis added). [One goes about the analysis of an organized body as one would analyze *a very complicated machine.* Movement comes no longer from the vital force but from an amount of heat produced by combustion.] These reflections on evolution are not the first on the idea of mechanical man in Flaubert; as early as 1847, he spoke of the human body as a machine, following the long French tradition: "Convenons que l'homme (ou la femme; l'un et l'autre vaut mieux) est une triste machine" (To Louise Colet, 23 September 1847, *Correspondance,* 1 [1973]: 473). [Let's agree that man (or woman; man and woman is better) is a sad machine.]

This theme of the machine appears most frequently in Flaubert's realist novels about the society contemporaneous with his own, and it is particularly prevalent in *L'éducation sentimentale,* which begins with a description of a machine, a steamboat. As the steamboat carries Frédéric and the reader into his life voyage, a kind of analogy develops between him and the boat based on the thermodynamic metaphor of breathing, heat, and combustion, a metaphor cited above in Flaubert's notes on Darwin and frequently used in scientific contexts of the time.[16] Frédéric "poussa un grand soupir" [let out a great sigh] to accompany the "respiration" of the machine, which "crachait avec un râle lent et rythmique son panache de fumée noire" (*L'éducation sentimentale,* 2:8) [spit out its plume of black smoke with a slow and rhythmic groan]. The resemblance between Frédéric

16. The grand metaphor is of man the steam engine, or, as Coleman calls it, an "energy conversion device" (Coleman, *Biology in the Nineteenth Century,* 123). Lavoisier summarized the working of this energy machine: "The animal machine [. . .] is governed by three main regulators: respiration, which consumes oxygen and carbon and provides heating power; perspiration, which increases or decreases according to whether a great deal of heat has to be transported or not; and finally digestion, which restores to the blood what it loses in breathing and perspiration" (quoted in Jacob, *Logic of Life,* 43). Serres discusses the metaphors involved in the human steam engine in *Feux et signaux de brume,* as does Dolf Sternberger in *Panorama of the Nineteenth Century,* trans. Joachim Neugroschel (New York: Urizen Books, 1977).

and the steamboat is further emphasized by the similarity in their names: Moreau is contained in the name of the boat, *Ville de* Mon*te*reau. The breathing that forms the basis of the similarity actually seems better performed by the machine, which "fumait à gros tourbillons" [emitted great whirls of steam], whereas the people arrive "hors d'haleine" [out of breath] (2:8).[17] Frédéric then starts out the text and his voyage as a metaphorical representative of man's mechanical nature.

This mechanical nature is most basically our physical nature, our body. In the 1845 version of *L'éducation sentimentale,* Jules bemoans the bodily (animal) mechanisms that make of him a kind of puppet blindly pushed here and there by external and internal forces: "Je n'ai plus ni espérance, ni projet, ni force, ni volonté, je vais et je vis comme une roue qu'on a poussée et qui roulera jusqu'à ce qu'elle tombe, comme une feuille qui vole au vent tant que l'air la soutient, comme la pierre jetée, qui descend jusqu'à ce qu'elle trouve le fond—*machine humaine* qui verse des larmes et sécrète des douleurs, chose inerte qui se trouve là sans cause, créée par une force incompréhensible et qui ne comprend rien à elle-même" (*L'éducation sentimentale,* 1845 ed., 1:314; emphasis added). [I have no more hope, nor project, nor force, nor will; I go and I live like a wheel that has been pushed and that will roll until it falls over, like a leaf that flies in the wind as long as the air holds it up, like the stone dropped that falls until it finds the bottom—*a human machine* that sheds tears and secretes pains, an inert thing that finds itself here without cause, created by an incomprehensible force, and that understands nothing of itself.]

Powerless and subject to unknown forces, humans can function mechanically also when they are subject to unconscious routine and habit; one becomes a kind of automaton or marionette. There is, for instance, the oft-commented automatic life of Félicité, who "toujours silencieuse, la taille droite et les gestes mesurés, semblait une femme en bois, fonctionnant d'une manière automatique" (*Trois contes,* 2:166) [always silent, with straight posture and measured gestures, seemed to be a wooden woman functioning in an automatic manner]. When Emma is stunned by her predicament at the end of *Madame Bovary,* she functions like an automaton: "Quatre heures sonnèrent; et elle se leva pour s'en retourner à Yonville, obéissant comme un automate à l'impulsion des habitudes" (*Madame Bovary,* 1:675). [Four o'clock struck, and she got up to return to

17. It is tempting to conjure up the presence of the steamship in *L'Ève future* later, and its sinking at the end of the novel, a shipwreck that parallels the demise of the machine-woman.

Yonville, obeying like an automaton the force of habit.] The human-automaton receives a more literal embodiment in an early text, "Rêve d'enfer," dating from 1837, the same year as "*Quidquid volueris.*" This text describes a kind of automaton that has a body and mind but no heart: "on eût dit, à le voir ainsi sérieux et froid, un automate qui pensait comme un homme" ("Rêve d'enfer," 1:90) [one would have said, to see him so serious and cold, he was an automaton that thought like a man].[18]

Thus, in Flaubert's world, we humans are material objects, machines or puppets, animated by forces of which we know little. It is significant that readers contemporary with Flaubert discerned a kind of mechanical universe in his works; they believed that "he sees in human action only the inevitable operation of implacable laws" (Weinberg, *French Realism,* 161). This theme of our mechanical nature participates in the century's fascination with various manifestations of actions that we undertake without volition or consciousness. Flaubert, like Balzac, knew about mesmerism and occasionally included it in his works, such as in *Bouvard et Pécuchet,* where it receives extended and comical treatment.

The Flaubertian twist given to mesmerism, however, picks up on its suspiciously sexual nature. It both reveals mechanical processes at work and is frequently linked to sexual attraction or seduction, as if our animal nature (sexual instinct) appeared to make us function automatically (mechanically).[19] In the early "Passion et vertu," Ernest makes Mazza, the woman he seduces, believe in magnetism, thus seducing her in two ways, intellectually and sexually ("Passion et vertu," 1:114). And both Frédéric and Rodolphe attempt to justify illicit sexual relations by means of magnetic attractions and special affinities. Here is Frédéric: "Une force existait qui peut, à travers les espaces, mettre en rapport deux personnes, les avertir de ce qu'elles éprouvent et les faire se rejoindre" (*L'éducation sentimentale,* 2:79). [A force existed that could put two people in touch with each other across a distance,

18. According to Sartre, Flaubert saw himself as the "nonspeaking animal" and his brother, Achille, as the "robot" (Sartre, *Family Idiot,* 1:25). Dominick LaCapra has noted how Flaubert enjoyed the marionette theater at the Rouen fair and how Bouvard and Pécuchet resemble the slapstick marionettes that pleased Flaubert there. Dominick LaCapra, *Madame Bovary on Trial* (Ithaca: Cornell University Press, 1982), 102.

19. As we saw in the Introduction, mesmerism was suspected of being some kind of illicit form of seduction. In a letter to Louise Colet, Flaubert describes the animal nature of his own love: "Oui je me sens maintenant des appétits de bêtes fauves, des instincts d'amour carnassier et déchirant, je ne sais pas si c'est aimer" (8–9 August 1846, *Correspondance,* 1:282). [Yes, I now feel I have the appetites of wild beasts, the carnivorous and rending instincts of love; I don't know if that is to love.]

alert them to what they were feeling, and draw them together.] It is most significant that Rodolphe speaks to Madame Bovary about the inevitability of their magnetic love at the same time that Monsieur Derozerays describes our emergence from our animal origins, thus linking the mysteriously mechanical nature of sexuality with evolution (determinism, mechanistic processes) contextually if not substantively: "Rodolphe, avec madame Bovary, causait rêves, pressentiments, magnétisme. Remontant au berceau des sociétés, l'orateur nous dépeignait ces temps farouches où les hommes vivaient de glands, au fond des bois. Puis ils avaient quitté la dépouille des bêtes, endossé le drap, creusé des sillons, planté la vigne" (*Madame Bovary,* 1:624). [Rodolphe, with Madame Bovary, was speaking of dreams, presentiments, and magnetism. Harking back to the cradle of civilization, the orator described to us those savage times when men lived on acorns in the depths of woods. Then they left off wearing animal skins, donned cloth, dug furrows, planted the vine.] The droning voice of Léon, who reads poetry to Emma—poetry being the seducer par excellence for her—seems to hypnotize her into automatic actions: "Emma l'écoutait, en faisant tourner machinalement l'abat-jour de la lampe" (1:607). [Emma listened to him while mechanically turning the lamp shade]. Is it then by chance that Emma becomes aware of the sexual attraction that exists between Léon and her when they go to see a new mill being built, with its mechanical "roues d'engrenages" (1:608) [gear wheels]?

Finally, all these elements of man's animal and mechanical natures—sexuality, monkeys, automatism—work together in one scene in *L'éducation sentimentale* when Deslauriers dances with a woman at the Alhambra: "Les musiciens, juchés sur l'estrade, dans des postures de *singes,* raclaient et soufflaient, impétueusement. Le chef d'orchestre, debout, battait la mesure d'une façon *automatique* [. . .] Deslauriers *pressait contre lui la petite femme,* et, gagné par le délire du cancan, se démenait au milieu des quadrilles comme *une grande marionnette*" (*L'éducation sentimentale,* 2:34; emphasis added). [The musicians, perched on the stage in *monkey*-like postures, strummed and blew furiously. The conductor beat time *automatically* (. . .) Deslauriers *pressed the little woman against him,* and, swept up in the frenzy of the cancan, flailed about in the middle of the quadrilles like *a big marionette.*] Thus our sexual instincts appear to be a kind of mechanical animality, a representation that unites reproduction (sexual instincts) and mechanistic functions in a vision of the human being as a product of material, physical processes. Flaubert's interest in automatism and in mesmerism's relationship to seduction shows his preoccupation with the way in which physical and mental processes that function independently of consciousness can direct bodies and minds.[20]

Mechanical Substitutions

Through this network of themes involving humankind's animal and mechanical nature, Flaubert's works explore the ambiguities of human identity and form an essential part of his particular form of the crisis of distinction. Flaubert's own brand of this crisis I describe as substitutability: a human and an animal, and a human and a machine, are so similar as to permit their substitutability. How do we distinguish humans from these other two categories? This crisis fans out into many of the most basic elements of Flaubert's works. I shall review some of these well-worn topics here—particularly those of commoditization, prostitution, and cliché—while weaving them into our particular context of mechanical animality and substitutability, in order to give quick shape to the effects of the crisis Flaubert articulates and would want to remedy.

The basic question at the heart of the crisis of human identity in Flaubert is: Am I a unique individual or am I so like others that I can easily be replaced by someone or something else? What defines me as a particular human being? What is my role, a role that will make me distinct from my neighbor, from an animal, from a machine, from the bourgeois horde?[21] Am I merely a cog in a machine of determinism and repetition that controls me? This is similar to the anxiety of the upper classes described by Bourdieu, the fear that one may "fall into the homogeneous, the undifferentiated," which betrays "an obsessive fear of number, of undifferentiated hordes indifferent to difference" (Bourdieu, *Distinction,* 469). Flaubert wants to retain the distinction, as shown when he praises Taine for exalting "l'individu si rabaissé de nos jours par la démocrasserie" (5? November 1866, *Correspondance* 3 [1991]: 548) [the individual, so disparaged today by "democrassery"].

20. One could imagine that Flaubert's bouts with seizures most likely reinforced his view of the human body as subjected to unknown forces and actions.

21. Ross Chambers clearly delineates the attempt of post-1848 French writers to distinguish their discourse from the bourgeois "words of the tribe," to establish that their works are different from clichés, because these writers experience "the anxiety of difference." See Introduction. In her excellent *Flaubert: Writing the Masculine,* 115, Orr looks at the problem of becoming a male individual and distinguishing oneself in that way in Flaubert's works. She goes so far as to say that Flaubert in his works creates the "individualization of certain male characters as against the clone-like reproductions of others."

This anxiety appears early when Flaubert the adolescent tries to map out his future. He would like to be unique, but he complains that there is perhaps no distinctive road for him to take, only well-trodden paths to follow: "Je serai un homme honnête, rangé et tout le reste si tu veux, je serai comme un autre, comme il faut, comme tous, un avocat, un médecin, un sous-préfet, un notaire, un avoué, un *juge* tel quel, une stupidité comme toutes les stupidités, un homme du monde ou de cabinet ce qui est encore plus bête. Car il faudra bien être quelque chose de tout cela et il n'y a pas de milieu" (to Ernest Chevalier, 23 July 1839, *Correspondance,* 1:49). [I will be an honest man, steady and all the rest if you please; I will be like another, as I am supposed to be, like everyone, a lawyer, a doctor, an official, a notary, an attorney, a plain old *judge,* a stupidity like all stupidities, a man of the world or of the office, which is even stupider. For one must be a part of all that and there is no middle ground.] Flaubert's choice of a writing career at least allowed him to pursue an identity different from those listed; he is not substitutable for one of those undesirables.[22]

This anxiety about identity and substitutability can be found to a greater or lesser degree in general in Flaubert's work, but it occurs most famously, once again, in *L'éducation sentimentale,* which one might be tempted to call the novel of mechanical substitutions. People substitute for other people as they take one another's places: Rosanette circulates among a good number of male characters in the novel. Deslauriers tries to take Frédéric's place in his relationship with women. Frédéric sees one woman and dreams of another. Hussonnet takes over Arnoux's journal.[23]

More insidious, perhaps, is the fact that because persons are materially determined objects they are, then, like things, and things can take over the role of a human being. As we see Madame Arnoux through Frédéric's eyes, it seems that she *is* her things and that selling her clothes means tearing up her very body: "[L]e partage de ces reliques, où il retrouvait confusément les formes de ses membres, lui semblait une atrocité, comme s'il avait vu des corbeaux déchiquetant son cadavre" (*L'éducation sentimentale,* 2:158).[24] [The distribution of these relics, in which he could still vaguely make out the forms of her limbs, seemed an atrocity to him, as if he had seen crows tearing up her corpse.] Léon feels that he is stepping on a person if he treads on Emma's dress (*Madame*

22. See Bourdieu's *Rules of Art* for an analysis of Flaubert's quest for distinction in the literary field.

23. In "Un coeur simple," Félicité manages to substitute her Loulou for the Holy Spirit, and in another instance goes so far as to become, in her own mind, Virginie: "[I]l lui sembla qu'elle était elle-même cette enfant" (*Trois contes,* 2:170). [It seemed to her that she was herself that child.]

24. This reminds one of Emma's figural dissection when her things are sold off.

Bovary, 1:607). In what is perhaps the most humorous example (replete with an ironic exclamation point of outrage) of the substitution and devaluation of individuals and the valorization of things, Sénécal takes Frédéric's place in relationship both to Deslauriers, the person, and to Arnoux's *things:* "Deslauriers lui apprenait qu'il avait recueilli Sénécal; et depuis quinze jours, ils vivaient ensemble. Donc Sénécal s'étalait, maintenant, au milieu des choses qui provenaient de chez Arnoux!" (*L'éducation sentimentale,* 2:42).[25] [Deslauriers informed him that he had taken in Sénécal and that for the last two weeks they had been living together. So Sénécal was now sprawled out amid the things that had come from Arnoux's place!]

Prostitution as the ultimate commodification of the human being has often been discussed in Flaubert. Almost everyone in *L'éducation sentimentale* seems to have a price. Linked to this degradation of people through selling is the degradation of art, especially as represented in *L'éducation sentimentale,* which becomes more and more commercial. Art, the one thing that might provide a means of escape for Flaubert from crass bourgeois uniformity, turns out to be a thing too, a thing whose worth is calculable and that is ever more valued for the amount of money that it can bring. Again, very early in his writing career, in the essay of 1839, "Les arts et le commerce," Flaubert shows disappointment about the way art is becoming devalued in a society that appreciates only commerce and profit ("Les arts et le commerce," 1:184–86). *L'éducation sentimentale* posits this degradation of art in the values of Arnoux, a name one might complete as "Art-nou-veau," the new, bourgeois, knick-knack conception of utilitarian art, ceramics and "le sublime à bon marché" (*L'éducation sentimentale,* 2:22) [the sublime at a cheap price]. Arnoux's journal, appropriately entitled *L'art industriel,* signifies a kind of industrialization, mechanization, and commoditization of art.[26] Indeed, this kind of art is itself described as a type of marketing machine by Flaubert in a letter to Louise Colet in which he laments "la

25. This theme of the commodification and reification of the human being appears in a bizarre way in a project in which Flaubert envisioned a house as being a subject, an individual, just like a person (*Carnets de travail,* 238). That clothes can be more durable, more lasting and "real" than the person who wears them, appears in an image in "Un coeur simple" where Virginie's clothes still hold the folds made by her body long after her death: "Le soleil éclairait ces pauvres objets, en faisait voir les taches, et des plis formés par les mouvements du corps" (*Trois contes,* 2:173). [The sun shone on those poor objects, showing their stains and the creases formed by the body's movements.]

26. J. A. Hiddleston, "Flaubert and *L'art industriel,*" *French Studies Bulletin,* Summer 1985, 4–5, notes that in the same journal in which parts of *La tentation de saint Antoine* were published (*L'artiste*), and at approximately the same time (1856–57), a new publication was annexed to each number of this journal. Its title was *Les arts industriels,* and its purpose was to "inform its readers about works in bronze, jewelry, engravings, prints, photography, furniture," which it did in three articles entitled "L'art industriel."

mécanique! la mécanique!" ["the mechanics! the mechanics!"] in speaking of Dumas, who wants to sell to the most consumers (15–16 September 1846, *Correspondance,* 1:343). Art, then, like humans, becomes a marketable, mechanically produced and clichéd object.

In the context of the crisis of distinction, the question of art for Flaubert comes back to the vexed nature of identity. Is the work of art a manifestation of the unique talents, mind, and will of the individual artist (a question taken up by Proust later), or is it a mechanically generated product of a particular body and environment? In a letter of 1864, Flaubert writes an interesting sentence that formulates this question of art in the context of the determinism of his era. Does art come from a "personal" source, either from the genius of individual will or from the divine, falling from the sky as inspiration; or is it merely mechanically produced without an individual creative or divine source? This is Flaubert's answer: "Autrefois, on croyait que la littérature était une chose toute personnelle et que les oeuvres tombaient du ciel comme des aérolithes. Maintenant, on nie toute volonté, tout absolu. La vérité est, je crois, dans l'*entre-deux*" (To Edma Roger des Genettes, 20 October 1864, *Correspondance,* 3:411; emphasis added). [In the past, it was thought that literature was something completely individual and that works fell from the sky like meteorites. But now any idea of the will, of the absolute, is denied. The truth is, I think, somewhere *in between.*] Flaubert finds that there is a certain amount of the automatic, the nonindividual, in art, but also that the individual or the inspirational exists. That the two are mixed together in an *entre-deux,* that there is not a clear answer, corresponds well to the crisis of distinction we have been discussing.

Art and the individual, substitutability and creativity, the crisis of distinction—all perhaps come down to the central problem in Flaubert's universe: language. Substitution *is* the rhetorical function of language. Because of similarities, equivalences, we make metaphors and similes, we connect disparate things. One thing then stands in for another, people for things, words for life, metaphors for the literal. It is because of the similarity between the dove, as religious icon representing the Holy Spirit, and the parrot, that Félicité substitutes the one for the other, real object for symbol, the ridiculous for the sublime (consequently blurring them together). In the following quotation from *L'éducation sentimentale,* it is clear that human substitutability, here that of one woman for another in Frédéric's life and thoughts, has its foundation in the suggestions given by words (here a name) and situations. Frédéric is at the Dambreuse house, where he entertains the possibility of taking Madame Dambreuse as a mistress. He then, through associations he makes when Monsieur Dambreuse mentions a name, goes through a list of other women in his life who substitute one for the other in his thoughts: "Le financier n'en était pas surpris, d'après tous les éloges que faisait de lui M. Roque. A ce nom, Frédéric revit la petite Louise, sa maison, sa chambre; et il se rappela des nuits pareilles, où il restait à sa fenêtre, écoutant les rouliers qui passaient. Ce souvenir de ses tristesses amena la pensée de Mme Arnoux; et il se taisait, tout en continuant à marcher sur la terrasse" (*L'éducation sentimentale,* 2:67). [The financier was not surprised by this, after all the praise that Monsieur Roque had lavished on him. At the mention of this name, Frédéric pictured little Louise, his house, his room; and he remembered other such nights when he stayed by his window listening to the cart drivers as they passed by. This memory of his sorrows led him to think of Madame Arnoux, and he remained silent while continuing to stroll on the terrace.] Indeed, it is almost as if substitutability takes on a life of its own; it becomes a kind of runaway machine of association that takes Frédéric with it. Other readers of Flaubert have also noted this rather fearsome mechanics of substitutability. Tony Tanner (*Adultery in the Novel,* 316), for instance, describes how the word *comme* makes everything run together, and Leyla Perrone-Moisés ("*Quidquid volueris,*" 152) says of Flaubert, "He lets himself slip into comparisons and shows that the word *like* can engender an automatic and infinite discourse."

Not only do we succumb to this mechanical substitutability of language and thought, we also use language mechanically, without understanding, just as the telegraph operator maneuvers his lines, manipulating, literally, the machine of language, without understanding it: "Quelle drôle de vie que celle de l'homme qui reste là, dans cette petite cabane à faire mouvoir ces deux perches et à tirer sur ces ficelles; rouage inintelligent d'une machine muette pour lui, il peut mourir sans connaître un seul des événements qu'il a appris, un seul mot de tous ceux qu'il aura dits. Le but? le but? le sens? qui le sait? [...] Un peu plus, un peu moins, ne sommes-nous pas tous comme ce brave homme, parlant des mots qu'on nous a appris et que nous apprenons sans les comprendre" (*Par les champs et par les grèves,* 2:484).[27] [What an odd life, that of the man who stays there, in that little shack, moving those two poles and pulling on those lines; mindless cog in a machine that is silent for

27. Jonathan Culler comments on this quotation in *Flaubert: The Uses of Uncertainty* (Ithaca: Cornell University Press, 1985), 166. This must have been the Chappe telegraph that had a post in Nantes.

him, he can die without knowing one single event that he reported, a single word out of all of those that he will have said. The purpose? The purpose? The meaning? Who knows? (. . .) A bit more or less, are we not all like this good fellow, speaking words that we have been taught and that we learn without understanding?]

This certainly makes it difficult to see how language/literature would save us from mechanical processes, because speaking is often itself an automatic process. In *L'éducation sentimentale,* Frédéric answers "mechanically"; several speakers at the clubs go on like talking machines: "[L]'orateur continuait comme une machine" [the speaker continued like a machine]; and the Spaniard, who continues speaking even though no one can understand him because he is speaking in Spanish, rolls his eyes "comme un automate" (*L'éducation sentimentale,* 2:75, 119–20) [like an automaton]. Most significant, this Spaniard was first described as "une espèce de singe-nègre" [a kind of monkey/black man]—here the monkey/human of "*Quidquid volueris*" merges with the speaking automaton to mock human intellect in this chaotic "Club de l'Intelligence" (2:118, 119). A human is a kind of automatic talking machine that can merely repeat, copy, and significant for our context, "ape" a language that others have used and that is not original.[28] Human language is always and necessarily repetition and thus cliché—even literary language.

One particular, very familiar scene can help draw together the many threads involved in this Flaubertian crisis of distinction. Are we mere animals, or something more? Are we machines, or do we have free will and independence? Is literature a manifestation of the individual, or is it a mere mechanical product? Our context of the crisis of distinction allows us to see various elements of the following well-known scene in a different light; it brings out the image of a monkey dancing in a kind of "art" machine:

> Une valse aussitôt commençait, et, sur l'orgue, dans un petit salon, des danseurs hauts comme le doigt, femmes en turban rose, Tyroliens en jaquette, singes en habit noir, messieurs en culotte courte, tournaient, tournaient entre les fauteuils, les canapés, les consoles, se répétant dans les morceaux de miroir que raccordait à

28. This thematization of the automatism of language has interesting links to Richard Terdiman's analysis of the "potential toward automatism" of the dominant discourse in his analysis of nineteenth-century France. See Richard Terdiman, *Discourse/Counter-Discourse: The Theory and Practice of Symbolic Resistance in Nineteenth-Century France* (Ithaca: Cornell University Press, 1985), 61.

leurs angles un filet de papier doré. L'homme faisait aller sa manivelle, regardant à droite, à gauche et vers les fenêtres. De temps à autre, tout en lançant contre la borne un long jet de salive brune, il soulevait du genou son instrument, dont la bretelle dure lui fatiguait l'épaule; et, tantôt dolente et traînarde, ou joyeuse et précipitée, la musique de la boîte s'échappait en bourdonnant à travers un rideau de taffetas rose, sous une griffe de cuivre en arabesque. (*Madame Bovary,* 1:596)

[A waltz immediately began, and, on the organ, in a small sitting room, dancers the size of a finger, women in pink turbans, Tyrolians in jackets, monkeys in dress coats, gentlemen in knee breeches, were turning, turning among the chairs, the sofas, the consoles, their images repeated in pieces of mirror connected at their corners by a strip of gold paper. The man turned the crank, looking right, left, and toward the windows. From time to time, while he spat a long jet of brown saliva onto the boundary stone, he used his knee to lift his instrument, whose hard strap strained his shoulder; and, at times sad and sluggish, or joyful and hurried, the music escaped from the box, droning through a pink taffeta curtain, under a brass claw in arabesque style.]

The machine is the organ-grinder's instrument that makes the music and makes the miniature dancers turn. Thus here, figural representations of both art (music) and human action (dance) are mechanically produced and repeated by the continuous turning of the handle.[29] Art also becomes a kind of mechanical repetition at the meta-textual level in the sense that this very passage of the text, this miniature ball scene, "repeats" the earlier ball scene of the Vaubyessard, albeit in a "diminished" and degraded form that symbolizes the degradation of the repetitious nature of language as cliché. Moreover, one important word in this mini-ball scene is repeated from the original ball scene and is itself repeated in this scene, a word that itself expresses repetition: "tournaient, tournaient." Flaubert's art constructs and symbolizes itself here as repetition, and repetition that is thus

29. There is an odd similarity between this scene and that analyzed above from *L'éducation sentimentale,* in which Deslauriers dances like an automaton to music directed by a mechanical maestro and played by monkey-like men.

subject to the degradation of cliché. What better symbol of this repetition than the small mirror in the box that repeats the image of the toy dancers who themselves repeat the actions of the real waltzers of the Vaubyessard? Perhaps only that of the monkeys who, dressed in men's clothes, dance with the humans in the box. Thus monkeys figure here the determinist foundation of our human nature, the fact that we are a product of implacable natural laws, that we are "mechanical" productions of evolution. And our simian nature is also our *bêtise,* our reliance on the tawdry, "aping" clichés of a degraded culture and its language. This is then what Flaubert might want to change.

The Origins of the Problem

The origin of humankind's simian nature as outlined by evolution is related in Flaubert to human origin in another sense: the conception and birth of the individual human being.[30] In several representations of primal scenes, Flaubert describes the actual act of physical human creation. These scenes manifest an attitude of disgust with reproduction, perhaps in part as a kind of condemnation of this simian, miming nature. In *Mémoires d'un fou,* the narrator represents the "primal scene" of the insemination, gestation, and birth of his imaginary reader/interlocutor, an origin described with repulsion and that emphasizes our bestial nature: "[T]u es donc né fatalement, parce que ton père un jour sera revenu d'une orgie, échauffé par le vin et des propos de débauche, et que ta mère en aura profité, qu'elle aura mis en jeu toutes les ruses de femme poussée par ses instincts de chair et de bestialité que lui a donnés la nature [. . .] Quelque grand que tu sois, tu as d'abord été quelque chose d'aussi sale que de la

30. Indeed, the new ideas provided by evolution about the origins of the human species were accompanied by changes in the scientific understanding of the physical origin of each individual human: in 1827 the mammalian egg was verified by von Baer, and in 1843 the presence of sperm within the egg was observed. Early nineteenth-century embryology proved that development was the "production in a cumulative manner of increasingly complex structures from an initially more or less homogeneous material" (Coleman, *Biology in the Nineteenth Century,* 37, 35). Flaubert was also interested in the cell and the origins of life, for example, as shown in an unusual scene when he meets one of the Goncourt brothers on the street and says that the defeat of the saint is due to "the scientific cell" in reference to the end of *La tentation de saint Antoine* and the birth of life. Edmond de Goncourt, *Journal des Goncourt: Mémoires de la vie littéraire,* vol. 4: *1870–71* (Paris: Fasquelle Charpentier, 1911), 352 (18 October 1871).

salive et de plus fétide que de l'urine; puis tu as subi des métamorphoses comme un ver, et enfin tu es venu au monde" (*Mémoires d'un fou,* 1:244–45). [You were thus inevitably born, because your father one day came back from an orgy, fired up by wine and debauched talk, and because your mother took advantage of that, because she put into play all the wiles of a woman pressed by the bestial instincts of her flesh, which nature gave to her (. . .) However great you are, you were first something as foul as saliva and as fetid as urine; then you underwent metamorphoses like a larva, and at last you came into the world.] In a letter to Louise Colet, Flaubert similarly criticizes his own parents and the act that created him one night: "D'ailleurs je ne peux pas m'empêcher de garder une rancune éternelle à ceux qui m'ont mis au monde et qui m'y retiennent, ce qui est pire. Ah, parbleu! c'était de l'amour aussi ça, sans doute. La belle chose! ils s'aimaient! ils se le disaient et une nuit ils m'ont fait, pour leur plus grande satisfaction. Et quant à la mienne ils ne s'en souciaient guère. Maudit soit l'homme qui crée, maudit l'homme qui aime" (To Louise Colet, 21 January 1847, *Correspondance,* 1:430). [For that matter, I can't help but harbor eternal resentment toward those who brought me into the world and who keep me here, which is worse. Ah, naturally, that was love too, doubtless. What a beautiful thing! They loved each other! They said so to each other and one night they made me, to their great satisfaction. And as for mine, they scarcely worried about that. Cursed be the man who creates, cursed be the man who loves.]

This criticism and disgust spill over to the idea that he might himself become a father: "L'idée de donner le jour à quelqu'un *me fait horreur*" (To Louise Colet, 11 December 1852, *Correspondance,* 2:205) [The idea of giving life to someone *horrifies me*], a sentiment expressed by Frédéric as well: "L'idée d'être père, d'ailleurs, lui paraissait grotesque, inadmissible" (*L'éducation sentimentale,* 2:139) [The idea of being a father, moreover, seemed grotesque to him, intolerable]. It is significant that in *Novembre* becoming a father is deemed worse than being a murderer, and the procreative act after marriage, in which a man takes a virgin because the law allows him to, is so abhorrent that it has no equivalent in *monkey* groups: "Il pensait sérieusement qu'il y a moins de mal à tuer un homme qu'à faire un enfant [. . .] A ses yeux, celui qui, appuyé sur le Code civil, entre de force dans le lit de la vierge qu'on lui a donnée le matin, exerçant ainsi un viol légal que l'autorité protège, n'avait pas d'analogue chez les singes" (*Novembre,* 1:273). [He seriously thought that it was not as bad to kill a man as to make a baby (. . .) In his eyes, someone who, backed by the Civil Code, forcibly enters the bed of a virgin given to him that morning, thus exercising a legal rape that the authorities protect, had no parallel in monkeys.] It would seem safe to say that the idea of natural generation and procreation is linked to disgust in Flaubert's texts; our animal origin is condemned.[31]

This disgust directs itself for the most part toward the figure of the mother. A web of images weaves itself around our problematic origin in her: the process of maternal reproduction, which is viewed as disgusting; the malformation of her offspring; the inability of culture and civilization to heal this abhorrent creation; and, most significant, that odd association of mothers with monkeys. Several of these images appear together in one rather remarkable, somewhat delirious passage in a letter composed by Flaubert at the time of the writing of "*Quidquid volueris.*" Here, human civilization is a mother who is a kind of ill-formed prostitute who sells her kisses (steamboats and railroads also make an appearance in this passage):

> [L]a civilisation, cet avorton ridé des efforts de l'homme a marché, trottiné sur ses trottoirs, du port elle a regardé les bateaux à vapeur, le pont suspendu, les murailles bien blanches, les bordeaux protégés par la police et chemin faisant ivre et gaie, elle a déposé au coin des murs avec les écailles d'huîtres et les tronçons de choux quelques-unes de ses croyances, quelque lambeau bien fané de poésie et puis détournant ses regards de la cathédrale et crachant sur ses contours gracieux, la pauvre petite fille déjà folle et glacée a pris la nature, l'a égratignée de ses ongles et s'est mise à rire et à crier tout haut, mais bien haut, avec une voix aigre et perçante: *J'avance.*—Pardon de t'avoir insultée—ô pardon, car tu es une bonne grosse fille qui marches tête baissée à travers le sang et les cadavres, qui ris quand tu écrases, qui livres tes grosses et sales mamelles à tous tes enfants et qui as encore la gorge toute cuivrée et toute rougie des baisers que tu leur vends à prix d'or—Ô cette bonne civilisation, cette bonne pâte de garce qui a inventé les chemins de fer. (To Ernest Chevalier, 24 June 1837, *Correspondance,* 1:23–24)

31. This disgust with natural procreation links Flaubert with the Decadents. The performative function of language, however, does not seem overtly thematized in the works of the Decadents, and so I have not pursued those works here, although that would warrant further study.

> [Civilization, that wizened runt of man's efforts, walked, scurried along her sidewalks; she looked at the steamboats in the port, at the suspension bridge, at the walls so white, at the bordellos[32] protected by the police, and on her way, drunk and cheerful, she shed some of her beliefs, some withered scrap of poetry, at the foot of walls with their oyster shells and pieces of cabbage. Then turning her gaze away from the cathedral and spitting on its gracious contours, that poor little girl, already insane and cold as ice, took hold of nature, scratched her with her fingernails and began to laugh and scream loudly, very loudly, with a shrill and piercing voice: "I advance!"—I am sorry to have insulted you, oh sorry! Because you are a good, fat slut who walks with her head down through blood and corpses, you laugh when you crush someone, you give your fat and dirty breasts to all your children, that chest all yellow and red from the kisses that you sell for a handsome sum. Oh, that good civilization, that sweet easy gal who invented trains.]

What is significant here is the uniting of certain images related to the mother: she is herself an ill-formed offspring, an "avorton" (like Djalioh and, later, Zola's humans);[33] she represents civilization, what distinguishes humans, but in a nefarious way; she is disgusting, a kind of dirty prostitute who charges for kisses; and she is responsible for the modern mechanical

32. The word *bordeaux* is ambiguous; it could either mean wine or be an old form of the word for bordello.

33. The image of the monstrous offspring of the mother reaches a fever pitch in *Salammbô*, 1:718: "Des serpents avaient des pieds, des taureaux avaient des ailes, des poissons à têtes d'homme dévoraient des fruits, des fleurs s'épanouissaient dans la mâchoire des crocodiles, et des éléphants, la trompe levée, passaient en plein azur, orgueilleusement, comme des aigles. [. . .] Ils avaient l'air, en tirant la langue, de vouloir faire sortir leur âme; et toutes les formes se trouvaient là, comme si le réceptacle des germes, crevant dans une éclosion soudaine, se fût vidé sur les murs de la salle. Douze globes de cristal bleu la bordaient circulairement, supportés par des monstres qui ressemblaient à des tigres. Leurs prunelles saillissaient comme les yeux des escargots, et courbant leurs reins trapus, ils se tournaient vers le fond, où resplendissait, sur un char d'ivoire, la Rabbet suprême, l'Omniféconde."

[Snakes had feet, bulls had wings, fish with human heads devoured fruit, flowers bloomed in the jaws of crocodiles, and elephants, trunk raised, went by in the azure, proudly, like eagles (. . .) They seemed, as they thrust out their tongues, to be trying to expel their soul; and every form could be found there, as if the receptacle of germs, giving way in a sudden blossoming, had burst open onto the walls of the room. Twelve blue crystal globes, supported by monsters that looked like tigers, bordered the wall in a circle. Their eyes protruded, like those of snails, and twisting their strong, compact loins, they turned toward the back, where the supreme Rabbet, the Omnifecund, was shining in an ivory chariot.]

and industrial nature of culture. Here the mother and the products of her reproduction anchor Flaubert's condemnation of our human "civilized" identity.[34]

However, the clearest association of the mother with our deformed nature resides in those strange fantasies of "*Quidquid volueris.*" In the primal scene of Djalioh's origin, his human/simian nature begins in a perverted mating process, gestation, and parturition, which are graphically represented as being located in a specific woman's body:

> Moi, j'avais à me venger d'une petite sotte de négresse, et voilà qu'un jour, après mon retour de la chasse, je trouve mon singe, que j'avais enfermé dans ma chambre avec l'esclave, évadé et parti, l'esclave en pleurs et toute ensanglantée des griffes de Bell. Quelques semaines après, elle sentit des douleurs de ventre et des maux de coeur. Bien! Enfin, cinq mois après, elle vomit pendant plusieurs jours consécutifs; j'étais pour le coup presque sûr de mon affaire. Une fois, elle eut une attaque de nerfs si violente qu'on la saigna des quatre membres, car j'aurais été au désespoir de la voir mourir; bref, au bout de sept mois, un beau jour elle accoucha sur le fumier. Elle en mourut quelques heures après, mais le poupon se portait à ravir. ("*Quidquid volueris,*" 1:108)

> [As for me, I had to take revenge on a little fool of a black slave woman, and so one day, after my return from the hunt, I found that my ape, which I had locked in my room with the slave, had

34. In *Mémoires d'un fou,* 1:243, we find again the combined image of anomalous birth (the word *avorté*), man, and civilization (art being its highest form), with, in addition, the context of the monkey: "Tout me semble borné, rétréci, *avorté* dans la nature. *L'homme,* avec son génie et son *art,* n'est qu'un misérable *singe* de quelque chose de plus élevé" (emphasis added). [Everything seems to me to be limited, shrunken, *aborted* in nature. *Man,* with his genius and his *art,* is but a miserable *ape* of something higher.] Again the insufficiencies of nature are related to an unsatisfactory physical birth, our material origin; and man, who aims for more, achieves only a mechanical aping of the ideal. In *Bouvard et Pécuchet,* at the other end of Flaubert's oeuvre, we find again an example of the monkey linked to the malformation of man and to procreation (sex). Bouvard is petrified when he sees the young Victorine lying down, presumably having "mated," with the malformed "bossu," Romiche, whose hand holds her leg and looks like "celle d'un singe" (*Bouvard et Pécuchet,* 2:299) [that of a monkey]. Disgust with the mother and with birth runs through many other Flaubert texts. In "*Quidquid volueris,*" 1:108, the slave woman gives birth to Djalioh on a manure pile. In *Salammbô,* the goddess is associated with fecundation as well as with putrefaction (and a monkey is present in the scene) (*Salammbô,* 1:708). Thus mothers give birth to the fallen nature of material man; her physical body grows the deficient human being, the disgusting *avorton.*

> escaped and run off, and that the slave was in tears and all bloodied by Bell's claws. Several weeks later, she felt pains in her belly and nausea. Fine! Well, five months later she vomited for several consecutive days; I was almost sure this time of my affair. Once she had a nervous attack that was so violent that they bled her copiously, because I would have despaired to see her die; in sum, at the end of seven months, one fine day she gave birth on a manure pile. She died several hours later, but the baby was thriving.]

In this strange "scientific" fantasy, Flaubert locates the origin of the problematic identity of Djalioh, the ambiguous man/beast, in this vivid primal scene of birth from a woman. As Sartre says, the discovery of the self in Flaubert is of "a congenital defect" (Sartre, *Family Idiot,* 1:327). Woman and birth from woman thus figure the origin, as it does later in Zola, of our animal, determined, hereditary nature, our powerlessness in relation to it, and of our origin in the body, in the animal.

The mother's link to our animality strengthens in that rather strange, obsessive image in Flaubert's texts that ties mothers to monkeys. At times it is the recurring image of a mother and child who sit next to a monkey, here in *La tentation de saint Antoine:* "Cependant, il distingue de l'autre côté du Nil, une Femme—debout au milieu du désert. Elle garde dans sa main le bas d'un long voile noir qui lui cache la figure, tout en portant sur le bras gauche un petit enfant qu'elle allaite. A son côté, un grand singe est accroupi sur le sable" (*La tentation de saint Antoine,* 1:557). [However, on the other side of the Nile he makes out a Woman standing in the middle of the desert. In one hand she holds in place the bottom of a long black veil that hides her face, while she holds in her left arm a small child that suckles. Next to her, an ape squats on the sand.] This literary episode parallels an event that Flaubert recounts in a letter of 1850—to his own mother: "Une femme balançait un enfant suspendu dans un hamac à un arbre.—A côté, par terre, était assis un gros singe" (To his mother, 7 October 1850, *Correspondance,* 1:696). [A woman rocked a child in a hammock hung from a tree.—Next to her, on the ground, sat a large ape.] It surely must be important that the woman whom Flaubert saw nursing a child on the beach and who inspired in Flaubert a love that affected him all his life was named Elisa Schle*singe*r. It is almost as if that particular nursing mother conjured up "metonymically," through the letters of her name, the monkey/*singe* that is metonymically next to the nursing mother in the textual images.[35] The mother-monkey link thus seems to posit the origin of man's deficient nature in his emergence from the mother, in his physical origin in woman's material, simian-related body.

Male Birth

As a kind of symbolic resolution of this problem of man's lowly nature, Flaubert represents the fantasy of the male takeover of the procreative process. One could read *Salammbô* as a kind of dramatization of this battle for the control of procreation in the struggle that takes place between female reproduction and male creation. Salammbô, a woman, worships a female goddess; Schahabarim, a weakened, emasculated male who begins by worshiping the goddess, shifts allegiance to a male god who represents "le principe mâle exterminateur" (*Salammbô,* 1:753) [the male exterminating principle]. The theft of the veil of Tanit figures the shift in power from the female to the male, and in the scene in which Mâtho purloins the veil, the description of the goddess, Tanit, is particularly telling. As the goddess of fecundity, a kind of ur-mother, she wields superlative procreative powers and is called the "Omniféconde" (1:718). Physically, she is embodied in a giant machine (which ties in with our theme of mechanical, material reproduction). As the men enter her chambers, they step on a sort of treadle that sets in motion an artificial, mechanical universe that seems to animate the statue of the goddess: "Mâtho fit un pas; une dalle fléchit sous ses talons, et voilà que les sphères se mirent à tourner, les monstres à rugir; une musique s'éleva, mélodieuse et ronflante comme l'harmonie des planètes; l'âme tumultueuse de Tanit ruisselait épandue. Elle allait se lever, grande comme la salle, avec les bras ouverts" (1:718).[36] [Mâtho took a step; a paving stone gave way under his heels, and just then the spheres began to turn, monsters to roar; music rose, melodious and humming like the harmony of the planets; the tumultuous soul of Tanit poured out in streams. She was about to get up, as tall as the room, with open arms.] Mâtho and Spendius confront the "machine" of woman's fecundity, and they proceed to steal the symbol of this woman, her

35. Biasi, editor of the *Carnets de travail,* also sees in the mother-monkey link an obsessive image. Janson has noted that in the Renaissance there was a "trendy" image of Mary with Christ and a monkey. H. W. Janson, *Apes and Ape Lore in the Middle Ages and the Renaissance* (London: Warburg Institute, University of London, 1952), 151. One wonders whether Flaubert saw such an image in his travels in Italy.

36. This art-producing machine (music is generated by it) that sets the world in motion echoes the organ grinder's machine in *Madame Bovary* that makes the tiny dancers spin.

veil: the men "take over" Tanit's powers.[37] In another sense, it is the men who, by tripping the treadle, give life to this universe and who seem to bring the statue to life, thus doubly stealing the female procreative function. In fact, natural reproduction has already been usurped, because the mother here is already a machine, an unnatural, technological construct.

Thus, the triumph of the male principle in *Salammbô* represents the takeover of woman's creative power, and indeed, the male principle has the upper hand at the end of this text: "[L]a tyrannie du principe mâle prévalait ce jour-là dans toutes les consciences, et la Déesse était même tellement oubliée, que l'on n'avait pas remarqué l'absence de ses pontifes" (*Salammbô,* 1:779). [The tyranny of the male principle prevailed that day in every mind, and the goddess herself was so completely forgotten that no one noticed the absence of her pontiffs.] Salammbô, the worshiper of Tanit, dies. Most important, however, the male god who triumphs *engenders himself,* as the high priest of Moloch chants: "Hommage à toi, Soleil! roi des deux zones, *créateur qui s'engendre, Père et Mère,* Père et Fils, Dieu et Déesse, Déesse et Dieu!" (1:780; emphasis added).[38] [Homage to you, Sun! King of the two zones, *creator who engenders himself, Father and Mother,* Father and Son, God and Goddess, Goddess and God!] Here, the defeat of the goddess, of maternal procreation, and the triumph of the male principle result in the advent of the male creator, who plays the role of both man and woman.

This sheds new light on Flaubert's reference to his writing of *Salammbô* as his attempt to give a kind of second life to Carthage, to "resuscitate Carthage," in his words (To Ernest Feydeau, 29 November 1859, *Correspondance,* 3:59). Flaubert's creative act of writing this text and of making something come (back) to life parallels the thematic content that depicts the male act of engendering life and rewriting woman's role. It is significant that on the day of the triumph of the male principle, the priests present real children, the offspring of real mothers, to the horrible, artificial statue of the god to which they will be sacrificed. The statue is a kind of automaton, an artificial artistic product, a man-made machine with moving

37. Mary Orr refers to what she calls the current-day priests of Moloch as those who attempt to steal the woman's role in an even darker way; they are "intent to valorize gynophobic acts which ultimately only imitate the womb as a (phallic) glass test-tube or gas chamber" (Orr, *Flaubert: Writing the Masculine,* 202).

38. The idea of self-creation appears in *Mémoires d'un fou,* 1:245, in the form of a desired impossible: "Es-tu le créateur de ta constitution physique et morale? Non, tu ne pourrais la diriger entièrement que si tu l'avais faite et modelée à ta guise" [Are you the creator of your physical and moral constitution? No, you would be able to direct it entirely only if you had made it and shaped it as you pleased.]

hands that it clasps to its *ventre,* the place from which children would be born from the mother; but here, before the male god, they will be destroyed. Their sacrificial destruction signifies the elimination of natural procreation:

> De minces chaînettes partant de ses doigts [de la statue] gagnaient ses épaules et redescendaient par derrière, où des hommes, tirant dessus, faisaient monter, jusqu'à la hauteur de ses coudes, ses deux mains ouvertes qui, en se rapprochant, arrivaient contre son ventre [...]
>
> Enfin un homme qui chancelait, un homme pâle et hideux de terreur, poussa un enfant; puis on aperçut entre les mains du colosse une petite masse noire; elle s'enfonça dans l'ouverture ténébreuse. (*Salammbô,* 1:780)[39]
>
> [Slender chains went from the fingers (of the statue) up to the shoulders and fell back down behind, where men pulled on them to raise the two open hands up to the level of the elbows, while the hands came together against the belly (...)
>
> Finally a man who staggered up, a man pale and hideous with terror, pushed a child; then between the hands of the colossus could be seen a small black mass; it disappeared down into the dark opening.]

Flaubert's creative act of writing may indeed reflect the thematic content that depicts the male takeover of the act of creation when artificial, man-made structures rewrite the function of the *ventre* and destroy (the products of) natural reproduction.[40] As Margaret Cohen has shown, realist authors created their genre by means of a kind of destruction or takeover of the sentimental and female form of the novel.[41]

Once again, it is not surprising that literary creation should be equated with procreation—it is a common metaphor, which we have seen already in Balzac and which Flaubert takes up. In a letter to Feydeau, and referring to the Bible, Flaubert places the brains of men in opposition to the wombs of women: "'Femme qu'y a-t-il de commun entre vous et moi?' est un mot qui me semble

39. This image is one that appears in a slightly different form in *La tentation de saint Antoine,* 1:551. There the animal gods take on a form that is more and more human until one of them turns into a kind of large statue that devours children: "Il y en a un, tout en fer rougi et à cornes de taureau, qui dévore des enfants." [There is one, all of red-hot iron with bull's horns, that devours children.]

40. Geoffrey Wall reminds us that Flaubert did distance himself from women at certain points of his life. Flaubert associated sexual desire with his own animality (he becomes a wild beast). *Flaubert, A Life* (New York: Farrar, Straus & Giroux, 2002), 77, 106).

41. Margaret Cohen, *The Sentimental Education of the Novel* (Princeton: Princeton University Press, 1999).

plus beau que tous les mots vantés dans les histoires. C'est le cri de la pensée pure, la protestation du cerveau contre la matrice" (*Correspondance*, 11 January 1859, 3:4–5).[42] ["Woman, what have I to do with thee?" is a saying that seems to me more beautiful than all the sayings praised in stories. It is the cry of pure thought, the protest of the brain against the womb.] This metaphor becomes, in a sense, more literal and less abstract when it conjures up physical images of the male birth process. *Par les champs et par les grèves* makes a very literal equation between gestating a baby and gestating an idea: "Rien ne dira les gestations de l'idée ni les tressaillements que font subir à ceux qui les portent les grandes oeuvres futures; mais on s'éprend à voir les lieux où nous savons qu'elles furent conçues, vécues, comme s'ils avaient gardé quelque chose de l'idéal inconnu qui vibra jadis" (*Par les champs et par les grèves*, 2:546).[43] [Nothing can express the gestations of the idea, or the shuddering that great future works impose on those who carry them within; yet we love to see the places where we know they were conceived, lived, as if they had retained something of the unknown ideal that resonated there before.] Flaubert thought of Bouilhet as his "*accoucheur*, celui qui voyait dans ma pensée plus clairement que moi-même"[44]

42. An example of the superior quality of artificial creation can be found in a letter to Hippolyte Taine: "C'est l'idée qu'il (l'individu) se fait de l'ensemble des choses et la *manière* de l'exprimer, laquelle est une Création égale, sinon supérieure à celle de la nature" (5? November 1866, *Correspondance*, 3:548). [It is the idea that he (the individual) makes of the whole, and the *manner* of expressing it, which is a Creation that is equal, if not superior, to that of nature.]

43. Jules, in the 1845 version of *L'éducation sentimentale*, uses a metaphor that ties writing to the labor of childbirth when he says that he is "heureux de sentir s'achever mon oeuvre, et déjà orgueilleux d'elle, comme la jeune mère qui, à travers ses douleurs, entend les vagissements vigoureux de son premier nouveau-né" (*L'éducation sentimentale, version de 1845*, 1:300) [happy to feel my work being completed, and already proud of it, like a young mother who, through her pains, listens to the vigorous wails of her first newborn baby].

44. Two other literary critics have noted these images, specifically in *La tentation de saint Antoine*. Marthe Robert, *Roman des origines et origines du roman* (Paris: B. Grasset, 1972), 336, observes in *La tentation* the elimination of maternal procreation and the accompanying fantasy of male childbirth: "To put oneself at the origin of life—this delirious desire of Antoine presupposes the abolition of the natural laws of procreation." Czyba, *Mythes et idéologie de la femme dans les romans de Flaubert* (Lyon: Presses Universitaires de Lyon, 1983), 321, similarly perceives that male childbirth stems from a kind of disgust with a natural reproduction that is "sullied" (just as we saw the importance of the link of disgust with mothers) and "the refusal of the natural laws of life whose origins are irreparably sullied, the megalomaniacal dream of Saint-Antoine–Flaubert to give birth to himself, to be the God of his being." If Flaubert does take rather literally this metaphor of male procreation, then Tony Tanner's analysis of Charles's cap is particularly apt here, and I quote it at length: "I can perhaps approach it indirectly by pointing out that the word *sac* is also used for the amniotic sac; the word *cordon* is also used for the umbilical cord; and the word *gland*, while undoubtedly meaning 'tassel,' as the standard translations indicate, is also used in anatomy to refer to the glans and is even now used colloquially to refer to the testicles [. . .] What the cap seems to contain among all the other things mentioned is a fragmented recapitulation of the period in the womb and the birth process" (Tanner, *Adultery in the Novel*, 239).

(To George Sand, 12 January 1870, *Correspondance,* 4:153; emphasis added) [*midwife* (in the masculine form), the one who could see into my idea more clearly than I myself].

Galatea

In a more generalized extension of this fantasy of male powers of creation that is similar to Balzac's new Pygmalion, Flaubert dramatizes in some of his texts the abandonment of the "real" woman/mother for the artificial, dream woman of man's own making. This is the core of the novel *L'éducation sentimentale.* Frédéric dreams of Madame Arnoux, in fact, imagining her life for her, creating a life in his mind (as does Balzac's Raphaël and, later, the narrator of Proust's *La prisonnière*). When he is at last given the opportunity to be with the real Madame Arnoux at the end of the novel, he decides against possessing a living woman and opts instead to perpetuate and venerate his ideal creation: "[T]out à la fois par prudence et pour ne pas dégrader son idéal, il tourna sur ses talons et se mit à faire une cigarette" (*L'éducation sentimentale,* 2:161). [Simultaneously out of prudence and a desire not to degrade his ideal, he turned on his heel and began to roll a cigarette.] Is it by chance that his rejection of this woman is a rejection of an incestuous situation that is repellent, a kind of rejection of the *mother*? "Cependant, il sentait quelque chose d'inexprimable, une répulsion, et comme l'effroi d'un inceste" (2:161). [However, he felt something inexpressible, a repulsion, and something like the fear of incest.] Czyba describes this strategy that is, according to her, concocted to "keep the woman at a distance while dreaming, while granting her the timelessness of myth and substituting fetishistic contemplation for carnal contact" (Czyba, *Mythes et idéologie,* 46). At the very least, it is clear that Frédéric's dreams have displaced and "distanced" the real woman: "Par la force de ses rêves, il l'avait posée en dehors des conditions humaines" (*L'éducation sentimentale,* 2:70). [Because of the strength of his dreams, he had placed her beyond human conditions.] A close look at the first meeting between Madame Arnoux and Frédéric shows that, in fact, "in the beginning" was the dream, not the woman. Before their first encounter on the steamboat, Frédéric sits already engrossed in dreams that involve, significantly, passion and art: "Frédéric pensait à la chambre qu'il occuperait là-bas, au plan d'un drame, à des sujets de tableaux, à des passions futures" (2:9). [Frédéric thought of the room he would live in there, of a plan for a play, of subjects for paintings, of future loves.] From dreams of artistic creation, the woman seems to appear as in a vision, almost as a kind of hallucination: "Ce fut comme une apparition: elle était assise, au milieu du banc, toute seule" (2:9). [It was like an apparition: she sat, in the middle of the bench, all alone.] The origin of Madame Arnoux is, in a way, literature: "elle ressemblait aux femmes des livres romantiques" (2:11). [She resembled the women in romantic books.]

In this dream-come-true, Madame Arnoux is a mother who, in our context of "*Quidquid volueris*," appears with a black servant woman. This combination of motherhood with the black slave/servant evinces the problematic ambiguities of "*Quidquid volueris*" with its slave woman as mother; indeed, at this moment the text seems to distance the real woman when Frédéric orientalizes Madame Arnoux: "Il la supposait d'origine andalouse, créole peut-être; elle avait ramené des îles cette négresse avec elle?" (*L'éducation sentimentale,* 2:10).[45] [He supposed her to be of Andalusian origin, Creole perhaps; had she brought this black woman back with her from the islands?] An item belonging to her takes Frédéric completely away from her presence as it plunges him back into his dreams: "Cependant, un long châle à bandes violettes était placé derrière son dos, sur le bordage de cuivre. Elle avait dû, bien des fois, au milieu de la mer, durant les soirs humides, en envelopper sa taille, s'en couvrir les pieds, dormir dedans!" (2:10). [However, a long shawl with purple stripes was placed behind her back, on the brass railing. Many times, in mid-ocean, on damp evenings, she must have wrapped herself in it, covered her feet with it, slept in it!] The brief appearance by the "real" woman seems to provide a mere pretext for continuing to create a fantasy. Frédéric thus first dreams of love, then anchors his artificial creation in the real Madame Arnoux, finally to prefer his own "creation" to the real thing.

Certainly Frédéric is not being held up as some wonderful example to be emulated, yet he is one of the few characters in this novel who do value something beyond crass materialism, so he is, in a sense, somewhat valorized. Even though Frédéric is not a real "artist," he still seeks elevation in an ideal, artificial creation that would be better than the degraded reality that surrounds

45. Several critics discuss this tendency to distance women. Czyba, *Mythes et idéologie,* 158, speaks of a less-literal distancing, one effected by representing man's gaze at the woman, "this distancing by the gaze, which is a constant in the Flaubertian corpus, from *Mémoires d'un fou* to *Madame Bovary,* and which will become a privileged perspective in *L'éducation sentimentale* of 1869." Mary Orr, "Reading the Other: Flaubert's *L'éducation sentimentale* revisited," *French Studies: A Quarterly Review* 46, no. 4 (October 1992), 412–23, goes so far as to interpret Frédéric's life as an attempt to separate himself, distance himself, from his mother.

him. In *L'éducation sentimentale,* where people are ultimately substitutable for one another, where Frédéric lacks control and is passively bounced around from episode to episode, from person to person, from identity to identity, he does take control of one thing: he creates a woman to love in his imagination, a woman who, although based in the real, is his artificial dream, a woman shaped to his desires. When faced with the choice between his dream and reality, he decides to remain with his dream woman, his fictional construction. This would appear to give Frédéric control over the script of his creation; even if he has no control over his own real life, he can invent and control a dream.

Thus Flaubert taps into the myth of Pygmalion: the male "artist" creates an artificial woman—in a statue, in a dream, in a mythic story—and falls in love with his own creation. In *Mémoires d'un fou* (1:246), the narrator states specifically that he loves his created woman and not the real woman: "Comment aurait-elle pu en effet voir que je l'aimais, car *je ne l'aimais pas alors,* et en tout ce que je vous ai dit, j'ai menti; *c'était maintenant que je l'aimais,* que je la désirais; que, seul sur le rivage, dans les bois ou dans les champs, *je me la créais là,* marchant à côté de moi, me parlant, me regardant" (emphasis added).[46] [How could she in fact see that I loved her, because *I didn't love her then,* and in all that I told you, I lied; *it was later that I loved her,* that I desired her; alone on the shore, in the woods, or in the fields, *later that I created her there for myself,* walking next to me, speaking to me, looking at me.] How apt, then, that Flaubert supposedly kissed a statue in Italy (Wall, *Flaubert, A Life,* 92).

This dream covers, however, only the first part of the myth of Pygmalion, because the fictional creation of woman remains just that. Frédéric's Galatea does not come to life. The author/artist merely lives in his fiction and bypasses the real woman. It is here, however, that science might suggest a way to complete Pygmalion's work, a way to make the dream become real, to "realize" the myth. Science posits the possibility of gaining control over the body and reproduction. Paul, the "scientist" creator in "*Quidquid volueris,*" claims that he has, in fact, made a child by unusual, "scientific" means: "[J]'ai fait un enfant par des moyens inusités" ("*Quidquid volueris,*" 1:108). [I made a child by extraordinary means.] It is his intellectual work that gives birth to Djalioh, work for which he receives the "croix d'honneur" from the Institute. Science might then offer the possibility of a revised reproduction that puts the mother in a secondary place.

46. Wall, *Flaubert, A Life,* 74, 105, conjures up the image of Flaubert in Pradier's studio watching the relays between beautiful women and statues.

Indeed, two scientists for whom Flaubert expressed enthusiastic admiration take up this theme of the generation of life. Haeckel deals with the mechanics of reproduction and various odd types of generation, some of which do not involve the typical, two-parent variety. Most important of these odd types of procreation is spontaneous generation, the ability of life to come into existence without reproduction: "Bear in mind first that we mean by this the production of an organic individual without parents, without the help of a generating organism" (Haeckel, *Histoire de la création,* 299). For Haeckel, spontaneous generation explains how life began at the very start. In Flaubert, we can see how the possibility of reproduction without parental participation would be intriguing.

Spontaneous generation is also the research topic of Félix-Archimède Pouchet, a doctor from Rouen with whom Flaubert retained ties and whom he liked quite a bit. As Benjamin Bart states: "Pouchet was an interesting scientist who, like Flaubert, lived a monastic existence dedicated to his work."[47] When Pouchet's wife died suddenly, Flaubert attended the funeral and planned to use Pouchet's grief as a model for Charles Bovary.[48] Jean Borie explains that he was the "student of Flaubert's father, friend of Flaubert's brother (at whose house Michelet met him), cousin of Gide's maternal grandmother."[49] The family friendship continued with Pouchet's son, Georges. Flaubert worked to try to get the son, who was also a scientist, several posts in Paris; Flaubert

47. Benjamin Bart, *Flaubert* (Syracuse, N.Y.: Syracuse University Press, 1967), 457.

48. "Comme il faut du reste *profiter de tout,* je suis sûr que ce sera demain d'un dramatique très sombre et que ce pauvre savant sera lamentable. Je trouverai là peut-être des choses pour ma *Bovary.* Cette exploitation à laquelle je vais me livrer, et qui semblerait odieuse si on en faisait la confidence, qu'a-t-elle donc de mauvais? J'espère faire couler des larmes aux autres avec ces larmes d'un seul, passer ensuite à la chimie du style. Mais les miennes seront d'un ordre de sentiment supérieur. Aucun *intérêt* ne les provoquera et il faut que mon bonhomme (c'est un médecin aussi) vous émeuve pour tous les veufs. Ces petites gentillesses-là, du reste, ne sont pas besogne neuve pour moi et j'ai de la méthode en ces études. Je me suis moi-même franchement disséqué au vif en des moments peu drôles" (To Louise Colet, 6 June 1853, *Correspondance,* 2:346). [Because one must, moreover, *profit from everything,* I'm sure that tomorrow will be very darkly dramatic and that this poor scientist will be pathetic. I will perhaps find something there for my *Bovary.* This exploitation, in which I will indulge and which would seem odious if one were to confess it, what is wrong with it? I hope to make others cry with the tears of one man, to go on afterward to the chemistry of style. But mine will be of a superior order of feeling. No *interest* will provoke them and my good man (he is a doctor, too) must move you for all widowers. These little kindnesses, moreover, are not a new task for me and I have a method in these studies. I have boldly dissected myself alive in certain unhappy moments.]

49. Jean Borie, *Mythologies de l'hérédité au XIXe siècle* (Paris: Éditions Galilée, 1981), 41 n. 10.

stayed with him at Concarneau in 1875; and it was this Georges Pouchet who gave Flaubert lessons, significantly, on fish dissection.

The elder Pouchet's book on his experiments with spontaneous generation, *Hétérogénie; ou, Traité de la génération spontanée, basé sur de nouvelles expériences,*[50] received a good review from Flaubert: "Je lis maintenant le volume de mon ami le docteur Pouchet sur l'*Hétérogénie,* cela m'éblouit. Quelle quantité de splendides bougreries il y a dans la nature!" (To Ernest Feydeau, 5 August 1860, 3:101). [I am now reading the work of my friend Doctor Pouchet on *Heterogeny;* it dazzles me. What a great quantity of splendid oddities there are in nature!] Pouchet (who disagreed with Pasteur's idea that microorganisms develop from other microorganisms) believed that he had proof of spontaneous generation when he saw microorganisms growing in water when they had not been visible before. His experiments seem quite zany for us in a post-Pasteur world—he adds to water various strange materials, such as a piece of the skull-bone of an Egyptian from the necropolis of Sakkara—and when microorganisms are produced, he believes it has generated new and different life (*Hétérogénie,* 152).

Pouchet believed that what was produced was an ovule just exactly as an ovule would be formed in the tissues of an ovary; it developed from surrounding organic matter. Thus spontaneous generation was like sexual generation, and one could conclude that women did not have any real role in the making of the new child: "The mother does not make her egg any more than she makes her fetus" (Pouchet, *Hétérogénie,* 329). Pouchet actually uses a metaphor taken from the world of art to describe the self-formation of the child: "We will say again that it is not the mother who sculpts it (her product), but that it is the product that sculpts itself" (334). Taken to its limits, this odd understanding of reproduction makes women superfluous in reproduction because new life can be formed without her (and as in Pouchet's experiments, a formation aided by the scientist): "This generation, as expressed by Burdach, as the manifestation of a being deprived of parents, is consequently a primordial generation, a Creation!" (1).

Flaubert himself, in another place, seemed interested in this Frankenstein-like experimentation with nature; in Flaubert's case it is the way to make a dead creature return to life in order to show the material (rather than spiritual) basis of life (and one that is oddly similar to

50. Félix-Archimède Pouchet, *Hétérogénie; ou, Traité de la génération spontanée, basé sur de nouvelles expériences* (Paris: J. B. Baillière & Fils, 1859).

Balzac's brain-replacement fantasy): "On décapite un animal, on le laisse mourir complètement. Mais après cette mort, nous injectons dans la tête du sang d'un autre animal de [la] même espèce battu et chauffé au degré nécessaire, et cette tête revit, ouvre les yeux, et ses mouvements nous prouvent que son cerveau, organe de la pensée, fonctionne de nouveau et de la même manière comme avant la décapitation" (*Carnets de travail,* 492). [One decapitates an animal and lets it die completely. But after its death, one injects into its head blood from another animal of the same species, mixed and warmed to the necessary degree, and the head comes back alive, opens its eyes, and its movements prove to us that its brain, the organ of thought, functions again and in the same manner as before the decapitation.] In the science of the time, then, the way was open for imagining new ways of tinkering with life, and even of creating it without the need of a female.

Flaubert explores this potential of science in several works. For instance, when reflecting on various inventions of the fantastic, Flaubert says that science alone creates, "la Science, seul *créant*" (*Carnets de travail,* 266) [Science, alone *creating*]. In the early text, "Passion et vertu," Ernest, a chemist, brings Mazza's sensuality to life, and thus, in a certain way, as Sartre says, "Ernest has given birth to her [. . .] a man wanted it to happen, made it the object of a consciously concerted enterprise" (Sartre, *Family Idiot,* 1:192–93). Sartre goes on to summarize several instances of man's "creation" of woman and of his replacement of the mother: "The absence of the mother is noteworthy; in the novellas we are studying, the sons are engendered but not born. A man awakens Mazza from a lethargic sleep. A man determines the crossbreeding that will produce Djalioh—the black slave woman, an indispensable receptacle, disappears after the birth [. . .] *Rêve d'enfer,* by making its characters issue directly from the Creator, is relieved of resorting to the mediation of a female belly" (1:248).

In Flaubert, however, this fantasy of a kind of material creating of a human, specifically of a woman, is really a curious, significant, but secondary part of his work. A much more important representation of an artificially created woman pursues, in a certain sense, the opposite path from this material one and goes back instead to Frédéric's immersion in his dreams. On this other path, it is the concept of the real, the material itself, and thus the real woman, that is put into question. As we have seen, for Flaubert, human beings are passive constructions of biological and mechanical processes. And for Flaubert, this idea of the constructed nature of the human goes beyond the physical to the social construction of persons. A now-famous letter to Louise Colet exemplifies in a specific and important way this fabricated nature of female social identity, which, as we saw in the first chapter, echoes Balzac: "*Dieu a créé la femelle, et l'homme a fait la femme;* elle est le résultat de la civilisation, une oeuvre factice" (To Louise Colet, 27 March 1853, *Correspondance,* 2:284). [*God created the female, and man made woman;* she is the result of civilization, an artificial work.] Other examples of this awareness of the constructed nature of woman abound. In the *Carnets,* Flaubert describes a scenario in which a woman plays a kind of artificial role; she is a "type" who follows certain fashion codes. After a time, however, when the style of this role no longer suits her, she does not stop playing it, but continues, as though she had "become" the role: "Une femme qui dans sa jeunesse a été 'un type' reste victime du type. Il faut qu'elle s'habille et se coiffe d'une certaine façon.–Et, même quand ce genre de coiffure et d'habillement ne va plus à sa personne, elle continue" (*Carnets de travail,* 571). [A woman who, in her youth, was a "type" remains the victim of this type. She has to wear her hair, and she must dress in a certain way. And even when this type of hairdo and clothing no longer goes with her person, she continues.] In a curious way, Madame Arnoux's bourgeois identity as a charitable "lady of the leisure class" seems to create her very real hands: "[S]es petites mains semblaient faites pour épandre des aumônes" (*L'éducation sentimentale,* 2:60).[51] [Her tiny hands seemed made for the distribution of alms.]

And this construction can take place linguistically, as we see in *Madame Bovary,* when motherhood itself, the most "natural" identity of women, is a role that one plays; in Emma's case it is a literary role: "Elle déclarait adorer les enfants; c'était sa consolation, sa joie, sa folie, et elle accompagnait ses caresses d'expansions lyriques, qui, à d'autres qu'à des Yonvillais, eussent rappelé la Sachette de *Notre-Dame de Paris*" (*Madame Bovary,* 1:610). [She declared that she adored children; that was her consolation, her joy, her folly, and she accompanied her caresses with lyrical effusions, which, to any but the people from Yonville, would have called to mind la Sachette of *Notre-Dame de Paris.*] As Czyba says of the way in which Emma is formed by novels: "By showing the heroine to be a victim of books, of the education she received in the convent, the novel leads the reader to put in question the myth of a feminine 'nature'; Emma

51. In her *Ladies of the Leisure Class,* Bonnie Smith has discussed the role of charity in the definition of the bourgeois woman (Princeton: Princeton University Press, 1981).

is what she was made to be" (Czyba, *Mythes et idéologie,* 111–12). Tanner too identifies Emma's constructed nature as a principal theme of the book: "Emma is caught and lost, caressed and violated, created and destroyed in and by the language into which she is born—a signal victim of the privileged discourses of the time" (Tanner, *Adultery in the Novel,* 312).[52] Flaubert was concerned about the education of his niece because he saw the importance of the way in which education constructed a woman and affected her entire life: "On apprend aux femmes à mentir d'une façon infâme. L'apprentissage dure toute leur vie [. . .] J'ai peur du corset moral, voilà tout. Les premières impressions ne s'effacent pas, tu le sais. Nous portons en nous notre passé" (To his mother, 24 November 1850, *Correspondance,* 1:711). [Women are taught to lie in a despicable way. This apprenticeship lasts all their lives (. . .) I fear the moral corset, that's all. First impressions can't be erased, you know that. We carry our past within us.]

Thus, in Flaubert, codes and language inscribe our identity, as they do in Balzac's world. Human "nature" is really a coded, repetitive, mechanical inscription. And because woman in particular is singled out as being constructed, she becomes the representative of both biological determinism (as we have seen, natural reproduction and heredity, monkeys and mothers) and social predetermination and bourgeois leveling (the social formation of the individual in society). Woman, in Flaubert, collapses the normally opposed realms of nature and culture in her embodiment of our constructed and coded animal and mechanical nature.

Flaubert, then, acknowledges that there is no "real" woman (or man for that matter) and that women's identities are assigned by societal convention. Indeed, this is at the heart of all that Flaubert decries: the inane clichés of bourgeois society that mold people and their possibilities. His entire being strives against these clichés, strives to forge a distinctive identity for himself as the literary hermit of Croisset, over and against those bourgeois codes, just as he strives against the bourgeois moral corset that would adversely define his niece.

A kind of recurring literary situation in Flaubert, from his early projects to his last works, is one in which language becomes reality, just as societal codes form identity. It is a kind of representation of the fact that reality *is* a construction of language. In a project for the "féerie théâtrale" [fairy-tale theater, a kind of extravaganza], Flaubert wanted to write a text in which

52. In my "Emma's Distinctive Taste," *Australian Journal of French Studies* 43, no. 2 (2006), 121–37, I explore this social formation of Emma through the theories of Bourdieu.

idiomatic expressions would "realize" themselves, come true literally. In this scenario, the expression "Prendre la lune avec les dents" [To take the moon with one's teeth], which means to dream of the impossible, becomes the quest of the hero who attempts a trip in a balloon. When he reaches the moon, however, his teeth stay there and he can no longer eat, for he has no more teeth. In an odd and comical way, the clichéd expression is literalized for this character.[53] In *Madame Bovary,* Emma's literary dreams do come true, even in their tiniest details.[54] In *Salammbô* (1:772) mention is made of words "ayant par eux-mêmes un pouvoir effectif" [having their own real power], and the same words describe Mannaëi in "Hérodias": "croyant que les mots avaient un pouvoir effectif" (*Trois contes,* 2:188) [believing that words had a real power]. In *L'éducation sentimentale* (2:89), the power of language over thought is expressed by the fact that Frédéric ends up believing in the lies he proffers. And there is the case of Bouvard and Pécuchet, who try to turn various ideas from books into their reality with little success and who end by copying codes, by making the reproduction of discourse their task in real life.[55]

If language and codes make up our reality, then the fantasy would be that literature, our fictional creation of a new world, might actually realize itself, might eventually become our "reality." Literature's performative power—"take the moon with one's teeth"—might change the world, might make our ideal fantasies become our "reality," one that can in any case only ever be constructed, coded. Why might we not be able to control coded constructions by manipulating language and the codes that make us?[56]

This brings us back to our opening example of the surgical operation on Hippolyte, which provides an extended representation of the power of language, here scientific language, to become real and serves to express once again the crisis of distinction. The tragedy of Hippolyte shows the

53. Marshall C. Olds has conducted an extensive study of the *féerie théâtrale,* in which this literalization of figural language is a crucial element. He mentions specifically the moon example. See Olds, *Au pays des perroquets: Féerie théâtrale et narration chez Flaubert* (Atlanta, Ga.: Rodopi, 2001), 59.

54. See my analysis of Madame Bovary in my *Fictional Genders: Role and Representation in Nineteenth-Century French Narrative* (Lincoln: University of Nebraska Press, 1989) and my "Teaching *Madame Bovary* Through the Lens of Poststructuralism," in *Approaches to Teaching Flaubert's "Madame Bovary,"* ed. Laurence M. Porter and Eugene F. Gray (New York: MLA Publications, 1995), 90–97.

55. Could we see the name *P-ou-chet* in the two names, B-*ou*-vard and *P*-écu-*chet*?

56. Terdiman sees a similar fantasy in Baudelaire: "In thus projecting *control* over automatized language, Baudelaire fantasized an antidote to involuntary and endless reproduction of the banal" (Terdiman, *Discourse/Counter-Discourse,* 211).

danger of the power of language that, machine-like, turns words into reality in ways that we cannot control and did not envision. Emma and Homais (significantly, a "bad mother" and a "scientist") push Charles to perform the operation that he reads about in texts; he aims to transform those linguistic signs into a new and better reality for Hippolyte. Here malformed nature, figured by Hippolyte's deformed foot, might be transformed into the ideal if the words could guide Charles's knife (the pen is indeed the surgeon's knife here). He attempts to accomplish this with the help of that strange machine, the *moteur mécanique,* which ties in with the mechanical language that automatically becomes our reality. Homais calls Charles's surgical performance "art" (*Madame Bovary,* 1:634); Charles is the artist/scientist who might create a new, improved version of man, a kind of human engineer.

Charles's operation fails and ends in the amputation of Hippolyte's leg; Charles "performed" the words, but their realization went awry. Although Charles wanted the machine, and figuratively the performative mechanics of language, to turn Hippolyte's leg into a beautiful, new, and improved nature, ironically the *moteur mécanique* and the use of the indecipherable language of the clubfoot turns his leg into an artificial construction, the prosthetic device that becomes necessary after the amputation. For, as we saw, the *moteur mécanique* (representing the artificial mechanics of language) becomes Hippolyte's very identity when Charles turns him into a sort of human machine or cyborg with his fancy mechanical leg (given to him by Charles): "Le pilon en était garni de liège, et il avait des articulations à ressort, une *mécanique compliquée* recouverte d'un pantalon noir, que terminait une botte vernie" (*Madame Bovary,* 1:638; emphasis added). [The wooden leg was adorned with cork, and it had spring joints, a *complicated mechanism* covered by a black pant leg, ending in a patent leather boot.] If Flaubert imagines controlling the power of words to make the real, the failure of the operation shows the danger of the power of language that, machine-like, turns words into reality in uncontrollable and unimagined ways. In the case of Hippolyte, we might fantasize controlling the power of codes that form us, but we remain riveted in our *bêtise* and are ultimately the victims of the unpredictable machinations of language. Flaubert, like Balzac, can imagine the possibility of creating reality through words, but that dream brings with it grave anxieties.

To conclude, we could summarize, then, a certain scenario that underlies Flaubert's texts. Man is passively born of woman. He has no control over this physical, animal origin, no control over the mechanical nature of this material existence. This animality problematizes and contaminates identity in various ways: man is part animal, part thinker; a male born from woman; a machine that wills to have free choice. To distance oneself from this lowly identity as passive machine, as animal, formed by mechanical processes and social coding, one must distance oneself from that corrupt origin, from woman, and create a new "origin," write a new birth, and in one specific sense write a new artificial woman born from man. One might manipulate the performative power of language to make this new fiction a "reality."[57] This Flaubert's texts attempt to do both thematically in their representations and in their very writing: thematically in Frédéric's dream woman, and by his texts themselves as they performatively make us see the realities of our nature and the shackles of our codes, and beyond this, to imagine the exciting yet dangerous possibilities of manipulating those codes.

57. This possibility of transformation and re-creation fits well with Lawrence Rothfield's notion of the Flaubertian self as being susceptible to transformation, in his *Vital Signs: Medical Realism in Nineteenth-Century Fiction* (Princeton: Princeton University Press, 1992), 30.

3

REWRITING REPRODUCTION: ZOLA

Il est indéniable que le roman naturaliste, tel que nous le comprenons à cette heure, est une expérience véritable que le romancier fait sur l'homme. [It is undeniable that the naturalist novel, as we understand it at this time, is a real experiment that the novelist carries out on man.]

—ZOLA, LE ROMAN EXPÉRIMENTAL

It seems ironic that Émile Zola's novels, which Zola proclaims to be highly scientific and experimental, abound with the richest and most complicated network of metaphors of the four authors studied here, almost as if the reassuring controlled surface of a scientific and epistemological intent permitted the wild circulation of underground images. The corpus of his works is like a vast body (or thermodynamic machine, as Serres would say) connected by the arteries of metaphors that flow freely from one text to the next, giving life to a kind of subtextual circulatory system. In this textual body, it is the *matrice,* the woman's womb, that will be the organ of choice for us, and here I would like to take one of Naomi Schor's small, toss-away comments (which in so many cases in her works contain profound implications) as a kind of structural principle for our exploration of these metaphors in Zola. We shall explore Schor's comments both in their literal sense and in their figurative sense of the meaning of *matrices* (as both womb and original form or pattern) and generation: "What Zola does, then, is to take ready-made associations and *generate* fiction from these stereotyped *matrices.*"[1] And we shall examine just how Zola mixes together symbolic material, preexisting *matrices* of metaphors, specifically those that define woman's nature, which he takes from science, culture,

1. Schor, *Zola's Crowds,* 162; emphasis added. Noiray, in his thorough, excellent study, *Le romancier et la machine,* has superbly analyzed many of the important mechanical metaphors in Zola. His work is a crucial foundation for many ideas here; our main difference lies in my emphasis on the *ventre* not as a digestive system but as womb.

and his own psyche.[2] These preformed, symbolic *matrices* place woman's identity in nature as biological reproducer; they define her by her *matrice*. After showing the flaws in natural reproduction as it must take place through woman, Zola then can *generate* his own fantasy of a better means of creation. Zola's textual *matrice* presents the fantasy that it can itself *generate* a new being. As do our other authors, Zola taps into the idea that culture and language generate the possibilities of reality, and he explores the fantasy of the role that language and his own text might play in that new generation.

The central *matrice* for us in Zola is the Halles as they appear in *Le ventre de Paris,* the novel whose focus is the merchants and workers who supply the growing alimentary needs for the bellies, *ventres,* of an increasingly populated Paris. This vast market area that supplies food for consumption to the human *ventres* of Paris is represented as an organic entity, itself a giant metaphorical abdomen, a stomach. But it is not only that; it is a hybrid construction in two ways in that it is both a stomach and a giant womb, and it is organic only metaphorically because it is actually an artificial human construction, a technological product. In his image of this artificial womb, Zola uses the *matrice* of folklore in another "natural" image, the myth of the cabbage patch (a role played by the stork in English). Marjolin is in fact "born" in the Halles—he is found in the cabbages amassed there: "Marjolin fut trouvé, un matin, par une marchande, dans un tas de choux, et [. . .] il poussa sur le carreau, librement. Quand on voulut l'envoyer à l'école, il tomba malade, il fallut le ramener aux Halles. Il en connaissait les moindres recoins, les aimait d'une tendresse de *fils*" (*Le ventre de Paris,* 1 625; emphasis added).[3] [Marjolin was found one morning by a woman vendor in a heap of cabbages, and (. . .) he grew up freely on the market floor. When they tried to send him to school he became ill and had to be brought back to the Halles. He knew their smallest recesses, loved them with a *son's* tenderness.] Cadine and Marjolin are the children, the idyll of this giant technological womb: "Et les Halles semblaient sourire de ces deux gamins qui étaient la chanson libre, l'idylle effrontée de leur ventre géant" (1:771). [And the

2. Serres, *Feux et signaux de brume,* 114, comments on this network of relays among meanings when he describes how three ideas of science (heredity, heat, and dynamics) "border on, in their turn, cultural formations already in place, mythic constellations, religious symbols, embedded rules of social organization."

3. All citations of Rougon-Macquart novels are to *Les Rougon-Macquart, histoire naturelle et sociale d'une famille sous le Second Empire,* ed. Lanoux and Mitterand. 5 vols. (Paris: Gallimard, 1960–67).

Halles seemed to smile on these two children, who were the free song, the impudent idyll, of their giant belly.]

Thus Zola creates a bizarre image of an artificial womb that manages to produce real, "natural" children. These two children could also be viewed as similar to the natural "products" that are sold in the Halles, similar to the cabbages among which they are found. Indeed, Schivelbusch (*Railway Journey,* 41) describes this very phenomenon when he discusses the process whereby the products brought from their point of origin in nature to a new, artificial location, such as the Halles, appeared not to be products of nature but rather creations of the marketplace itself: "No longer was [the product] seen in the context of the original locality of its place of production but in the new locality of the market-place: cherries offered for sale in the Paris market were seen as products of that market." Cadine and Marjolin, like the cabbages for sale in the Halles, are symbolic "products," offspring of the artificial space of the modern marketplace.

Moreover, this giant, artificial organ that gives birth to Cadine and Marjolin is also described as a giant machine:[4]

> Et Florent regardait les grandes Halles sortir de l'ombre, sortir du rêve, où il les avait vues, allongeant à l'infini leurs palais à jour. Elles se solidifiaient, d'un gris verdâtre, plus *geántes* encore, avec leur mâture prodigieuse, supportant les nappes sans fin de leurs toits. Elles entassaient leurs masses géométriques; et, quand toutes les clartés intérieures furent éteintes, qu'elles baignèrent dans le jour levant, carrées, uniformes, elles apparurent comme *une machine* moderne, hors de toute mesure, quelque *machine à vapeur,* quelque chaudière destinée à la digestion d'un peuple, *gigantesque ventre de métal,* boulonné, rivé, fait de bois, de verre et de fonte, d'une élégance et d'une puissance de *moteur mécanique, fonctionnant* là, avec la chaleur du chauffage, l'étourdissement, le branle furieux des roues." (*Le ventre de Paris,* 1:626; emphasis added)
>
> [And Florent looked at the great Halles as they emerged from darkness, from dream, where he had before seen them stretching out their infinite airy palaces. They solidified, a greenish-gray, even more *gigantic,* with their prodigious mast-like frames supporting

4. See Noiray, *Le romancier et la machine,* 1:236–37, for an analysis of this machine-like aspect of the Halles.

> the endless surfaces of their roofs. They piled up in geometric masses, and when all the interior lights had been extinguished, when, square and uniform, they bathed in the dawning light, they seemed like a modern *machine,* beyond all measure, some sort of *steam engine,* some boiler meant for the digestion of a people, *a gigantic metal belly,* bolted, riveted, made of wood, glass, and cast iron, with the elegance and power of a *mechanical motor running* there with the temperature of a furnace, with the astounding and furious turbulence of wheels.]

I shall take the mechanical womb as a symbolic, nodal organ for exploring the rich and complicated circulation of Zola's metaphors, which will give us access to his fantasy of artificially creating a woman, indeed, the fantasy of man's technological takeover of a woman's ability to give birth. This mechanical womb appears in other figures throughout Zola's works, other images of giant products of human technology that are equated with wombs and that generate humans. In *Germinal,* for instance, it is the mine, specifically in its cavernous, womblike structure similar to that of the Halles and in images of germination and gestation.[5] The first visual description of the mine shows it as a giant, dark space that contains humans in a kind of a cold, damp womb, a vision seen by Étienne after his long descent in the elevator shaft, into the depths of the earth: "Le froid devenait glacial, on enfonçait dans une humidité noire, lorsqu'on traversa un rapide éblouissement, la vision d'une caverne où des hommes s'agitaient, à la lueur d'un éclair" (*Germinal,* 3:1159). [The cold was becoming glacial; they were sinking into a black dampness, when in a flash of light they passed by a fleeting, dazzling sight: the vision of a cave where men bustled about.] For Zola, this artificial womb is, as we shall see, the mechanical nature of gestation, birth, and heredity.

The path that we follow throughout the overall body of Zola's works will be, first, the continued presence of our familiar crisis of distinction of man from his technological products and of man from animal, a crisis that generates the possibility that the mechanical nature of organic man might allow the control of his identity; second, Zola's depiction of the

5. Other critics who discuss the womb-image of the mine in *Germinal* are Nichola Ann Haxell, "Childbirth and the Mine: A Reading of the Gaea-Myth in Zola's *Germinal* and the Poetry of Marceline Desbordes-Valmore," *Neophilologus* 73, no. 4 (1989), 522–31; and Rachelle A. Rosenberg, "The Slaying of the Dragon: An Archetypal Study of Zola's *Germinal,*" *Symposium,* Winter 1972, 349–62.

nefarious, uncontrolled effects that man's technological products already have on the formation of human identity, effects that demonstrate that human identity can indeed be constructed; and third, the anxieties produced by these effects of technology and by hybridism itself; and finally Zola's fantasy cure.

The Animal Machine

For Zola, the crisis of distinction between the natural and the technological is heightened by refined theories of evolution and the increased industrialization of France,[6] and he pursues even more profoundly the Balzacian and Flaubertian image of man as machine. Serres has, of course, analyzed the structuring thermodynamic principle at work in Zola's texts, whereby everything—body, machine, railroad system, text—is a motor; and Noiray has thoroughly mapped the image of the machine, and specifically the man-machine, in Zola's works. For our purposes, in Zola's fiction, bodies of men and bodies of machines function in similar ways, a similarity that is manifested in a remarkable little detail in *Germinal* (3:1253): the revolutionary Souvarine was a medical student, who studied human bodies, before he became a *machineur,* a caretaker of machines in the mine.[7] The mechanical metaphor of the marionette also appears in Zola (continuing the metaphors of Balzac and Flaubert), when routine or uncontrollable actions make puppets of humans. In *L'assommoir* (2:401), washerwomen have "des profils anguleux de marionnettes" [the angular profiles of marionettes]; and the alcoholic Coupeau at the end of the novel dances uncontrollably, "un vrai polichinelle, dont on aurait tiré les fils, rigolant des membres, le tronc raide comme du bois" (2:787) [a veritable puppet, whose strings were being pulled, flailing his limbs, his trunk stiff as a board]. For Zola, then, mechanization has become man's being.

In the science of the time as well, the old conception of the man/machine gained new force; Haeckel, for example (whose works Zola read and who was admired by Flaubert), creates an image of the body as a collection of gearlike organs that work together to make activity possible: "In fact, when it comes to

6. Schor, *Zola's Crowds,* xi, analyzes the "*anxieties* of origin and difference." David Baguley, *Naturalist Fiction: The Entropic Vision* (New York: Cambridge University Press, 1990), 210, also speaks of the "crisis of forms and distinctions."

7. In speaking of Pascal and his project, Serres, *Feux et signaux de brume,* 61, claims that "the doctor is an engineer."

living beings, the word 'organism' implies an animate body, composed of organs, of dissimilar parts, which, like the parts of *an artificial machine,* mesh with each other like gears and act together to produce the activity of the whole" (Haeckel, *Histoire de la création,* 164; emphasis added). Zola echoes this idea in *Le roman expérimental,* where he states that the body is a machine whose cogs can be manipulated by the scientist/machinist: "Quand on aura prouvé que le corps de l'homme est une machine, dont on pourra un jour démonter et remonter les rouages au gré de l'expérimentateur, il faudra bien passer aux actes passionnels et intellectuels de l'homme."[8] [When we will have proven that the body of man is a machine, whose gears we can one day take apart and put back together at the will of the experimenter, then we shall have to move on to the passionate and intellectual acts of man.] The resemblance goes the other way too: machines are like men. In science it is the image of thermodynamics, and in literature it is the metaphor of respiration (also found in Flaubert), when machines seem to breathe like living beings: "[U]ne seule voix montait, la respiration grosse et longue d'un échappement de vapeur" (*Germinal,* 3:1134). [One lone voice rose up, the deep and long breath of steam escaping.]

This intensified view of the mechanical nature of man does not preclude his Balzacian and Flaubertian animality, of course, for if, in Zola's world, man was a kind of machine, evolution continued to situate him through his physical body in the animal realm as well, where he is mechanically determined by his instincts and bodily functions. The title of *La bête humaine* itself expresses this animal heritage from the distant past that breaks out in humans, mainly Jacques Lantier, but in that book also Roubaud, who must try to appease the "bête hurlante au fond de lui" (*La bête humaine,* 4:1017) [beast roaring in his depths]. Indeed, in Zola these two metaphors join to form a new image of the human being as a kind of organic machine regulated by its internal hereditary pulleys and gears–including the tares of the *Rougon-Macquart*—and thrown into an environment to which it reacts in mechanical ways, life and the experimental novel itself.[9] The miner in *Germinal* (3:1276) is both brutish beast and machine: "le mineur vivait dans la mine comme une brute, comme une machine"

8. Zola, *Le roman expérimental; Les romanciers naturalistes,* vol. 32 of *Oeuvres complètes* (Paris: Cercle du Bibliophile, 1968?), 34. Claude Bernard, one of the major scientific influences on Zola, used the metaphor of a gun factory to illustrate the working together of various parts of a living organism (Jacob, *Logic of Life,* 189).

9. Sternberger, *Panorama of the Nineteenth Century,* 79, considers the concepts of evolution and natural selection that developed at that time as another kind of "brutal automatism." Andreas Huyssen, *After the Great Divide: Modernism, Mass Culture, Postmodernism* (Bloomington: Indiana University Press, 1986), 70, concludes that nature itself became a vast machine.

[a miner lived in the mine like a brute, like a machine]. In *Au Bonheur des Dames,* the department store, symbol of man's new world of modern consumer culture, is frequently presented as an enormous beast, yet it figures also as a machine. Here, the text performs a complicated interweaving of animal and machine metaphors, where brutish human evolutionary battles to "consume" one's rivals in the survival of the fittest help to maintain the giant new machine of "consumer" society: "Tous, d'ailleurs, dans le rayon, depuis le débutant rêvant de passer vendeur, jusqu'au premier convoitant la situation d'intéressé, tous n'avaient qu'une idée fixe, déloger le camarade au-dessus de soi pour monter d'un échelon, le manger s'il devenait un obstacle; et cette lutte des appétits, cette poussée des uns sur les autres, était comme le bon fonctionnement même de la machine" (*Au Bonheur des Dames,* 3:542). [For that matter, everyone in the department, from the apprentice dreaming of becoming a salesperson, to the department head coveting a role in the business, everyone had one obsession: to dislodge the worker above in order to move up a rung, to eat him if he became an obstacle; and this battle of appetites, this pushing one against the other, was actually like the good functioning of the machine.] In this combined view of man as an animal subjected to modern mechanical and/or evolutionary processes, such as the survival of the fittest and the new institutions of mass consumerism, humans are passive players in a drama of desolate hereditary and environmental mechanisms.[10] Evolution and animality, determinism, and mechanical functioning have been thoroughly integrated into the problematic definition of human identity for Zola.

Mechanical Reproduction and Reproduction by Machine

In Zola, the technological reproduction figured by the Halles applies more generally to human reproduction as well, because, for him, procreation is another mechanical function of the man/machine. Pauline in *La joie de vivre* teaches herself reproductive anatomy by reading Lazare's medical books, and in this way she discovers the functioning of her own mechanical female

10. As Baguley, *Naturalist Fiction,* 216, puts it: "[Naturalist novelists] tended to seize upon a view of man subjected to irrepressible drives, reacting mechanistically to biological urges, motivated by the basic instincts for food, sex, violence, ruled by environmental, hereditary and even primeval impulses, spurred on or defeated in the ruthless competitiveness of life. For the naturalists the human species itself was being subsumed into the animal species." This mechanistic vision of the laws of heredity is seen as a "fatal, disruptive force," in David Baguley's *Émile Zola, L'assommoir* (New York: Cambridge University Press, 1992), 33.

organs: "[E]t elle n'avait pas de honte, elle était sérieuse, allant *des organes qui donnent la vie* aux organes qui la règlent, emportée et sauvée des idées charnelles par son amour de la santé. La découverte lente de *cette machine humaine* l'emplissait d'admiration" (*La joie de vivre,* 3:854; emphasis added). [And she felt no shame, she was serious, moving from *the organs that give life* to the organs that regulate it; she was carried away, and saved from carnal thoughts, by her love of health. The slow discovery of *this human machine* filled her with admiration.] The woman's womb, like the Halles, is a kind of organic machine that churns out its product, as in the infamous scene in which Louise gives birth, where her body is a reproductive mechanism that acts even when she is unconscious: "Cependant, les efforts du ventre et des reins tâchaient encore de le chasser; même évanouie, la mère poussait violemment, s'épuisait à ce labeur, dans le besoin *mécanique* de la délivrance" (3:1096; emphasis added). [However, the exertions of her belly and loins were still trying to expel it; even when she fainted, the mother kept pushing violently, exhausted herself in this labor, in the *mechanical* need for delivery.][11] If woman is generally associated with nature, for Zola the mechanical laws of the animal body make of woman and "natural" reproduction an organic motor that automatically produces its products.

This mechanistic understanding of reproduction is associated with heredity as well and is manifested in the scientific literature consulted by Zola. Haeckel claimed that heredity proceeded in a mechanical way in reproduction: "In the current state of physiology, it can be shown, in an incontestable way, that the phenomena of heredity are absolutely natural occurrences, that they are due to *mechanical causes*" (Haeckel, *Histoire de la création,* 163; emphasis added). Man, like all other animals, begins as a simple cell, and the process of the generation and growth of a new individual comes down to the automatic nature of cell-division and multiplication (305, 178). Zola too describes his version of heredity as a law, a mechanism, one that regulates the generation of his own text: "Au lieu d'avoir des principes (la royauté, le catholicisme) j'aurai des lois (l'hérédité, l'énéité [*sic*]) [. . .] Je me contenterai d'être savant [. . .] Point de conclusion d'ailleurs. Un simple exposé des faits d'une famille, en montrant le mécanisme intérieur qui la

11. Noiray, *Le romancier et la machine,* 1:397, notes that woman in Zola *is* a kind of machine: "More important, woman is subjected to biological determinism; she is a machine, so to speak, in her interior, in her very nature, in her nerves, and even more precisely, in her sex." Susie Hennessy, *The Mother Figure in Émile Zola's "Les Rougon-Macquart": Literary Realism and the Quest for the Ideal Mother* (Lewiston, N.Y.: Edwin Mellen Press, 2006), provides an interesting analysis of the link between mothers and the mechanical.

fait agir" ("Différences entre Balzac et moi" (5:1737). [Instead of having principles (royalty, Catholicism) I will have laws (heredity, *innéité*) (...) I will be content to be a scientist (...) No conclusion however. A simple exposition of the facts about a family, while showing the interior mechanism that makes it function.]

Just as human bodies then seemed to be constructed in mechanical, organic ways, the increasing mechanization of the everyday world seemed to be able to transform those human bodies and identities. The actions of the man/machine, for instance, are determined by the environment, as in *Germinal,* where mechanized work and the integration of humans into this cultural routine make humans function like the machines that surround them: "[I]l était accepté, regardé comme un vrai mineur, dans cet écrasement de l'habitude qui le réduisait un peu chaque jour à une fonction de machine" (*Germinal,* 3:1249–50).[12] [He was accepted, viewed as a real miner, in that crush of habit that reduced him a little each day to the function of a machine]. Schivelbusch, in his analysis of the effects of mechanization on man, emphasizes this aspect of industrialization felt by those subjected to "the noise of the machinery at work, the interaction, characteristic of large industries, of gigantic machine complexes that make human beings appear as 'mere living appendages' of themselves" (*Railway Journey,* 120).

Noiray takes this one step further when he claims that the growing presence of machines in everyday life in Zola's age transformed the quotidian reality of human beings and superimposed on it a new surreality of the artificial and the mechanical: "these new machines superimposed a different, radically strange form of existence on the natural realm" (Noiray, *Le romancier et la machine,* 1:16). Industrialization was, as Schivelbusch (*Railway Journey,* 2) states, "a complex process of denaturalization" as the worker became more separated from his product because of the division of labor, and as the materials used in production became ever more removed from nature (wood was replaced by iron and coal). Steam power itself seemed to be artificial, "independent of outward nature and capable of prevailing against it—as artificial energy in opposition to natural forces" (10). This new, artificial world superimposed onto the real became what Schivelbusch terms "second nature" (130), it became the new normal, the new natural, the new real, as it transformed

12. See Noiray, *Le romancier et la machine,* 1:462–67, for a detailed analysis of the work of the human body-machine in *Le docteur Pascal.*

the old "natural" ways of life. Nature then becomes what is always already transformed by man's technological work.

The giant mechanical wombs of Zola would then seem to be linked to the modern in the sense of the industrialization of France (machines) and a sprawling urbanism (Paris) because they are linked either to machines and work (the mine in *Germinal*) or to work and life in the modern city (*Le ventre de Paris*). Even a home in Paris can be transformed into the image of a giant womb when that home is a large apartment building. In *Pot-Bouille,* the poor pregnant "piqueuse de bottines" [boot stitcher], with her "ventre énorme de femme enceinte" (*Pot-Bouille,* 3:253–54) [enormous belly of a pregnant woman], seems to expand to fill the entire apartment building with a kind of contagious presence: "Et son ventre avait grossi sans mesure, hors de toute proportion [. . .] Le ventre, maintenant, lui semblait jeter son ombre sur la propreté froide de la cour, et jusque sur les faux marbres et les zincs dorés du vestibule. C'était lui qui s'enflait, qui emplissait l'immeuble d'une chose déshonnête, dont les murs gardaient un malaise. A mesure qu'il avait poussé, il s'était produit comme une perturbation dans la moralité des étages" (3:254). [And her belly had grown exorbitantly, beyond all proportion (. . .) The belly, now, seemed to him to cast its shadow on the cold cleanliness of the courtyard, and even onto the false marble and gilded zinc of the vestibule. It was what swelled out, what was filling up the apartment building with something dishonest; the walls retained a malaise from it. As it had expanded, a kind of disruption in the morality of each floor of the building had taken place.] Her womb, which becomes homologous to the entire building as it casts its shadow and contaminates, links this organic reproduction to the city (the large apartment building) and thus to technological production.

Schivelbusch makes some fascinating speculations about the role of these new, gigantic buildings that were made possible because of iron and glass materials. Huge constructions of "transit and storage" (*Railway Journey,* 45), such as the Halles and the department store, worked to transform not only the perception of the world by the people who entered those spaces but also the identities and functioning of these people in a more profound way: "Social rules and technologically produced stimuli structure the individual in a similar manner, regularizing, regulating, shaping him according to their inherent laws" (168).[13] For Zola, this

13. Noiray, *Le romancier et la machine,* 1:236–53, provides another view of the modern building as machine.

transformation becomes a kind of creation by the new industrial order as when, for example, the coal from the mine seeds the old, natural order of the womb/earth, perhaps to create a new hybrid nature: "Et, sous le ciel livide, dans le jour bas de cet après-midi d'hiver, il semblait que tout le noir du Voreux, toute la poussière volante de la houille se fût abattue sur la plaine, poudrant les arbres, sablant les routes, *ensemençant la terre*" (*Germinal,* 3:1192; emphasis added). [And, under the livid sky, in the low light of this winter afternoon, it seemed that all the black of the Voreux, all the blowing coal dust, had descended onto the plain, powdering the trees, sanding the roads, *sowing the earth.*] One might say that the giant constructions of modern industrialism described by Zola do indeed create the bodies, lives, and identities of the people who live in and use them through a kind of generation by contamination.

Thus does Zola imagine how the large, hollow, artificial space of the mine or the marketplace could be a kind of womb where a new type of human is formed. The mine physically changes the living beings who work inside her; it "rewrites" them, as shown in the sallow complexions of the miners and the generation of albino spiders.

Dangerous Wombs

These mechanical wombs give rise to horrible anxieties. If the mine in *Germinal,* like the Halles in *Le ventre de Paris,* is a belly that represents both gestation and digestion, in *Germinal* the connotation of eating becomes the sinister possibility that the mine might collapse and "devour" the humans in it, just as the rich owners symbolically consume the miners: "Aussi les riches qui gouvernent, avaient-ils beau jeu de s'entendre, de le vendre [le mineur] et de l'acheter, pour lui manger la chair: il ne s'en doutait même pas" [*Germinal,* 3:1276-77). [So the rich who controlled things could easily agree with each other, could buy and sell him (the miner) in order to consume his flesh; he never even had the faintest inkling about it.] And the mine does bear the voracious name "Le Voreux."[14]

14. David Bellos, "From the Bowels of the Earth: An Essay on *Germinal,*" in *Forum for Modern Language Studies* 15 (1979), 35-45, associates the mine with digestion. And Zola certainly was obsessed with food, as Albert Sonnenfeld amply demonstrated in his "Émile Zola: Food and Ideology," *Nineteenth-Century French Studies* 19, no. 4 (1991), 600-611.

In order to explore the anxieties created by these wombs, I would like to make a digression through a psychoanalytical understanding of the devouring womb as another of Schor's stereotyped metaphoric "matrices" of culturally shared meanings that ground Zola's image of the mechanical womb and from which he makes his fiction. Most striking in the case of Le Voreux is its resemblance to certain images in common childhood fantasies described by Melanie Klein. Klein speaks first of the monsters that inhabit children's dreams: "the man-eating wolf, the fire-spewing dragon, and all the evil monsters out of myths and fairy-stories [that] flourish and exert their unconscious influence in the phantasy of each individual child [who] feels itself persecuted and threatened by those evil shapes."[15] In *Germinal,* the mine, with its ventilators like lungs and its capacity to engulf human beings, seems to be a living, mechanical monster from these bad dreams of children: "Cette fosse [. . .] lui semblait avoir un air mauvais de bête goulue, accroupie là pour manger le monde [. . .] Il s'expliquait jusqu'à l'échappement de la pompe, cette respiration grosse et longue, soufflant sans relâche, qui était comme l'haleine engorgée du monstre." [This mine (. . .) seemed to him to have the sinister look of a gluttonous beast, crouching there to eat the world (. . .) He thus understood even the sound of the pump exhaust, that heavy, drawn-out respiration, panting continuously, like the congested breathing of the monster.] "Pendant une demi-heure, le puits en dévora de la sorte, d'une gueule plus ou moins gloutonne, selon la profondeur de l'accrochage où ils descendaient, mais sans un arrêt, toujours affamé." [For half an hour, the shaft devoured them in that way, with a mouth more or less gluttonous depending on the depth of the work area to which they descended, but ceaselessly, always ravenous.] (*Germinal,* 3:1135–36, 1154.)

The man-eating, giant stomach/womb (one thinks of the child-eating monster in *Salammbô*), this voracious monster, would be, according to Klein, a typical image of the child's parents, as she goes on to explain: "But I think we can know more than this. I have no doubt from my own analytic observations that the real objects behind those imaginary, terrifying figures are the child's own parents, and that those dreadful shapes in some way or other reflect the features of its father and mother, however distorted and phantastic the resemblance may be" (Klein, *Love, Guilt, and Reparation,* 249). Thus Zola perhaps draws these images of

15. Melanie Klein, *Love, Guilt, and Reparation, and Other Works* (New York: Free Press, 1975), 249.

monstrous, mechanical mothers' wombs from common fantasies that surface in the descriptions of fearful childhood chimeras of mothers (and fathers).[16]

This phantasmic image of the devouring womb itself generates a "matrice" of interrelated fantasies in Zola, one of which includes the fantasy of not being able to be born, of not being able to escape the womb. Étienne, for instance, imagines in a fever-based dream that he is not able to squeeze his body through a narrow passage of the mine: "[U]ne fièvre éphémère qui le tint quarante-huit heures au lit, les membres brisés, la tête brûlante, rêvassant, dans un demi-délire, qu'il poussait sa berline au fond d'une voie trop étroite, où son corps ne pouvait passer" (*Germinal,* 3:1248). [A short-lived fever kept him in bed for forty-eight hours, his limbs weak, his head burning, while he dreamed, half delirious, that he was pushing his cart at the end of a tunnel that was too narrow, where his body could not get through.] Mouret uses a similar image when he speaks with Albine in the Paradou about his previous life, before he was "born" to his new life with her: "C'est étrange, avant d'être né, on rêve de naître ... J'étais enterré quelque part. J'avais froid. J'entendais s'agiter au-dessus de moi la vie du dehors. Mais je me bouchais les oreilles, désespéré, habitué à mon trou de ténèbres" (*La faute de l'abbé Mouret,* 1:1343–44). [It is strange; before one is born, one dreams of being born ... I was buried somewhere. I was cold. I heard the life outside stirring above me. But I blocked my ears, desperate, accustomed to my dark

16. In Zola's texts, as in Klein's descriptions, this devouring mother's womb can in turn be eaten by the creatures that it devours. In the following quotation from Zola, it is the word *morsure* that makes the link between digging and biting: "[O]n aurait pu, l'oreille collée à la roche, entendre le branle de ces insectes humains en marche, depuis le vol du câble qui montait et descendait la cage d'extraction, jusqu'à la *morsure* des outils entamant la houille" (*Germinal,* 3:1163; emphasis added). [With an ear against the rock, one could have heard the bustling activity of these human insects on the move, from the flight of the cable that raised and lower the extraction cage, to the *bite* of the tools cutting into the coal.]

In *Le ventre de Paris,* 1:689, in a most strange and horrible scene of a human actually being devoured by animals, Florent tells how this person's stomach, the ventre, the organ that devours, was itself being *devoured* by crabs: "Quand ils revinrent à l'écueil ils virent leur compagnon étendu sur le dos, les pieds et les mains dévorés, la face rongée, le ventre plein d'un grouillement de crabes qui agitaient la peau des flancs, comme si un râle furieux eût traversé ce cadavre à moitié mangé et frais encore" [When they came back to the reef, they saw their companion lying on his back, his feet and hands devoured, his face gnawed away, his *belly filled* with a swarm of crabs that shook the skin of his sides, as if a furious death rattle had coursed through this half-eaten and still fresh corpse.] Uncannily, these belly-crabs appear in a description of an actual child's fantasy, in Klein, *Love, Guilt, and Reparation,* 241: "When I described the fight which in phantasy John had inside the mother's body with his father's penises (crabs)–actually with a swarm of them–I pointed out that the meat-house, which had apparently not been broken into and which John was trying to prevent them from getting into, represented not only the inside of his mother's body but his own inside."

hole.] In *L'assommoir* (2:438), Madame Gaudron displays her giant pregnant stomach, "étalant son ventre de femme enceinte" [displaying her belly of a pregnant woman] in the infamous parade of Gervaise's wedding party to and around the labyrinthine rooms of the Louvre: metonymy links the giant pregnant stomach with the fearful trap of the Louvre's endless corridors from which the wedding party cannot escape. Finally, Zola himself claimed to have had a similar nightmare of being trapped in a tunnel/birth canal: "He is not afraid of being buried alive, but sometimes on a train he was beset by the idea of being stopped in a tunnel whose two ends caved in" (Toulouse, *Enquête médico-psychologique,* 260).

The threat of being devoured or trapped by the womb thus represents certain anxieties about the ability of such giant, modern structures, such as mines and department stores, to take over and transform man's nature, to imprison him in his new identity. The department store in fact appears to generate a new humanity: "Un monde poussait là, dans la vie sonore des hautes nefs métalliques" (*Au Bonheur des Dames,* 3:612). [A world was growing there, in the sonorous life of high metallic naves.] Le Voreux indeed does "devour" human beings when they lose their lives in her body, and, as we saw earlier, those spiders and workers who spend day after day there are transformed into new and weakened, sallow beings. If in Balzac and Flaubert artificial reproduction is valorized (although with attendant anxieties), Zola seems to break with their representations to criticize these dangerous mechanical wombs.

Zola's rhetoric becomes specifically obstetric, and its subject becomes more nefarious, when the mine actually "creates" an *avorton,* a misshapen offspring, Jeanlin, symbol of the deformities that it inflicts on the workers.[17] Étienne, who wants to manipulate the creation of new miners and change it for the good, has the following perception of Jeanlin: "Il le regardait, avec son museau, ses yeux verts, ses grandes oreilles, dans sa dégénérescence d'*avorton* à l'intelligence obscure et d'une ruse de sauvage, lentement repris par *l'animalité* ancienne. *La mine, qui l'avait fait, venait de l'achever,* en lui

17. The children of two of these wombs resemble each other. Zola himself indicated the connection between the children of the "ventre de Paris" and those of the mine in his sketches for *Germinal.* He specifically lumps together Cadine and Marjolin with Jeanlin and hopes to hide this connection when he reminds himself to avoid too much similarity among them: "Pour éviter la ressemblance avec l'épisode de Marjolin et de Cadine, il faut absolument que je mette mon enfant seul au fond de la mine" [In order to avoid the similarity with the episode with Marjolin and Cadine, it is absolutely necessary that I put my child alone in the depths of the mine] (quoted in Philip Walker, "The Ébauche of *Germinal,*" *PMLA* 80, no. 5 [December 1965]: 576). All three children seem to be the products of the giant, modern constructions they inhabit, the offspring of mechanical reproduction.

cassant les jambes" (*Germinal,* 3:1370; emphasis added). [He looked at him, with his snout, his green eyes, his big ears, with the degeneracy of a *runt* with dim intelligence and the cunning of a savage, who was being taken over slowly by an ancient *animality. The mine, which had made him, had just completed him* by breaking his legs.] Alzire too would seem to have inherited her deformed back with its *bosse* [hump] from the mine/mother with its own *bosses* that can injure inattentive workers (3:1161).

Furthermore, Zola's giant wombs threaten illness and death. The most sinister of these poisoning wombs is perhaps the still in *L'assommoir.* Described as a large, fearsome machine with underground tubes and corridors, almost in an image of the mother's internal sex organs, it serves up its poisonous cuisine: "Mais la curiosité de la maison était, au fond, de l'autre côté d'une barrière de chêne, dans une cour vitrée, l'appareil à distiller que les consommateurs voyaient fonctionner, des alambics aux longs cols, des serpentins descendant sous terre, une cuisine du diable devant laquelle venaient rêver les ouvriers soûlards" (*L'assommoir,* 2:404). [But the special feature of the place was in the back, on the other side of an oak barrier, in a glassed-in area; it was the distilling apparatus that the customers would watch as it worked, still heads with long necks, spiral tubes going underground, a devil's kitchen in front of which drunken workers came to dream.] It is significant that Mes-Bottes wants to attach his mouth to the opening of the tube, like a baby at the breast: "Lui, aurait voulu qu'on lui soudât le bout du serpentin entre les dents, pour sentir le vitriol encore chaud, l'emplir, lui descendre jusqu'aux talons, toujours, toujours, comme un petit ruisseau" (2:411). [As for him, he would have liked to have the end of the spiral tube welded between his teeth, in order to feel the still-warm alcohol fill him up, descend to his heels, on and on, like a small river.] This liquid source threatens to inundate all of Paris with its lethal secretions: "L'alambic, sourdement, sans une flamme, sans une gaieté dans les reflets éteints de ses cuivres, continuait, laissait couler sa sueur d'alcool, pareil à une source lente et entêtée, qui à la longue devait envahir la salle, se répandre sur les boulevards extérieurs, inonder le trou immense de Paris" (2:411–12). [The still, with no fire or cheer reflected in its dull brass, continued quietly, letting its alcoholic sweat flow, like a slow and stubborn spring, which eventually must invade the room, overflow to the outer boulevards, flood the immense hole of Paris.] The maternal liquid from this womb/machine is what ruins Coupeau and turns him into a marionette, a machine like itself, his artificial "mother."[18]

18. Janet Beizer analyzes women and fluidity in Zola in her *Ventriloquized Bodies: Narrative of Hysteria in Nineteenth-Century France* (Ithaca: Cornell University Press, 1994).

Thus Zola does indeed seem to condemn the nefarious effects of the growing mechanization of life and man in his metaphoric representations of the powers of technology to poison human beings.

As a kind of solution to this problem, in *Germinal,* Zola envisions the destruction of the injurious Voreux. If, as Mark Seltzer notes, in the naturalist novel in general, mining carries overtones of a kind of violent obstetrics that man perpetrates on the earth,[19] in *Germinal* (3:1530) this violent obstetrics is reversed when Souvarine employs its methods to destroy the mine by attacking its *ventre:* "La bête avait sa blessure au ventre." [The beast had its belly wound.] His strategy works; the machine of the mine seems to be a giant woman trying to rise up as she dies (the feminine form of the *elle* contributes to this effect): "Et l'on vit alors une effrayante chose, on vit la machine, disloquée sur son massif, les *membres* écartelés, lutter contre la mort: *elle* marcha, *elle* détendit sa bielle, son *genou* de *géante,* comme pour se lever; mais *elle* expirait, broyée, engloutie" (3:1546; emphasis added). [And then they saw a frightening thing: they saw the machine dislocated from its mount, its *limbs* spread out, fighting against death: *she* walked, *she* stretched out her rod, her *giant's knee,* as if to get up; but *she* expired, broken, swallowed up.] The artificial, mechanical womb meets a violent, eviscerated end in this case, as Souvarine attempts to end the mine's devastating effects on the humans who work in it and to pave the way for creating a new world. (Similarly, Jacques's female machine, la Lison, ends up being *éventrée,* eviscerated [*La bête humaine,* 4:1260].)

Dangerous Reproduction

It would be a mistake, however, to isolate these images of threatening mechanical wombs from the female characters in the novels, for their characteristics parallel each other in case after case. The enormous size of the mechanical wombs parallels the very common Zola image of the massive bulk and power of many female characters, represented as giants towering over small, vulnerable men. Florent thinks of la Normande as a giant to be feared: "Elle lui semblait colossale, très lourde, presque inquiétante, avec sa

19. Seltzer, *Bodies and Machines,* 34: "[The] activities of these men, explicitly allied to the technologies of mining, to the force and 'black smoke' of the steam machines, constitute a two-fold assault on the mother-earth by her 'progeny': a violent ingestion and assimilation and an extraction from her 'vitals' that resembles a violent obstetrics."

gorge de géante; il reculait ses coudes aigus, ses épaules sèches, pris de la peur vague d'enfoncer dans cette chair" (*Le ventre de Paris,* 1:738). [She seemed colossal to him, very heavy, almost alarming, with the bosom of a giant; he drew in his sharp elbows, his scrawny shoulders, beset by the vague fear of sinking into that flesh.] Tante Phasie, in her life-and-death struggle with her husband, Misard, is a "colosse devant l'insecte dont il se sent mangé" (*La bête humaine,* 4:1031) [colossus before the insect that it feels devouring it]; the man as insect on the body of a giant woman appears also in the mechanical context when Jacques is called "un insecte rampant" (4:1165) [a crawling insect] on his woman/machine, la Lison. Most amazing is that when Nana is compared to a giant human construction area replete with machines and danger, it is Nana who seems larger and more nefarious to Mignon: "À Cherbourg, il avait vu le nouveau port, un chantier immense, des centaines d'hommes suant au soleil, des machines comblant la mer de quartiers de roche, dressant une muraille où parfois des ouvriers restaient comme une bouillie sanglante. Mais ça lui semblait petit, Nana l'exaltait davantage [. . .] [T]oute seule, sans ouvriers, sans machines inventées par des ingénieurs, elle venait d'ébranler Paris et de bâtir cette fortune où dormaient des cadavres" (*Nana,* 2:1467). [In Cherbourg, he had seen the new port, an immense construction site, with hundreds of men sweating in the sun, with machines filling in the sea with large chunks of rock, erecting a wall where sometimes workers lay like a bloody pulp. But it seemed small to him, Nana exalted him more (. . .) All alone, with no workers, with no machines invented by engineers, she had just shaken Paris and built that fortune in which corpses slept.] Nana's immense power parallels that of the mine in *Germinal* that can devour, swallow up, the men they both dominate. Nana accomplishes this by consuming men's property: "À chaque bouchée, Nana dévorait un arpent. Les feuillages frissonnant sous le soleil, les grands blés mûrs, les vignes dorées en septembre, les herbes hautes où les vaches enfonçaient jusqu'au ventre, tout y passait, dans un engloutissement d'abîme; et il y eut même un cours d'eau, une carrière à plâtre, trois moulins qui disparurent" (*Nana,* 2:1455). [With every mouthful, Nana devoured an acre. The leaves trembling in the sun, the tall ripe wheat, the golden vines of September, the tall grasses that rose to the cows' bellies: everything went into the devouring abyss; and even a stream, a quarry for plaster, and three mills disappeared there.] This final image parallels quite explicitly the description of the mine in *Germinal* that swallows up the canal and the buildings near it.

This hyperbolic image of giant wombs parallels as well the obsessive image of the exaggerated fertility and sexuality of many of Zola's female characters, their larger-than-life reproductive abilities, such as in the description of la Mouquette in *Germinal,* who is physically deformed by her excessive sexuality (the word *bosse* is also used for Alzire's hunchback): she is a "bonne fille dont la gorge et le derrière énormes crevaient la veste et la culotte [. . .] [E]lle promenait au milieu d'eux l'indécence de son costume, d'un comique troublant, avec ses bosses de chair, exagérées jusqu'à l'infirmité" (*Germinal,* 3:1155) [good gal, whose enormous bosom and behind were bursting her jacket and pants (. . .) In the midst of the miners, she paraded the indecency of her clothes, which were of a comic yet arousing nature, with her humps (*bosses*) of flesh, enlarged to the point of deformity]. Exaggerated fertility takes another, more positive turn in *Fécondité* (a positivity that is troubling given these images in the *Rougon-Macquart* series), when Marianne keeps producing new children like clockwork. La Maheude is a "bonne femelle qui produisait trop" (*Germinal,* 3:1333) [good female who had too many young]; the widow Désir is "une forte mère de cinquante ans, d'une rotondité de tonneau, mais d'une telle verdeur, qu'elle avait encore six amoureux, un pour chaque jour de la semaine, disait-elle, et les six à la fois le dimanche. Elle appelait tous les charbonniers ses enfants" (3:1267–68) [a strong fifty-year-old mother, as rotund as a barrel but with such vitality that she still had six lovers, one for each day of the week, she said, and all six on Sunday. She called all the coal workers her children]. There is definitely a Zola type: giant, sexually voracious mothers.

Women, their sexuality, and their reproductive roles thus exude danger in Zola's texts and, beyond their role as character types, serve to set the scene for man's helplessness and vulnerability as he is faced with both his biological and his technological formation. One must conclude that this association of giant women and artificial wombs does not present some kind of sunny utopian future for mankind, but rather a nightmarish vision of both heredity and the effects of industrialism on the human race, of the driving force of industrial and urban development that warps bodies and continues its runaway forward advance like the conductor-less train at the end of *La bête humaine.*

The tainted aspect of "mechanical reproduction," both by women and by the industrial, reflects the specific tainted nature of the mechanical process of heredity in Zola's *Rougon-Macquart* series, which many have noted is a dark and deleterious process that passes on murderous impulses, tendencies toward alcoholism, and insanity. At the base of this contaminated family tree, Zola posited a woman, Adélaïde, "Tante Dide," who passes on the originary *tare* [defect] of her illness to her offspring, who then manifest it in various ways. Certainly it takes two—or, in Dide's case, three—to make children, but it is also clear that Dide, rather than her partners, is the focus of the origin (all the children are hers; the men seem secondary). Hers is the first real story of the *tare,* the degeneracy of the family to come.[20] Thus, as in Flaubert, a warped, mechanical heredity is associated with a woman who, through reproductive processes, produces deformed, tainted children. Indeed, Zola, following the science of his time, did think that mothers were responsible for passing on certain problematic traits to their offspring—for instance, a pregnant woman who stole could pass that obsession on to her children ("Documents et plans préparatoires," 5:1702).

Dide as origin furthermore represents Zola's women more generally, who are cited as the origin of hereditary problems. *La bête humaine* (4:1044) asks specifically whether Jacques's hereditary malady is the fault of the women in his family's past: "Cela venait-il donc de si loin, du mal que les femmes avaient fait à sa race, de la rancune amassée de mâle en mâle [. . .]?" [Did it come from so far back, from the evil that women perpetrated on his race, from the rancor amassed from male to male (. . .)?] Louise's feebleness is attributed to her mother's debauchery and insanity in *La curée* (1:434): "Portée dans ces flancs malades, Louise en était sortie le sang pauvre, les membres déviés, le cerveau attaqué, la mémoire déjà pleine d'une vie sale." [Carried in that sick womb, Louise was born from it with thin blood, twisted limbs, an afflicted brain, her memory already filled with a filthy life.] Louise's problems then develop into a bizarre form of collective sexual unconscious shared between mother and daughter: "Parfois, elle croyait se souvenir confusément d'une autre existence, elle voyait se dérouler, dans une ombre vague, des scènes bizarres, des hommes et des femmes s'embrassant, tout un drame charnel où s'amusaient ses curiosités d'enfant. C'était sa mère qui parlait en elle" (1:434). [Sometimes she thought she confusedly remembered another existence, she watched bizarre scenes play themselves out in a vague obscurity: men and women kissing, an entire carnal drama that amused her childish curiosity. That was her mother speaking in her.] Once again, it is not surprising that, in Zola's time, heredity should be viewed as coming from the mother, because, after all, our physical origin is clearly located within the mother's body; it is there that the child forms, it is in her womb that heredity embodies itself. Sick heredity—by extension, heredity itself—becomes associated with the woman through the body of the mother.

Adelaïde's problems and their legacy may in fact be a manifestation of another general cultural perception, another of Schor's *matrices,* of Zola's

20. Beizer, *Ventriloquized Bodies,* 172, studies this matriarchal origin in Dide's body in the context of hysteria.

times. Yvonne Knibiehler and Catherine Fouquet state that "the eternal illness of women is a commonplace at the end of the eighteenth century" and that, later, woman's healthy gynecological physiology was perceived as being pathological, that woman was "an eternal invalid" (Knibiehler and Fouquet, *La femme et les médecins,* 107, 89). According to Ruth Harris, at the end of the nineteenth century, women were seen as being ill and feeble; as in Zola's case, frequently the locus of this illness was the womb, most famously in the way in which hysteria was understood.[21] Michelet, as an example, certainly seems to find the womb, particularly in its reproductive duties, to be both injured and nefarious in the following description of its postpartum state, written as a kind of warning to the male readers of his book: "Whoever has not been hardened, made indifferent to these miserable spectacles, is scarcely master of himself when he sees the exact depiction of the womb after birth. A trembling, spine-chilling suffering seizes hold of him . . . The incredible irritation of this organ, the foul torrent that exudes so cruelly from the devastated cavity—Oh, what horror! One pulls back" (Michelet, *L'amour,* 131). Here, the womb seems almost to contaminate the observer himself, let alone the poor human who might be born from it. In this context, it seems highly significant that Zola's character, Pascal, would develop his theories of heredity by studying the wombs of pregnant women who died of cholera, as if the general rules of heredity would be based on ill women as they reproduced. The perception that women and their wombs were sick may point to this general belief and anxiety, manifested by Zola, that women, through the mechanics of heredity, were passing on deleterious traits to their young. Female pathology also feeds into the larger anxiety about degeneration that permeated French and European society at the end of the nineteenth century.[22]

Most significant for Zola's world is that mental illness (including hysteria) is one of the *tares* that comes from the mother, as Zola asserts: "Le

21. Harris, *Murders and Madness,* 207, claims that Charcot, as the rest of his culture, seemed to lump all women together in a "unifying pathologization" and that in his studies he displayed a strange obsession with women: "Throughout this wide-ranging polemic (on hysteria and hypnotism) it is impossible to escape the obsession with women which permeated the discussion" (203). Schor, *Zola's Crowds,* 128, notes Zola's association of women with disease.

22. This differs from Seltzer's conclusions about other naturalist texts. In Seltzer's analysis of those works, the naturalist text *is* the machine that produces degeneration ("genesis as *de*generation"); here Zola seems to be moving in a slightly different direction, one in which the naturalist text generates degeneration in order to expose its origins and, as we shall see, to cure it (Seltzer, *Bodies and Machines,* 38).

système nerveux me paraît devoir dériver plus souvent de la femme. Les maladies mentales viennent surtout des mères" ("Documents et plans préparatoires," 5:1725). [It seems to me that the nervous system must come more often from the woman. Mental illnesses come mainly from mothers.] The *tare* of Adélaïde, the original mother of the *Rougon-Macquart* family, was a kind of mental/physical illness—hysteria, her *troubles hystériques,* which expressed themselves in various ways in her offspring.[23] In fact, Dide becomes crazier when she has children, and in this way the family *tare* of insanity is specifically related to childbirth: "Dès ses premières couches, elle fut sujette à des crises nerveuses qui la jetaient dans des convulsions terribles" (*La fortune des Rougon,* 1:44). [Since the delivery of her first child, she was subject to nervous attacks that sent her into terrible convulsions.] It is also perhaps pertinent to mention that Émile Zola was seen to have inherited a nervous condition from his mother, whose name was, significantly, Émilie.[24]

Hysteria provides the most important link between wombs and nervous illness, and it was believed in Zola's time that hysteria was hereditary.[25] Even though at the end of the nineteenth century, scientific evidence, such as the existence of male hysteria, showed that hysteria was not exclusively a disease of the womb, the illness continued to be linked essentially with women. Knibiehler and Fouquet argue that Charcot's

23. Noiray, *Le romancier et la machine,* 1:403: "One can thus see the necessary relation that Zola establishes—in this case and in each case when a woman or her imaginary equivalent is involved—between the woman's body, her mechanical metaphor, and the idea of the breakdown, from a sexual origin, of this human machine."

24. In that very strange but interesting book, Édouard Toulouse, who was head of a clinic at the Faculté de Médecine of Paris, interviewed and examined Zola and recorded the results of his examination. Even though some of his "scientific" observations are quite strange to us today, they are all useful in that they tell us what this doctor thought of Zola's mental state and what Zola himself might have thought. "Mr. Zola's mother [. . .] also had nervous attacks dating from her youth, which had diminished in intensity as she grew older. The characteristics of these crises were these: aura (the sensation of a lump in the throat), tonic convulsions with contractions, then more extended convulsions, without complete amnesia afterwards" (Toulouse, *Enquête médico-psychologique,* 112). Zola too had a number of what this doctor called nervous symptoms, some of which follow: "At present, the attacks are not as strong, but they have been replaced by a state of chronic discomfort, by nearly constant weakness and irritability. Often *gastric pains* are the occasion for or signal of nervous exacerbations [. . .] Being squeezed in a crowd during Lent once provoked an anxiety attack in Mr. Zola with serious pseudo-anginal characteristics [. . .] From this point of view and also because of certain morbid ideas [. . .] one has the right to say the Mr. Zola is really a neuropath because his pains appear to be independent of any perceptible organic change" (165–66; emphasis added). Could his digestive troubles—troubles of the *ventre*—be significant?

25. Yves Malinas, *Zola et les hérédités imaginaires* (Paris: Expansion Scientifique Française, 1985), 37–38, 98–100.

spectacles acted to display the power of the male doctor over the female patient: "Everyone admired the power and knowledge of the master, struggling with a patient who submitted to his will" (Knibiehler and Fouquet, *La femme et les médecins,* 224).

Hysteria along with its relationship to the female characters in Zola has already been the object of several thorough and interesting studies, and it is not central to our topic. What is most intriguing in our context is the use of hypnotism as a tool in the treatment of hysterical women. As we saw in the Introduction and in Balzac, mesmerism (and later hypnosis) could be used as a means to control and cure patients, generally women, who came under the physician's power. Charcot and the men who worked with him did use hypnotism as a tool to control pliable hysterical women, and they viewed women generally as weak-willed and controllable: "Despite this, his writings and, more particularly, the popular perception of hysteria almost always concentrated on women's passive or manipulative qualities and the ability of men to overpower and control them" (Harris, *Murders and Madness,* 203); "In this state, subjects seemed like human marionettes, dancing to the strings of the operator" (167). Both the practice of mesmerism in Balzac's time and that of hypnosis at the end of the century provide the "physician" with control of another human, most particularly of those women with their ill wombs.

The control that hypnosis gives the doctor allows him not only to attempt to help the patient but also to study hysteria in a kind of scientific experiment. One need only to remember the images of Charcot and his colleagues in the process of observing the contortions of hysterical women in the amphitheater. Indeed, as Ruth Harris (*Murders and Madness,* 166) has seen, Charcot's experiments on living women were part of the Bernardian ideal of experimental medicine; interventions such as hypnosis in the illness of hysterical women were called, most outrageously, "psycho-physiological vivisection," which implies scientific experimentation performed on living creatures, in this case women (here we return to the role of the dissection of women discussed in the Introduction).

The Hero Engineer

Faced with woman's voracious sexuality and her role in mechanical, organic reproduction and its tainted products, the hero, often portrayed as a kind of self-made savior, must attempt to obtain a new purity by immersing himself in his work, triumphing over the mechanical womb and/or distancing himself from the women associated with it. Jacques Lantier tries to purify himself by plunging himself into work and attempting to dominate his engine, la Lison, and by keeping himself away from real women.[26] The pure worker, Goujet, in *L'assommoir,* stays away from women. Most significant is that the two idealistic revolutionaries Florent and Étienne, possible engineers of a future society, eschew the opposite sex and fear the mechanical *ventre.* In *Le ventre de Paris,* Florent feels apprehensive toward the Halles and attempts to keep his distance from Lisa and other women; Étienne feels similar repugnance toward the mine in *Germinal* and attempts as well to keep away (ultimately unsuccessfully) from women. At the end of *Germinal,* Étienne survives Catherine, who might have been pregnant with his child (however brief and unlikely a pregnancy it might have been), and he survives even though the giant mine/womb is destroyed along with Catherine and the imagined product of her own, natural womb.

As in Flaubert and Balzac, the rejection of the woman and reproduction goes hand in hand with the fantasy of creating an artificial, new, ideal woman. For Zola, these idealist heroes see themselves as destroying the corrupt, impure world represented by woman and natural procreation and creating a brave new artificial and pure world where they are the creators of a new woman and/or a new reality. The real woman constantly comes up against the ideal, artificial woman in these texts, an idealism that can take the form of work, religion, revolution, art, or science.

Let us superimpose several of the stories of these heroes, a superimposition that will allow us to tell a more general tale about them. First, there is Étienne Lantier and the dismantling of the mechanical womb: his goal is to transform the nefarious mine's relationship to the miners, her "children," so she will no longer create such monsters as Jeanlin and such sad creatures as Alzire. In this text, for Étienne, the ideal is a purified future of prosperity for the miners, and it is described in terms of a new growth, a new birth so to speak, of people: a "régénération radicale des peuples" (*Germinal,* 3:1275) [radical regeneration of peoples]. Étienne, through his educative strategies, envisions the germination of the revolutionary "seed" he provides: "Mais, à présent, le mineur s'éveillait au fond, germait dans la terre ainsi qu'une vraie graine; et l'on verrait un matin ce qu'il pousserait au beau milieu

26. I analyze mechanical metaphors from a different, psychoanalytic and rhetorical viewpoint as a means of controlling woman's desire and male identity in *La bête humaine.* See my "Gender, Metaphor, and Machine: *La bête humaine,*" *French Literature Series* 16 (1989), 110–22.

des champs: oui, il pousserait des hommes, une armée d'hommes qui rétabliraient la justice" (3:1277). [But now, the miner was awakening in the depths, germinating in the earth like a real seed; and one morning we shall see what will grow in the midst of these fields: yes, men will grow, an army of men who will reestablish justice.] Thus it is through the power of his words, his ability to convince the miners to unite and to strike, that his new family, the offspring of his words, would be born. It is not surprising, then, that when the strike fails, it is described as a miscarriage: "Mais il faudrait vouloir, personne ne veut, et c'est pourquoi la révolution avortera une fois encore" (3:1481). [But one must want it, no one wants it, and that is why the revolution will abort once again.] However, even though the strike fails, Étienne emerges at the end of the novel from the destroyed machine womb to begin a new, unknown life; he is reborn from that destruction (and the destruction of Catherine). If in the beginning of the novel Étienne is seen as gestating the unknown consequences of his mother's illness, at the end he has escaped the natural mother that Catherine might be, the mechanical womb is destroyed by a process he set going, and he is reborn from that destroyed womb. He himself is the *inconnu* [unknown or stranger] that he *couvait* [was incubating] (1171).

In *La faute de l'abbé Mouret,* it is not the hero who gives birth to himself, but rather the hero who gives birth to a woman. This text contrasts the ideal woman, embodied in the image of the Virgin Mary and specifically linked to the mother, with the impure, "natural" woman Albine, as well as Serge Mouret's sister, Désirée. Serge Mouret flees natural reproduction and imagines himself as Mary's son in his image of himself in her body, drinking her milk: "[L]ui, soupirait après l'eau de cette fontaine; lui, habitait le bel intérieur de Marie, s'y appuyant, s'y cachant, s'y perdant sans réserve, buvant le lait d'amour infini qui tombait goutte à goutte de ce sein virginal" (*La faute de l'abbé Mouret,* 1:1289). [He thirsted for the water from that fountain; he dwelt in Mary's beautiful interior, finding support there, hiding there, losing himself there without reserve, drinking the milk of infinite love that fell drop by drop from that virginal breast.] Serge has separated himself from real women and reproduction and, in a kind of idealism, looks to the religious figure of Mary for a purer representation of woman and a purer kind of sexuality, an artificial, imaginary sexuality. Indeed, Zola, in his criticism of Catholic celibacy, represents Mouret's relationship to Mary in heavily erotic imagery; Serge calls her his "chère maîtresse" [beloved mistress]; she speaks to him "une langue d'amour" (1:1289) [a language of love]. This ideal, imaginary eroticism is reflected in

Mouret's fascination with the Immaculate Conception, as when he imagines reproduction without the body: "Oh! multiplier, enfanter, sans la nécessité abominable du sexe, sous la seule approche d'un baiser céleste!" (1:1313). [Oh! To multiply, to give birth, without the abominable necessity of sex, merely by the approach of a celestial kiss!]

When Mouret falls ill in the central section of the book and falls for Albine, she incarnates the ideal woman that the image of Mary represented. Albine is Mouret's dream come true, turned into a body. He claims in his illness that Albine came from his chest (a displaced womb) and from his mouth and his eyes in a revision of the story of Eve born from Adam's rib and in a reversal of his imagining himself in Mary's body: "Je rêvais de toi. Tu étais dans ma poitrine et je te donnais mon sang, mes muscles, mes os. Je ne souffrais pas. Tu me prenais la moitié de mon coeur, si doucement, que c'était en moi une volupté de me partager ainsi [. . .] Et je me suis réveillé, quand tu es sortie de moi. Tu es sortie par mes yeux et par ma bouche, je l'ai bien senti" (*La faute de l'abbé Mouret,* 1:1339). [I was dreaming of you. You were in my chest, and I gave you my blood, my muscles, my bones. I did not suffer. You took half of my heart, so gently, that it was for me a voluptuous pleasure to divide myself that way (. . .) And I awoke when you came out of me. You came out from my eyes and my mouth; I really felt it.] This is almost a combination of the story of Pygmalion (Mouret worships a statue of Mary, and Albine seems to be the incarnation of the statue) and that of Adam giving life to Eve, but with a twist, through his vision (his eyes) and his mouth (words) rather than through his rib. And this is our first connection to the notion of the artist or writer and his creation.

It is in *L'oeuvre* that the hero's quest for the ideal becomes a quest to give birth, and to give birth specifically to a woman. Claude Lantier, the painter, attempts to create the image of a woman on canvas that would be alive in the old dream of Pygmalion (and in a reference to Balzac's "Le chef d'oeuvre inconnu"). But Pygmalion is transformed when the text constantly labels his attempt to paint this woman as an "accouchement," "birth": "Il se brisait à cette besogne impossible de faire tenir toute la nature sur une toile, épuisé à la longue dans les perpétuelles douleurs qui tendaient ses muscles, sans qu'il pût jamais accoucher de son génie" (*L'oeuvre,* 4:245). [He was being broken by this impossible task of trying to make a painting hold all of nature; he was finally exhausted by the perpetual pains that tensed his muscles, without ever being able to give birth to his genius.] The various titles tried out by Zola show clearly the metaphoric equivalence between Claude's desire to create this living woman and the act of giving birth: "Faire un enfant. Faire un monde. Faire de la vie. Création. Créer. Procréer [...] Enfantement. Accouchement. Parturition. Conception. Enfanter [...] Les Couches saignantes [...] Les faiseurs d'hommes [...] Le siècle en couche [...] Les couches du siècle" (*L'oeuvre*: "Étude, Le texte," 4:1338). [To Make a Child. To Make a World. To Make Life. Creation. To Create. To Procreate (...) Childbirth. Delivery. Parturition. Conception. To Give Birth (...) Bloody Delivery (...) The Makers of Men (...) The Century Giving Birth (...) The Births of the Century.] Claude loves women's *ventres,* and his attempt to reproduce them on canvas represents his attempt to dominate the creative process and to create life. Indeed, as Dominique Jullien notes, when Claude paints his own dead child, he highlights the fact that he is choosing his own representation and creation over his biological child born from woman: "From that time on, the metamorphosis of the dead child into the painting has the overly simple logic of a phantasm: Claude gets rid of the product of Christine's belly in order to put in its place the product of his art."[27]

Perhaps the strangest, most fantastic representation in this text of the desire to give birth to a woman appears in the description of the fall of Mahoudeau's statue. He has labored long to create a colossal sculpture of a woman (it would seem to replace the giant, real women in Zola's texts) but has not had enough money to spend on a proper scaffolding for it. In the scene in which the statue of the woman collapses, she actually first appears to begin to move, like a giant mannequin or Galatea come to life. The artists watching her see her *ventre* move first; this place where women give birth, here artificial, is the first that the artist animates: "À ce moment, Claude, les yeux sur le ventre, crut avoir une hallucination. La Baigneuse bougeait, le ventre avait frémi d'une onde légère, la hanche gauche s'était tendue encore, comme si la jambe droite allait se mettre en marche" (*L'oeuvre,* 4:224). [At that moment, Claude, his eyes on her belly, thought he was hallucinating. The Bather was moving, her belly had quivered in a slight wave, her left hip had stretched out more, as if her right leg were about to begin walking.] Then the entire statue seems to walk, as if it has come to life: "Peu à peu, la statue s'animait tout entière. Les reins roulaient, la gorge se gonflait dans un grand soupir, entre les bras desserrés. Et, brusquement, la tête s'inclina, les cuisses fléchirent, elle tombait d'une chute vivante, avec

27. Dominique Jullien, "Le 'Ventre' de Paris: Pour une pathologie du symbolisme dans *L'oeuvre* d'Émile Zola," *French Forum* 17, no. 3 (September 1992), 295. Chantal Bertrand Jennings, in the chapter on Pygmalion in her *L'éros et la femme chez Zola: De la chute au paradis retrouvé* (Paris: Klincksieck, 1977), 121–26, touches on the tendency of Zola in his later works to refashion the woman and to eliminate her.

l'angoisse effarée, l'élan de douleur d'une femme qui se jette" (4:224).[28] [Bit by bit, the entire statue came to life. Her hips swayed, her breast swelled in a heavy sigh between her open arms. And suddenly, her head bent down, her thighs gave way, she collapsed in a living fall, with the frightened anguish and the impulsion of a woman who throws herself down in sorrow.]

The superposition of several Zola texts thus shows that, in the attempt to purify the world of the contamination brought about by women and machines, the hero, in a kind of *urtext* in Zola's world, attempts himself to "give birth" to a purer society, himself to give birth to a new kind of woman, to take over the role of procreation and at the same time create the ideal woman. This desire to take over the functions of the mother's body has profound links with Zola's naturalist and scientific project, specifically in the final text, *Le docteur Pascal,* where Pascal's scientific project of understanding and mapping the heredity of his family is the mimetic double of Zola's own project of the *Rougon-Macquart.* Here the anxieties and fascinations of Zola's character function in parallel with those of the writer, who wants to create a new world, and we are invited to read Pascal's project as an echo of Zola's own.

Pascal appears to be an apt representation of the experimental scientist lauded by Bernard and Zola. His quest is that of the man of science who wants to study nature, to learn her secrets, and to dominate and "treat" her. Just as in Zola's *Rougon-Macquart* this quest is for the acquisition of the power of female reproduction, so Pascal needs to understand the mechanics of birth, just what happens inside the woman's body, how a person is conceived. In some of Zola's other writings as well, this gaze aims more specifically at the physiological locus of reproduction—the woman's womb, where conception takes place—and at its mysterious functioning, which was poorly understood at the time. The following discussion by Virchow of the beginning of life, which centers on the timeless question of origins and the essence of human identity, as well as on the mechanics of the fertilization of the human egg, was singled out and copied by both Haeckel and Zola. Here is Haeckel's transcription: "To determine the link that the egg-cell has with the man and with the woman would be to explain almost all these mysteries. The origin and development of the egg-cell in the

28. Another man in this same text seems to complete an imperfect birth from woman. Dubuche must continue to "gestate" his children because his wife could not make them healthy: "[I]l achevait de les mettre au monde, par un continuel miracle de tendresse" (*L'oeuvre,* 4:316). [He finished bringing them into the world, by a constant miracle of tenderness.]

maternal body, the transmission of the particular physical and moral characteristics of the father to this cell by means of his semen, these are the facts that touch on all the questions that the human mind has asked about the essence of man" (Haeckel, *Histoire de la création,* 179–80).[29] The primal scene of our creation, and of artificially creating humans more generally, generated curiosity, even fascination, in Zola as it seemed to do in Flaubert. Zola's detailed notes reveal his interest in the way in which reproduction and heredity could make a new body, as he reviews various speculations about it, such as: "On a été jusqu'à se demander si le foetus n'était pas formé par deux corps entiers, l'un à la mère, l'autre au père" ("Documents et plans préparatoires," 5:1696). [They went so far as to wonder if the fetus was formed by two whole bodies, one from the mother, the other from the father].[30]

Pascal, like Zola, focuses his attention on heredity in his quest to understand reproduction, and on that place where heredity embodies itself, the woman's womb. The following lengthy quotation reveals some curious information about Pascal's, and symbolically Zola's, project:

> Ce qui avait amené le docteur Pascal à s'occuper spécialement des lois de l'hérédité, c'était, au début, des travaux sur la gestation. Comme toujours, le hasard avait eu sa part, en lui fournissant toute une série de cadavres de femmes enceintes, mortes pendant une épidémie cholérique. Plus tard, il avait surveillé les décès, complétant la série, comblant les lacunes, pour arriver à connaître la formation de l'embryon, puis le développement du foetus, à chaque jour de sa vie intra-utérine; et il avait ainsi dressé le catalogue des observations les plus nettes, les plus définitives. A partir de ce moment, le problème de la conception, au principe de tout, s'était posé à lui, dans son irritant mystère. Pourquoi et comment un être nouveau? Quelles étaient les lois de la vie, ce torrent d'êtres qui faisaient le monde? Il ne s'en tenait pas aux cadavres, il élargissait ses *dissections* sur l'humanité vivante, frappé de certain faits constants parmi sa clientèle, mettant surtout en observation sa propre famille, qui était devenue son principal champ d'expérience, tellement les

29. Quoted also in part in Zola's notes for *Le docteur Pascal,* 5:1578.

30. This relates to the distinct fascination with fecundity and birth shown by many of Zola's male characters. Mouret, in his flight from procreation, manifests an intense sensitivity to them. Then, just before Mouret's possession of Albine, the description of the garden is lavish and itself "fecund" (*La faute de l'abbé Mouret,* 1:1407–8).

cas s'y présentaient précis et complets. Dès lors, à mesure que les faits s'accumulaient et se classaient dans ses notes, il avait tenté une théorie générale de l'hérédité, qui pût suffire à les expliquer tous. (*Le docteur Pascal,* 5:944–45; emphasis added)

[What had led Doctor Pascal to concern himself with the laws of heredity in particular was, in the beginning, his work on gestation. As always, chance had played its part by furnishing him with a whole series of corpses of pregnant women who had died during an epidemic of cholera. Later he checked over the dead bodies, completed the series, filled lacunae, in order to familiarize himself with the formation of the embryo, then the development of the fetus in each day of its intrauterine life; and he had thus compiled the clearest, most definitive list of observations. From that moment, the problem of conception, at the heart of everything, posed itself to him in all its irritating mystery. Why and how a new being? What were the laws of life, that torrent of beings that made the world? He did not limit himself to cadavers, he expanded his *dissections* to living humanity, because he was struck by certain constants among his clientele and he observed above all his own family, which had become his principal experimental domain, since so many precise and concise cases came up there. From then on, as facts accumulated and were classified in his notes, he had attempted a general theory of heredity that might suffice in explaining them all.]

Here, in Pascal's experiments, we have represented a twofold destruction of the old womb, that locus of mechanical heredity in natural reproduction: first, the women and fetuses are dead, and, second, Pascal in his surgical autopsies then opens up and destroys the wombs to study them. In order to construct his ideal intellectual map of heredity, in order to understand the truths about and, in a certain way, control his own family, he must uncover the secrets of reproduction in the womb. Here Zola is perfectly in line with Jordanova's analysis of using dissection to descend into the depths of woman.[31] To open up the mystery of generation, to remove the obstructions to reach her truth, is to understand and control nature. Here we have a scientific enactment of the

31. "Three distinct issues can be discerned here: the evocation of an abstract femininity, the route to knowledge as a form of looking deep into the body, and the material reproductive processes associated with women" (Jordanova, *Sexual Visions,* 50).

destruction of the womb found in the word *éventrer,* which is the word used for Jacques's desire to kill and to kill women in *La bête humaine,* and the word used for the death of the mine/womb in *Germinal.* It is significant that Pascal is called not by his family name but only by his first name, as he, in his desired rewriting of reproduction, would no longer be a child of his family but a child only of himself.[32]

Through Pascal's investigation of the origins of human life and a family's heredity, Zola provides us with a parallel representation of his own project, the study of the nefarious heredity of various generations of a family with a woman at its origin. As Zola himself says in another context, he (like Pascal) plays the role of the surgeon who opens up bodies: "J'ai simplement fait sur deux corps vivants le travail analytique que les chirurgiens font sur des cadavres."[33] [I simply carried out on two living bodies the analytic work that surgeons carry out on cadavers.] Does the creation of the *Rougon-Macquart* series itself, like Claude's paintings of women's bellies, Étienne's word-created revolutionaries, or Pascal's improvement of heredity, echo the attempt to achieve the pure, male form of reproduction through the idea? Zola did view his naturalist project as a kind of scientific experiment, as we saw in our epigraph: "[L]e roman naturaliste, tel que nous le comprenons à cette heure, est une expérience véritable que le romancier fait sur l'homme" (*Le roman expérimental,* 30). [The naturalist novel, such as we understand it at this time, is a real experiment that the novelist carries out on man.]

To answer this question, a look at the experimental method that so influenced Zola can supply some information. This method aimed at experimenting on nature to improve it, to engineer it, to control it. In particular, Claude Bernard, the scientist at the center of Zola's concept of the experimental novel, has been associated with the development of this link of science with control and ultimately with creation. Bernard's new ideas on interventionist methods "have led a number of historians to describe Bernard as the crucial articulator of a biology organized around experimental control and devoted to technological powers" (Pauly, *Controlling Life,* 53). Pauly links

32. It is interesting also that in *Le ventre de Paris,* 1:725, Florent attempts to take on a kind of mothering role, first for his brother, then for la Normande's son: "Sa joie, son rêve secret de dévouement, était de vivre toujours en compagnie d'un être jeune, qui ne grandirait pas, qu'il instruirait sans cesse, dans l'innocence duquel il aimerait les hommes." [His joy, his secret dream of devotion, was to live forever in the company of a young person who would never grow up, whom he would constantly instruct, and through whose innocence he would love mankind.]

33. Émile Zola, Preface to the second edition of *Thérèse Raquin* (Paris: G. Charpentier, 1882), iii.

Bernard's work of the 1860s with the awakening interest in trying to create what does not yet exist in nature. Bernard actually "may have claimed that man could one day create new life."[34] Indeed, Bernard did imagine intervening in the development of an embryo with the goal of changing its nature and development: "Bernard similarly raised the possibility that 'by modifying the internal nutritional environment [of an embryo], and by holding the organized matter in some way in the nascent state, we may hope to change its direction of development and consequently its final organic expression'" (53).[35] Life could possibly be controlled artificially.

At the end of the nineteenth century in France, writers such as the strange Vacher de la Pouge were in fact championing the fashioning of a superior society through human manipulation and control. And Zola, through the words of Pascal, thinks about intervening in human life to improve it, all the while being cognizant of the dangers of this enterprise:

> Et, devant cette trouvaille de l'alchimie du vingtième siècle, un immense espoir s'ouvrait, il croyait avoir découvert la panacée universelle, la liqueur de vie destinée à combattre la débilité humaine, seule cause réelle de tous les maux, une véritable et scientifique fontaine de Jouvence, qui, en donnant de la force, de la santé et de la volonté, referait une humanité toute neuve et supérieure. (*Le docteur Pascal,* 5:949)
>
> [And faced with this discovery of the alchemy of the twentieth century, an immense hope opened up; he believed he had discovered the universal panacea, the elixir of life destined to combat human debility, the only real cause of all ills, a veritable scientific fountain of youth, which, in giving strength, health, and will, would remake a new and superior humanity.]
>
> Corriger la nature, intervenir, la modifier et la contrarier dans son but, est-ce une besogne louable? [. . .] Et rêver une humanité plus saine, plus forte, modelée sur notre idée de la santé et de la force, en avons-nous le droit? Qu'allons-nous faire là, de quoi

34. Stebbins, "France," in *The Comparative Reception of Darwinism,* ed. Glick, 136.

35. As Pauly has reported, this interest in the possibility of creating life was validated by such later feats as artificial parthenogenesis. At the turn of the century, Loeb, for example, succeeded in artificially inducing by chemical means embryological development in sea urchin eggs. Clearly, artificial parthenogenesis "represented an attack on the privileged status of natural modes of reproduction." See Pauly, *Controlling Life,* 94, 97–99.

> allons-nous nous mêler dans ce labeur de la vie, dont les moyens et le but nous sont inconnus? (5:1084)
>
> [To correct nature, to intervene, to modify it and oppose it in its aims, is that a laudable task? (. . .) And to dream of a humanity that is healthier, stronger, modeled on our idea of health and strength, do we have the right to do that? What will we be doing there, with what will we be meddling in this labor of life, whose means and ends are unknown to us?]

Zola indeed represents the possibility of a reengineering of humans that would cure the hereditary illness that comes from birth from woman's womb, and this reengineering is imagined in a variety of contexts in the science of the time.

One way that science might intervene would be to effect a change in breeding that would improve the human body; this possibility was reinforced by the continued belief held in some circles that acquired characteristics could be inherited. Once again we find the importance of Lamarck: "[B]ecause of the widespread belief in France in the Lamarckian theory of the inheritability of acquired characteristics, many would-be reformers saw great advantages in a theory maintaining that any physical improvements in the population would be passed to subsequent generations."[36] If improvements could be made that were inheritable, the human condition could be improved limitlessly. Here science took the road toward eugenics.[37]

Although it has generally been believed that France was not involved in eugenics in the late nineteenth and early twentieth centuries, this may be a problem of vocabulary; the concept of eugenics was there if the word was not (Schneider, *Quality and Quantity*, 4). The eugenics movement in France seems to have been fueled in part by the fin-de-siècle fear of degeneration and depopulation that has been thoroughly studied. As Schneider shows, this perception of decadence apparently prevented the French movement, at least at the beginning, from becoming a negative movement of purification, of the need to "eliminate undesirable elements in the population" because of the perceived need specifically to increase the quantity of the population. In France, eugenics instead took the position of improving both the size and the

36. William H. Schneider, *Quality and Quantity: The Quest for Biological Regeneration in Twentieth-Century France* (New York: Cambridge University Press, 1990), 8.

37. Interest in eugenics, viewed as a predominantly British, German, and American trend, appears to have been a more widespread presence in most industrial societies. See Schneider, *Quality and Quantity*, 3–4.

quality of the population (Schneider, *Quality and Quantity,* 8). If the decline of the French nation was caused by the influence and effects of cities, alcohol, misconduct, tuberculosis, and venereal disease (topics covered by Zola, which Schneider emphasizes [8-20]), then social control of these nefarious elements could improve the French populace.[38]

One way of controlling the quality of the population is represented by the movement called *puériculture,* which sought to improve the quality as well as the quantity of newborns–what Borie calls through Zola the "empire of babies" (Borie, *Mythologies de l'hérédité,* 162).[39] *Puériculture* used as its method the control of the bodies and habits of pregnant women, the beginnings of prenatal care (Schneider, *Quality and Quantity,* 67–68). Zola represented aspects of this theory in his later work, *Fécondité,* where a depopulated France seemed to have as its cause excessive abortions but some good news came in the fact that unwed mothers were cared for in special "hotels." This newly institutionalized care of women's pregnant bodies participated in the (continuing) takeover of obstetrics by doctors that proceeded in earnest in the nineteenth century as female midwifery

38. Bénédict-Augustin Morel, who influenced Zola and his times, viewed degeneration as a contagious illness that needed to be cured. Borie, *Mythologies de l'hérédité,* 104–5.

39. Although they appeared as early as 1858 in a paper by physician Alfred Caron, the ideas of puericulture did not catch on until much later in the century, when improvements in the survival of the mother allowed doctors to turn their attention to the improvement in the condition of the child (Schneider, *Quality and Quantity,* 64–65). At that time, interest in the mother began to be subordinated to interest in the child, and the mother, in a sense, was viewed as a tool with which to make good babies.

The eugenics movement, as it took more specific form in France at the beginning of the twentieth century, shows some remarkable links with many scientists and theories that relate both to our authors and to the ideas they explored. First, early proponents of puericulture moved on to eugenics, and Schneider has provided a useful list of these early eugenics proponents in France. On this list we find that the French consultative committee to the First Eugenics Congress in London, 1912, included Vice President Adolphe Pinard, a professor at the École de Médecine in Paris and the major backer of puericulture. Second, Jules Déjérine (whose 1886 book, *L'hérédité dans les maladies du système nerveux,* Zola read and used) joined in the eugenics movement and became another vice president of this First Congress. But what is perhaps the most surprising link is the link between mesmerism/hypnosis and eugenics. That Pierre Janet should also appear among the names of the members of the Congress creates a connection between the control and management of women and madness (hysterics), and the control and management of heredity in France. The Nobel Prize winner Charles Richet, a colleague of Charcot who worked in Jules Marey's lab (Marey is important in the Villiers chapter) and who was interested in spiritism, suggestion, somnambulism, and the hypnoid state, was also a vice president of the French Eugenics Society (Schneider, *Quality and Quantity,* 85–86, 99). Mesmerism happened on our ability to control the minds and bodies of others; eugenics, hypnotism, and psychiatry continued to plan this control in a more modern scientific context, one that had a history of taking women as its objects.

was replaced by male obstetrics.[40] Mark Seltzer, referring to the writings of Augustus Kinsley Gardner and of Graham Barker-Benfield, sees this general trend as one that aims to "'replace' female generative power with an alternative practice, at once technological and male, [. . .] 'to take charge of the procreative function in all of its aspects'" (Seltzer, *Bodies and Machines,* 27–28).[41]

This technological, male takeover of generation that appears in the scientific culture of the time thus parallels the fantasy we have seen represented in Zola's texts, where the male gives birth to a new form of human and gives birth to women: men have taken over the reproductive function and can rewrite the mechanics of heredity and determinism. Through modern theories, through the idea, through technology, they can control procreation. If Zola's representation of his heroes' attempts to rewrite reproduction coalesces with his own *Rougon-Macquart* experimental project, then the naturalist project would not collaborate with degenerate, natural reproduction but would attempt to cure it. Zola's words would thus activate the curative process; his texts would perform "surgery" on a deficient reality.

Roubaud, in one scene in *La bête humaine,* attempts to "cure" a deficient reality by rewriting it. First, when he discovers Séverine's infidelity, he is

40. Knibiehler and Fouquet, *La femme et les médecins,* 177–200, show the evolution in France from female midwife to male doctor.

41. A second direction taken by the early eugenics movement at the end of the nineteenth century was the perceived need to control who would reproduce. One of the strangest characters in the movement was Lapouge, who believed that artificial insemination was the way to control and improve the quality of human beings and that only a small number of males should have their hereditary material passed on (Schneider, *Quality and Quantity,* 62). This idea of artificial insemination in fact appeared in the 1884 novel *Le faiseur d'hommes* (by Ram Baud, pseudonym), in which a doctor artificially inseminates a woman with her husband's sperm. Lapouge labeled this process "Minerva replacing Eros" (Schneider, *Quality and Quantity,* 62), and it clearly shows man's interest in control—indeed, artificial control—of the creation of human life. Another aspect of puericulture seen in Zola is the idea that the physical and psychological state of the parents at the time of conception was an important element in the creation of negative qualities in the child. This state, it was believed, had an immediate hereditary effect on the child being formed: a cold, drinking, any negative influence, could adversely affect the child (Schneider, *Quality and Quantity,* 74–75). One need think only of Gervaise and the state of her parents at the time of her conception, and the relationship of that state to her limp (the origin of her limp is ambiguous and quite interesting; in any case; both parents were drunk, and they most likely were beating each other that night): "Conçue dans l'ivresse, sans doute pendant une de ces nuits honteuses où les époux s'assommaient, elle avait la cuisse droite déviée et amaigrie" (*La fortune des Rougon,* 124). [Conceived in drunkenness, doubtless on one of those shameful nights when her parents were beating each other, she had a twisted and withered right hip.] One way to reverse the degradation of the French population, then, would be to work to eliminate these influences on babies.

able to "read" the truth through the surface of her body: "Elle voyait qu'elle se perdait, qu'il lisait clairement sous sa peau, et elle aurait voulu revenir, ravaler ses paroles" (*La bête humaine,* 4:1012). [She saw that she was losing, that he was clearly reading under her skin, and she would have liked to go back, to swallow her words.] But after this, in a strange kind of effort to rewrite this revelation that will change their lives, he tries to beat words into her body: "'[T]u as couché avec! . . . couché avec! . . . couché avec!' Il s'enrageait à ces mots répétés, il abattait les poings, chaque fois qu'il les prononçait, comme pour les lui faire entrer dans la chair" (4:1013). ["You slept with him! . . . slept with him! . . . slept with him!" He became enraged by these repeated words, he slammed his fists down each time he said them, as if to make them enter into her flesh.] This is truly a strange and violent way to rewrite a woman.

However, in a novel that does not belong to the *Rougon-Macquart* series we find an uncanny embodiment of the fantasy in which the author/experimenter creates a new, real human being through a certain process of writing. That novel is *Madeleine Férat,* which contains an infamous example of one of Zola's (now dethroned) scientific ideas. Jacques, who is Madeleine's first lover in this text, does not impregnate her during the time of their affair, but when Madeleine, later, married to another man, has a child, it is not so much the offspring of her husband, Guillaume, as that of her first lover, Jacques. This is explained scientifically by Zola as a physiological process whereby the first male to possess a woman infiltrates her body and influences her later offspring. It is explained rhetorically by Zola as the process whereby the man *writes* his very being on the woman's body and in so doing transforms both her and her child; once again we have the notion of inscribing bodies and identities. Jacques's possession of Madeleine leaves traces on her being, a kind of writing, performed by his body, by his sexual relations with her, by his semen as a kind of ink, so that her child by another man bears the marks of her first lover, looks like him: "[S]a chair vierge avait pris *l'empreinte ineffaçable* du jeune homme"; "[I]l laissa la jeune femme éternellement *frappée à la marque* de ses baisers"; "[L]'effet charnel de la possession n'en gardait pas moins sa force; les *traces* de la liaison qui l'avait rendue femme, survivaient à son amour"; "[L]e sein de la jeune femme donnait à l'enfant les traits de l'homme dont il gardait *l'empreinte.*"[42] [Her virgin flesh had taken on the *indelible imprint* of the

42. Émile Zola, *Madeleine Férat* (Paris: C. Marpon & E. Flammarion, 18??), 181–82; emphasis added.

young man; He left the young woman eternally *stamped with the mark* of his kisses; The carnal effect of his possession did not lose any of its force; the *traces* of the relationship that had made her a woman survived her love; The woman's breast gave to the child the traits of the man whose *imprint* she retained.] What is important for us here is that Jacques's writing on Madeleine creates not only their child but also Madeleine herself. His semen, or his *sang* [blood], in Zola turns her into a new being; he "gestates" her, forms her into a new woman: "On eût dit que Jacques, en la serrant contre sa poitrine, la moulait à son image, lui donnait de ses muscles et de ses os [. . .] Elle se trouvait formée" (*Madeleine Férat,* 181–82). [One would have said that Jacques, holding her to his breast, was molding her in his image, giving her his muscles and his bones (. . .) She found herself formed.] Here we have the fantasy that Jacques would be the equivalent of the surgeon/writer, would through his "text" create, form a new woman. It is the allegory of writing, of imprint and trace, that links Zola with Jacques's creative process; of course, it is Zola himself who creates this very woman Madeleine through writing, in this book that tells of her formation.[43]

Thus through the image of the mechanics of heredity we find a haunting presence in Zola's works of a desire to eliminate natural reproduction and all its associated problems and to venture into a new world, one where males could create women and offspring. Serge's Madonna, who would come from his mouth; Claude's woman, who would emerge from the ideal painting; Jacques's Madeleine, who would be formed by his "writing"—a new woman and humankind would emerge from the artist's and writer's craft.

43. How apt that the mistress of the father of Madeleine's husband is science: "Son père lui avait jadis parlé de la science avec une jalousie sourde, une ironie amère. Il devait la considérer comme *une maîtresse* lubrique et cruelle qui le brisait de ses voluptés" (*Madeleine Férat,* 84; emphasis added). [His father had spoken to him in the past about science with a muted jealousy, a bitter irony. He must have thought of it as a lubricious and cruel *mistress* who exhausted him with her voluptuous pleasures.]

4

VILLIERS AND HUMAN INSCRIPTION

[L]'Esprit du siècle, ne l'oublions pas, est aux machines. [The Spirit of the century, let us not forget, is in machines.]

—VILLIERS, "LA MACHINE À GLOIRE"

[C]'est la statue attendant le Pygmalion créateur. [It is the statue awaiting the Pygmalion creator.]

—VILLIERS, *L'ÈVE FUTURE*

Woman's Ills

If the writers we have examined thus far use the fantasy of the artificial woman in different ways, their representations are similar because the creation of woman is not realized in a literal way in the narratives: there is no character who actually creates a real artificial woman. The fantasy appears rather in themes and structures scattered throughout their works that form a kind of subtext that figures the possibility of constructing a woman, social or physical. However, Villiers de l'Isle-Adam at the end of the century does represent the literal construction of an artificial woman. This author, who in *L'Ève future* refers both to Balzac's *La recherche de l'absolu* and to Flaubert's *Salammbô* (but who, disliking naturalism, would not give place of preference to Zola), seems to pick up disparate elements of his predecessors' texts, elements relating to this fantasy of creation, to inscribe them in the story of *L'Ève future,* in much the same way that Thomas Edison uses literary texts to help him manufacture, with the help of the desire of Lord Ewald and the spirit of Sowana, the voice of his perfect android woman.

In Villiers's novel, this creating of Hadaly is achieved by means of inscription: the perfect artificial woman can be made when the form of the body of a real woman is "inscribed" on an artificial machine/body by means of Edison's scientific encoding. Here a human-like machine, which on a more symbolic level is constructed by cultural codes in the other texts we have studied, is literally "built" in the creation of Hadaly. In this novel, it is science that enables man to inscribe new bodies.

To speak of Villiers's relationship to science is an enterprise fraught with danger, because his attitudes toward science and its creations are as paradoxical and ambiguous as was his life. This thinker, who was, as Henri de Régnier describes, "une protestation vivante contre l'esprit positiviste et réaliste de son temps" [a living protest against the positivist and realist spirit of his times], wrote this convincing and informed piece of science fiction about Thomas Edison and his inventions.[1] Villiers is a man who at one time favored the commune and who also believed firmly in the restitution of the monarchy. One must therefore approach Villiers's writings with an understanding of these contradictions and allow his conflicting images their right of place in his representations.[2] Indeed, Villiers's stance toward the crisis of distinction, the ambiguities feared and shunned by his predecessors, is quite different from theirs. Villiers exploits the crisis of distinction, between animate and inanimate, natural and artificial, and turns this ambiguity to his advantage.

Villiers rejected realism and naturalism in favor of his own brand of idealism. His fiction is, at heart, a desire to cure the illness of his contemporary world and to make the ideal real, a process in which his writing would participate. Villiers hoped for "a total regeneration of society" (Raitt, *Life of Villiers,* 118), which his *L'Ève future* suggested in its representation of the regeneration of woman. Thus, although he might reject the utilitarian nature to which the science of his time was being put, in this novel he changed the goals of science, bent its technologies to his idealist uses, and imagined science as an art that might work toward a reengineering or rewriting of that society, a refabrication of "nature" that would improve on it. In his attempt to rid the world of bourgeois values, to save a kind of aristocracy, he "used" the scientist, Edison (who ironically made possible, as Rhonda Garelick states, the levelings of mass culture[3]), to compose the story of the way this ignoble culture could go beyond itself.

1. Henri de Régnier, *Portraits et souvenirs: Portraits et souvenirs—pour les mois d'hiver* (Paris: Mercure de France, 1913), 23. Cited also in Alan Raitt, *The Life of Villiers de l'Isle-Adam* (New York: Oxford University Press, 1981), 368. John Anzalone, "Golden Cylinders: Inscription and Intertext in *L'Ève future,*" *L'Esprit créateur* 26, no. 4 (Winter 1986), 43, considers Edison a false positivist. See Noiray, *Le romancier et la machine,* 2:375–76, for another discussion of Villiers's ambivalent attitude toward science.

2. Rodolphe Gasché, "The Stelliferous Fold: On Villiers de l'Isle-Adam's *L'Ève future,*" *Studies in Romanticism* 22 (Summer 1983), 300–301, in fact, reads this ambiguity of *L'Ève future* as its aesthetic center.

3. Rhonda Garelick, *Rising Star: Dandyism, Gender, and Performance in the Fin-de-Siècle* (Princeton: Princeton University Press, 1998), 80–81.

Villiers's was a typical criticism of bourgeois culture, one he shared with Flaubert, whom he admired, in its rejection of commoditization. The real world in *L'Ève future* is a fallen one in which money has replaced old, superior values. It is Alicia Clary, the woman whom Lord Ewald loves, who represents all that is wrong with the times. A clear example of her base nature is that, having erred in her past, she feels not noble remorse or defiance but rather crass materialist regret: "Maintenant, ce que cette femme regrette dans sa faute, loin d'être l'honneur lui-même (cette abstraction surannée), n'est que le bénéfice que ce capital rapporte, prudemment conservé."[4] [Now what this woman regrets in her mistake, far from being honor itself (that antiquated abstraction), is but the profit that its capital yields, when it has been prudently preserved.] She is an alluring body impurely filled with bourgeois codes and identity, an ugly mix: "une Déesse bourgeoise" (*L'Ève future,* 1:804) [a bourgeois Goddess]. Like Flaubert, Villiers suggests that language itself is linked to this bourgeois identity in its mechanical repetition of coded forms. Language is a cliché, constantly repeated: "Improviser! . . . s'écria Edison: vous croyez donc que l'on improvise quoi que ce soit? qu'on ne *récite* pas toujours? [. . .] En vérité, toute parole n'est et ne peut être qu'une redite" (1:918). ["Improvise!" cried Edison. "Do you believe then that we can improvise anything? That we don't always *recite*? (. . .) In truth, every word is only and can be only a repetition."] The human being mechanically repeats and parrots.

Because Alicia's identity has been written by bourgeois codification, Ewald actually considers trying to rewrite Alicia's character himself; he would be another new Pygmalion.[5] Ewald recounts how he had hoped

4. Villiers de L'Isle-Adam, *L'Ève future,* in *Oeuvres complètes,* ed. Alan Raitt, Pierre-Georges Castez, Jean-Marie Bellefroid (Paris: Gallimard, 1986), 1:802. All references to Villiers's works are to this edition unless otherwise noted.

5. This is something that Jules Michelet had suggested in *L'amour; la femme* (Paris: Flammarion, 1985). According to Michelet, the young, newly married woman "veut commencer une vie absolument nouvelle, sans rapport avec l'ancienne. Elle veut renaître avec lui [son mari] et de lui: 'Que ce jour, dit-elle, soit le premier de mes jours! Ce que tu crois, je le crois: *Ton peuple sera mon peuple et ton dieu sera mon dieu.*' [. . .] Il faut [. . .] la [la femme] refaire, la renouveler, la *créer* [. . .] Nous sommes des ouvriers, créateurs et fabricateurs, et les vrais fils de Prométhée. Nous ne voulons pas une Pandore toute faite, mais une à faire" (75) [wants to begin an absolutely new life, without any relationship to the past. She wants to be reborn with him (her husband) and from him: "Let this day be," she says, "the first of my days! What you believe, I believe: *Your people will be my people and your god my god.*" (. . .) She [woman] must be (. . .) remade, renewed, *created* (. . .) We are the workers, the creators and the makers, and the true sons of Prometheus. We do not want a Pandora ready made, but one to be made]. For Michelet, the woman is a kind of child that one must educate: "La femme de dix-huit ans sera volontiers la fille, je veux dire, l'épouse docile, d'un homme de vingt-huit ou trente ans" (*L'amour; La femme,* 75). [The eighteen-year-old woman will willingly be the daughter, I mean to say, the docile spouse, of a twenty-eight- or thirty-year-old man.]

that he could succeed in turning Alicia into a mirror reflection of his own thoughts and self:

> Une femme! n'est-ce pas une enfant troublée de mille inquiétudes, sujette à toutes influences? [. . .] Une joie naturelle doit nous porter [. . .] à doucement reprendre, à transfigurer par mille transitions lentes—et dont elle nous aime davantage, les devinant,—à guider, enfin, un être frêle, irresponsable et délicat qui, de lui-même et par instinct, demande appui.—Donc, était-il sage de juger aussi vite et sans réserve une nature dont l'amour pouvait bientôt (et ceci dépendait de moi) modifier les pensées jusqu'à les rendre le reflet des miennes? (*L'Ève future,* 1:797)[6]

> [A woman! Is she not a child troubled by a thousand concerns, subject to any influence? (. . .) A natural joy must lead us (. . .) to reform her gently, to transfigure her by means of a thousand slow transitions (for which she, guessing them, loves us more), in a word, to guide this frail, irresponsible, and delicate being, who herself instinctively asks for support.—Thus, was it wise to pass judgment so quickly and completely on a nature whose thoughts could soon be modified by love (and this depended on me) to the point that they might become the reflection of my own?]

But this is not possible because the false bourgeois surface has become the very nature of Alicia's "soul." It was not that Alicia was playing the social role of the *bourgeoise;* rather, the social role, here symbolized by her career as an actress, had become her essence: "Que d'évidences, alors, il a fallu pour me prouver que la comédienne—*ne jouait pas de comédie!*" (*L'Ève future,* 1:807) [How much evidence, then, it took to prove to me that the actress—*was not acting!*]. In a sense, the artificial coding has become her nature, and Alicia is the creation of the bourgeois culture that has written her identity; she is a kind of mass-produced, common subjectivity. This real woman is but an artificial product of her surroundings; she is the artificial doll, "*la poupée*" (1:837).

Thus we have once again in Villiers's work the nineteenth-century theme of the constructed nature of human identity. However, it must be

6. Villiers actually acted a part in an informal representation of Charles Cros's play, which had a title that is particularly significant here: "La Machine à changer le caractère des femmes" (Raitt, *Life of Villiers,* 160) [The Machine That Changes Women's Characters].

said that in *L'Ève future* it is more particularly *woman's* identity that appears to be shaped by her bourgeois milieu; Lord Ewald and Thomas Edison, the two male main characters, seem to belong to an elite few who have a different, more noble identity, noble in its more modern, ungenealogical, Stendhalian sense. Thus, an inscribed, inferior bourgeois cultural identity becomes equated with woman.

Indeed, this insipid character of Alicia is not simply an unfortunate characteristic of one individual; it comes to represent all women in Edison's and Ewald's worlds, and women thus become the locus of imperfection. Many of the lengthy conversations between Ewald and Edison entail a litany of misogynist complaints, particularly in a chapter entitled "Dissection." Baudelaire's influence can be seen in this aspect of Villiers's thought, in which woman is the animal nature of humans: "C'est de la pure animalité" [It is pure animality], as opposed to man who "a l'air d'un dieu qui a oublié" (*L'Ève future,* 1:889) [has the look of a god who has forgotten].[7] This text calls forth familiar anxieties about the female body that are typical of the fin de siècle and of Flaubert's and Zola's texts: the contagion of seduction and the physical dangers of syphilis, the threat that woman will devour man, the threat of emasculation.[8] The only two women to have good qualities are not really whole persons: one has an ill body, and the other is bodiless. Mistress Anderson, who suffered a nervous attack after her husband's ruin and death, sleeps constantly. Her body is "inhabited" by the second good woman, Sowana, who is either a spirit or a kind of "multiple personality" of Mistress Anderson. And Edison believes that, of

7. Raitt, *Villiers de l'Isle-Adam et le mouvement symboliste* (Paris: José Corti, 1965), 79–81, links this idea of woman with Baudelaire's.

8. Edison found in Evelyn Habal's possession certain chemicals used to treat syphilis. Villiers de l'Isle-Adam, *L'Ève future,* ed. Nadine Satiat (Paris: Garnier Flammarion, 1992), 272 n. 168. Women are compared to man-eating birds (1:889) and to vampires and vipers (1:892), and they are poisoners (1:891). They are emasculators: Delilahs (1:807), petrifiers (1:818), and they freeze man's senses (1:820). Woman is a pestilential being: "Oui: telles sont ces femmes! jouets sans conséquences pour le passant, mais redoutables pour ces seuls hommes, parce qu'une fois aveuglés, souillés, ensorcelés par la lente hystérie qui se dégage d'elles, ces 'évaporées'—accomplissant leur fonction ténébreuse, en laquelle elles ne sauraient éviter elles-mêmes de se réaliser—les conduisent, *forcément,* en épaississant, d'heure en heure, la folie de ces amants, soit jusqu'à l'anémie cérébrale et le honteux affaissement dans la ruine, soit jusqu'au suicide hébété d'Anderson" (1:890). [Yes, such are these women: playthings of no consequence for the passerby, but fearful for these men alone; because once these men are blinded, sullied, bewitched by the slow hysteria that emanates from them, these "frivolous women"—accomplishing their dark task, through which they cannot themselves avoid becoming what they must be—lead these men *inevitably* (while heightening their insanity by the hour) either to the point of cerebral anemia and shameful fall into ruin, or to the dazed suicide of Anderson.]

the rest of women, the worst seducers should be summarily executed: "[J]e conclus que le droit, libre et naturel aussi, de cet homme sur elles [. . .] est la mort sommaire" (*L'Ève future,* 1:891). [I conclude that the unrestricted and natural right of this man over them (. . .) is a summary death.]

Thus, as in Zola's texts and to a certain extent in Flaubert's texts, behind the desire in *L'Ève future* to construct an ideal woman lie fear of and disgust for woman and her reproductive body. To construct an artificial woman would allow one to leave behind the dangers her real body poses. Let us not forget Léon Bloy's statement that "l'ombilic du poète singulier que fut l'auteur de *L'Ève future* [. . .] c'était son besoin vraiment inouï d'une restitution de la Femme"[9] [the central concern (umbilicus) of the singular poet who was the author of *L'Ève future* (. . .) was his truly unprecedented need for a restitution of Woman]. The ideal, artificial woman could negotiate man's desire without contact with the feared object—somewhat like a fetish.[10]

In fact, the text provides us with a remarkable symbol that combines Edison's murderous impulses toward woman and the ideal fetish. When Ewald contacts Edison by telegram to inform him of his upcoming visit, the telegram falls on a woman's arm lying on a table in Edison's workshop. When we first see this arm, the text suggests in the context of the passage either that it was the arm of a woman who had been in a train accident (which, significantly, was Edison's fault) or that it was a medical experiment carried out by Edison. The arm could be seen as a symbol of the woman as the object of the violence she threatens.

However, later we find out that this arm is in fact a preliminary experiment on Edison's part to construct artificial flesh. The arm, so surprisingly alive-looking, is a step in the process of creating the artificial ideal woman. It is the arm that could come to life and symbolically provide the missing arms to the Venus de Milo's perfect form to make Hadaly, the android that will perfect both art (the armless statue) and nature (Alicia), "une Vénus victorieuse [. . .] ayant retrouvé ses bras au fond de la nuit des âges et apparaissant au milieu de la race humaine" (*L'Ève future,* 1:810) [a Venus victorious (. . .) who has found her arms again in the depths of the

9. Léon Bloy, "La résurrection de Villiers de l'Isle-Adam," in *Histoires désobligeantes, l'oeuvre complète de Léon Bloy* (Paris: François Bernouard, 1947), 10.

10. Lathers's article "*L'Ève future* and the Hypnotic Feminine" gives an excellent interpretation of the fetish of the arm as well as a fine reading of the role of the arm in general: *Romanic Review* 84, no. 1 (January 1993), 43–54. Felicia Miller-Frank, "Edison's Recorded Angel," also discusses the fetish: *Jeering Dreamers: Villiers de L'Isle-Adam's "L'Ève" future at Our Fin de Siècle* (Atlanta, Ga.: Rodopi, 1996), 152–53.

night of ages and who appears in the midst of the human race]. The missing perfection of the female body—she is not a man, she has no phallic nature, she does not send back Ewald's reflection to him—can be repaired by a mechanical fetish/prosthesis, the artificial and superior (limb or android) (1:830–32).[11]

Science makes possible the invention of a prosthetic device that could change the imperfect real and improve on nature, which is, in this text and more generally in the cultural context of the time, a woman: "Et, entre nous, la Nature est une grande dame" (*L'Ève future,* 1:831). [And, between us, Nature is a great lady.] Early in the text, Villiers describes some of Edison's real inventions, machines and devices that improve on the imperfect abilities of human bodies. For example, he mentions (in information he most likely got from an article) the invention of a kind of hearing aid that allowed the somewhat deaf Edison not only to improve his hearing but also, according to Villiers, to hear better than a normal person.[12] Villiers describes Edison as "le magicien de l'oreille (qui, presque sourd lui-même, comme un Beethoven de la Science, a su se créer cet imperceptible instrument—grâce auquel, ajusté à l'orifice du tympan, les surdités non seulement disparaissent, mais dévoilent, plus affiné encore, le sens de l'ouïe)" (1:768) [the magician of the ear (who, nearly deaf himself, like a Beethoven of Science, managed to create for himself that imperceptible instrument—thanks to which, fitted to the orifice of the eardrum, deafness not only disappears, but also imparts, even more sharply, the sense of hearing].

A French scientist, Étienne-Jules Marey, who worked and published at the time Villiers was writing, pursued this ideal of the creation of technology to enhance human perception. A kind of medical engineer, Marey, like Villiers's Edison, recognized that machines could make up for the limitations of the human body. He invented equipment that went beyond the confines of human sense perception and that, as a kind of prosthetic supplement, could detect, relay, and record reality and thus

11. Here we might think of Flaubert's Hippolyte. See Lathers, "Hypnotic Feminine," 47–48, for an analysis of a different direction for this fetishism. Noiray, *Le romancier et la machine,* 2:287–88, gives a description of the prosthetic devices that were shown at the Exposition of 1878, which Villiers likely visited.

12. Seltzer, *Bodies and Machines,* 10, notes the prosthetic nature of these early technological breakthroughs: "the earliest typewriters were designed for and sometimes by the blind, as the first telephone and the first gramophone were designed by the nearly deaf (Bell and Edison)." John Anzalone ("Danse macabre, ou le pas de deux Baudelaire-Villiers: Essai sur un chapitre de *L'Ève future,*" in *Jeering Dreamers,* 118) pursues a similar analysis when he describes how Edison makes the invisible visible.

make possible the replication of events that unaided humans could not perceive. Many of his experiments involved the recording and replication of natural movement: the photography of motion, the inscription of the body's language, and the creation of artificial reproductions of movement. A brief detour through Marey's work, and Marey's presence on the scene of French science, will enrich our understanding of the context of Villiers's representations.

The Graphic Method

The Universal Exposition in Paris in 1889 attracted to its exhibits three important thinkers in our study. Villiers, at death's door, was taken around, perhaps in a wheelchair (Noiray, *Le romancier et la machine,* 2:281), to the exposition where Edison's inventions, from the light bulb to the phonograph, were displayed, as other Edison inventions had been displayed in the previous exposition that Villiers likely attended in 1878. In 1889, Villiers must have seen firsthand many of the devices he had described in *L'Ève future.* Edison attended that 1889 exposition in the company of our scientist and inventor, Marey.[13] After the 1889 exposition, Edison left Paris and returned to America, and out of this visit came Edison's famous kinetoscope (Braun, *Picturing Time,* 189), an invention similar to one that Villiers imagined in the novel he had completed a few years before.[14]

Marey's inventions and experiments had frequently appeared in the pages of the popular journal *La nature,* from which Villiers most likely gleaned much of the science needed for *L'Ève future,* and Villiers probably read certain issues of 1878.[15] In the issue of 28 September 1878, Marey published an article on "moteurs animés" [animated motors], which would certainly have been intriguing for Villiers and in which Marey describes what he called "physiologie

13. Marta Braun, *Picturing Time: The Work of Étienne-Jules Marey* (Chicago: University of Chicago Press, 1992), 189.

14. It is significant that Marey came close to creating moving pictures, another way of inscribing body movement, and is sometimes seen as one of the inventors of cinematography before Lumière: "But while the final 'trick' was due to Lumière's ingenuity, the spirit of a cultural machine that could bring the image to life came from Marey, who called for and designed it" (François Dagognet, *Étienne-Jules Marey: A Passion for the Trace,* trans. Robert Galeta with Jeanine Herman [Cambridge: Zone Books, 1992], 155). Dagognet's book is an excellent introduction to and resource for information on Marey.

15. See Noiray for a description of a number of inventions that appear both in *L'Ève future* and in the journal *La nature* (Noiray, *Le romancier et la machine,* 2:281–85).

graphique" [graphic physiology][16] and his "graphic method." This particularly interesting article contains illustrations of machines, graphs, horses, and, most significant, bas-reliefs of horses—in other words, artistic artifacts combined with "scientific" understandings of motion.[17]

In the same year of that journal, one finds an article on Edison's "tasimeter," which Villiers describes in his novel in a manner similar to that of the prose of the journal. Here is Villiers's description: "Cela sert à mesurer la chaleur d'un rayon d'étoile" (*L'Ève future,* 1:941) [It serves to measure the heat of a star's ray]; the author of the journal article states that Edison "espère arriver à mesurer la chaleur des étoiles et la lumière du soleil" [hopes to be able to measure the heat of stars and the light of the sun].[18] It certainly seems possible that Villiers, in looking through this and other 1878 issues, might have come across this Marey article (particularly because both appear in the same table of contents) and other articles by Marey; in any case, what is of real interest here is the dovetailing of their thoughts about the "scriptibility" and the "graphing" of the human body.

Marey had a profound influence on many aspects of French thought, including art and science; Dagognet asserts that, as a "physician, or more precisely a physiologist, [he] had a revolutionary effect on medicine, art, technology and culture" (Dagognet, *Étienne-Jules Marey,* 11). For our purposes, it is first the link between the animal and the machine in Marey's work that is important, as we see in the first pages of one of his well-known books: "Very often and in every era, living beings have been compared to machines, but it is only in our time that we can understand the scope and appropriateness of this comparison."[19] This comparison works, on the one hand, because the animal *is* a type of machine, as Marey's title, *La machine animale,* makes perfectly clear. It is movement or a kind of work produced by the animal body that Marey views as being machine-like: "Seen from this point of view [the production of movement], the animal organism differs from our machines only in its superior

16. Étienne-Jules Marey, "Moteurs animés, expériences de physiologie graphique," *La nature,* 28 September 1878, 273–78; 5 October 1878, 289–95.

17. Both Dagognet and Rabinbach emphasize the artistic aspects of Marey's works and his influence on the world of art. Marcel Duchamp credited Marey's photographs for inspiring his "Nude Descending a Staircase" (Rabinbach, *The Human Motor,* 115). Dagognet actually views Marey's work as residing somewhere between science and art (Dagognet, *Étienne-Jules Marey,* 132), just as Villiers at times represents Edison's work as both art and science in *L'Ève future.*

18. "Micro-tasimètre d'Edison," *La nature,* 27 July 1878, 135.

19. Étienne-Jules Marey, *La machine animale: Locomotion terrestre et aérienne* (Paris: Librairie Germer Baillière, 1873), v. The entire French text is available online from the Bibliothèque Interuniversitaire de Médecine, http://194.254.96.21/livanc/?cote=32624&do=chapitre.

efficiency."[20] On the other hand, he saw that the technical machines being created at that time went beyond mere pulleys and gears, that they were, in a sense, a kind of body: "Modern engineers have created machines much more precisely comparable to animated motors. These motors in fact, by means of a bit of fuel consumed, produce the force necessary to animate a series of organs and to make them carry out the most varied tasks" (Marey, *La machine animale,* v–vi). Thus Marey's interests clearly fall in line with the preoccupations of our previous authors—specifically, the amorphous border between man and machine.

In the context of Villiers's novel, the most important of Marey's goals was his desire to "record" nature, to inscribe its workings and the workings of the animal machine. He aimed to make raw, physical reality communicate its secrets by determining just how to transcribe it so that man could understand it. And he would do this by developing the appropriate machines for the task.

Some of his first experiments dealt with the attempt to record the human pulse. Clearly, vivisection (our surgical context) was not appropriate for the study of the living functions of the human body, so Marey decided to capture the rhythms of the body and figure out how to record them on paper so that they could be studied and understood. Around 1860 he developed what he called a "sphygmograph," which greatly improved on previous attempts to record pulse, and he was able to deduce from it important new information about the heart and blood flow. This was a device that translated the pulse to a stylus that actually wrote a line on paper, thus tracing the action of the human heart in a kind of body-writing. He developed a number of these inner-body recorders and later set to work to record the movements of the outer body through photographs and other means.

The basic principle for Marey is that bodies have their own language caused by movement (which for him is the essence of life), the "language of nature" (Dagognet, *Étienne-Jules Marey,* 43).[21] As Marey stated: "If a

20. Étienne-Jules Marey, *Du mouvement dans les fonctions de la vie: Leçons faites au Collège de France* (Paris: Germer Baillière, 1868), 69. The entire French text available online at BIUM: http://194.254.96.21/livanc/?cote=31057&p=3&do=page.

21. See both Rabinbach and Dagognet for fascinating analyses of this "language." Rabinbach further cites Benjamin's discussion of a "super-language," "nameless, non-acoustic languages . . . issuing from matter" (Rabinbach, *The Human Motor,* 95). The strangest instance of the connection of this brute body-language with a machine that would read it is noted by Kittler: Rilke fantasized the use of a phonograph needle to listen to the wavy lines that knit together the human skull. Friedrich Kittler, *Grammophon, Film, Typewriter,* trans. Geoffrey Winthrop-Young and Michael Wutz (Stanford, Calif.: Stanford University Press, 1999), 38–46.

metaphor were really necessary, I would prefer to compare the study of natural sciences to the work of archeologists who decipher inscriptions written in an unknown language, who try several meanings for each sign, one after the other [...] and succeed only at the end in understanding the principles which will help them to teach others how to decipher this language" (Marey, *Du mouvement,* 24). Attempts to observe and record this language by means of human senses alone were insufficient because the senses are limited and cannot come up to the task of observing many phenomena: "What makes the new method valuable is that it does away with most of the difficulties that the study of life phenomena presented in the past, that it makes up for the insufficiency of the senses, and that it introduces precise measurements in the domain of science that didn't seem to permit them"[22] (one thinks here of Villiers's description of Edison's hearing aid).

Machines, however, could be made to do this work for man. They could break down movement into smaller pieces that could be seen and analyzed. Movement was transformed into lines and nature inscribed itself in a "direct writing" of life (Dagognet, *Étienne-Jules Marey,* 20). By recording the body's movement in this way, Marey managed to unite "the body's own signs (pulse, heart rate, gait, the flapping of wings) with a language of technical representation" (Rabinbach, *The Human Motor,* 97). Marey even felt that this graphic language was one that everyone could understand—a kind of universal language, and one that is natural. We must add that Villiers's good friend Charles Cros was also an inventor who was interested in this same kind of body-tracing and in the understanding of the workings of the human machine.[23]

Once the natural phenomenon was recorded, the scientist had to decipher it, to "read" it, to continue Marey's own metaphor of the interpretation of the inscription of the language of the animal machine. Biology became an exegetical science, a "biogrammatology," and science became a kind of "writing-reading system" (Dagognet, *Étienne-Jules Marey,* 86, 52). How apt, then, that Marey was compared with Mallarmé (Rabinbach, *The Human Motor,* 88), another close friend of Villiers.

22. Étienne-Jules Marey, "Cinquante ans d'applications de la méthode graphique en physiologie," *Cinquantenaire de la Société de biologie: Volume jubilaire* (Paris: Masson & Compagnie, 1899), 39–47. The entire text available online at BIUM: http://web2.bium.univ-paris5.fr/livanc/?cote=21950&p=52&do=page.

23. See Dagognet, *Étienne-Jules Marey,* 150–51, on Cros's cylinder recordings.

It is here that Marey's thinking coincides so well with Villiers's. Villiers too, through Edison, described the natural world as a crude text that could be recorded: "les vibrations du son, autour de nous, s'inscrivent en traces que l'on peut fixer comme une écriture" (*L'Ève future,* 1:784) [the sound vibrations around us are inscribed in traces that can be set down like writing]. In Villiers, the human body is a kind of language. It is thus not only human social identity that is encoded, as we have seen in the fact that Alicia's identity was coded by her bourgeois milieu. Alicia's *physical* body also bears traces of encoding that can be read. Edison claims that Alicia's resemblance to the famous *Venus victrix* was brought about when the image of the statue was actually imprinted on her flesh, scripted, by some strange kind of family coding: Alicia does not see that "cette ressemblance avec la statue dont on reconnaît l'empreinte en la chair de cette femme, oui! que cette ressemblance—n'est que *maladive,* que ce doit être le résultat de quelque *envie,* en sa bizarre lignée" (1:969)[24] [this resemblance to the statue, whose imprint one can see on the flesh of this woman, yes! that this resemblance is only *pathological,* that it must be the result of some *desire* in her bizarre lineage]. Thus, although Alicia's body is "nature," it is always already inscribed, a transcription of another body/text (a human creation, the statue). In a sense, there is no nature, only text.

The same idea of inscription surfaces also in Villiers's *Claire Lenoir* (2:148), where, for the scientist Bonhomet, insect nerves are like "une écriture très ancienne" [a very ancient writing] and where images, both real and supernatural, can be physically inscribed on the body, specifically on the eye (the image of the murder imprinted on Claire's retina) or on the bodies of gestating babies: "Avez-vous réfléchi sur ces monstres humains tigrés de taches bicolores, de fourrures,—sur les céphalopodes, les hommes-doubles, les fautes horribles de la nature, enfin, provenues d'une sensation, d'un caprice, d'une *vue,* d'une IDÉE, pendant la gestation de la femme?" (2:193). [Have you thought about those human monsters with bicolor spots, with fur—of cephalopods, double-men, horrible mistakes of nature, in fact, who originated in a sensation, a caprice, a *vision,* an IDEA, during the woman's gestation?]

Because the body is a kind of written language, Villiers's Edison, like Marey, will use machines to record and transcribe the body language—in

24. Marie-Hélène Huet, *Monstrous Imagination* (Cambridge: Harvard University Press, 1993), 223, reads this imprint of the statue on Alicia's body as the "visible imprint of a mother's unsatisfied desire."

Villiers's case the body language of several women. This mechanical inscription of woman appears first in the celebrated "talking cinema" scene of the recording of Evelyn Habal's dance, which is described by Edison as a scientific experiment: "Miss Evelyn Habal était donc devenue pour moi le sujet d'une expérience ... curieuse" (*L'Ève future,* 1:896). [Miss Evelyn Habal had thus become for me the subject of an experiment that was ... curious.] Edison had taken pictures of the original dance in succession, "la photographie successive" [successive photography], thus breaking her performance into small parcels, "dissecting" it, just as Marey did in his photographic experiments in movement. All her movements reproduced *themselves,* as Villiers expresses it in the reflexive form of "se reproduisaient" (1:897). Thus Evelyn Habal's body has inscribed itself on the film.

As Edison looks at the film with Lord Ewald, he slowly enumerates the various body parts of Evelyn Habal, thus verbally repeating the original "dissection": "Quelles hanches! quels beaux cheveux roux! de l'or brûlé, vraiment! Et ce teint si chaudement pâle? Et ces longs yeux si singuliers? Ces petites griffes en pétales de roses [. . .]?" (*L'Ève future,* 1:897–98). [What hips! What beautiful red hair! Burnished gold, really! And this complexion so warmly pale? And these singular elongated eyes? These small nails like rose petals (. . .)?] In a second film Edison takes Evelyn Habal even further down the road of revelation when he completes the "dissection" and captures her without the accoutrements of artifice, without her makeup, hair, teeth. He has gotten down to the original language of her body, which he has recorded and which is repulsive.

Edison finally takes Evelyn apart one last time when he literally takes the artificial body parts previously "amputated" and enumerated, as well as the makeup that beautified Evelyn, out of the drawer for Ewald's contemplation. (These artificial body parts remind us again of that uncanny, lifelike arm.) This process of breaking down and enumerating parts is linked to language, the enumeration being called a "nomenclature" (*L'Ève future,* 1:902). For Villiers, the prosthetic attributes of Evelyn are themselves a language, as expressed when the transformations wrought by this artifice are described as a kind of translation in language: "Ce n'est plus qu'une question de vocabulaire; la maigreur devient de la gracilité, la laideur du piquant, la malpropreté de la négligence, la duplicité de la finesse, et caetera, et caetera" (1:899). [It is no more than a question of vocabulary; skinniness becomes slenderness, ugliness becomes piquancy, uncleanliness becomes nonchalance, duplicity becomes cleverness, etcetera, etcetera.] Evelyn translates her original body language into a new, artificial, more seductive one.

What becomes clear in Evelyn Habal's case (and she is a representative of all women) is that what is most desirable about her is what is most artificial, the dressed-up body, the prosthesis, "l'Artificiel illusoirement vivant" (*L'Ève future,* 1:904) [Artifice illusorily alive], an echo of Raphaël's tastes in *La peau de chagrin.* However, Villiers, through the voice of Edison, goes beyond the mere declaration of the desire for artifice to speculate that in fact there is only artifice (just as bodies are already texts). Villiers suggests through Edison that there is no difference between the real and illusion, that because everything is ultimately an illusion, all comprehension exists in the realm of ideas: "Nul ne sait où commence l'Illusion, ni en quoi consiste la Réalité" (1:789). [No one knows where Illusion begins, or of what Reality consists.]

Thus the real can never be known in itself; we have only artificial, duplicate ideas of the real. In that sense, then, everything is "artificial." Women, for Villiers, simply cover themselves with an artificial identity of their making that can better manipulate the illusions of the men they want to seduce. Edison suggests that instead of accepting these illusions created by women why not create an illusion oneself? "[P]uisqu'en un mot la Femme elle-même nous donne l'exemple de se remplacer par de l'Artificiel, épargnons-lui, s'il se peut, cette besogne" (*L'Ève future,* 1:905). [Since in a word, Woman herself gives us the example of replacing herself with the Artificial, let us spare her, if possible, that task.] Thus Villiers poses the question that if all is an illusion, why not choose the best illusion, one that is better than the one offered to us?[25] If all women are artificial, why not choose the perfect artificial woman for Ewald: "[C]himère pour chimère, pourquoi pas l'Andréide elle-même? [. . .] Essayons de changer de mensonge!" (1:905)? ["Chimera for chimera, why not have the Android herself? (. . .) Let us try to change lies!]

Indeed, after a time, the illusion will become second "nature," and Ewald will know instantly all the commands that make Hadaly work: "Avec un peu d'habitude [. . .] tout vous deviendra *naturel*" (*L'Ève future,* 1:858).[26] [With a bit of practice (. . .) everything will become *natural* to you.] Because the ideal Alicia would be the beautiful body filled with an

25. Franc Schuerewegen discusses a kind of "choice" of what is real, in "'Télétechné' fin de siècle: Villiers de l'Isle-Adam et Jules Verne," *Romantisme* 20, no. 69 (1990), 81; as does Raitt, *Villiers et le mouvement symboliste,* 248.

26. This reminds one of the way in which Bourdieu describes how artificial social constructs eventually are perceived to be natural.

equally beautiful soul, Edison's science gives him the ability to embody the ideal in this machine: "Je forcerai, dans cette vision, l'Idéal lui-même à se manifester, pour la première fois, *à vos sens,* PALPABLE, AUDIBLE ET MATÉRIALISÉ" (1:836). [I shall force, in this vision, the Ideal itself to appear, for the first time, *to your senses,* PALPABLE, AUDIBLE, AND MATERIALIZED.] In this way, the new artificial Alicia would become the "real" Alicia: "Eh bien! avec l'Alicia future, l'Alicia réelle, l'Alicia de votre âme, vous ne subirez plus ces stériles ennuis" (1:913). [Well then! With the future Alicia, the real Alicia, the Alicia of your soul, you will no longer endure these sterile problems.] In sum, because all is illusion, one should not be concerned to know which is the copy, which is the model, and one should pick the best illusion and take it for the real. Once again, there is no crisis of distinction here because the artificial has been declared the universal.

Thus Edison goes ahead with his experiment, and his machines (the camera and the phonograph) decode and record the language of Alicia's beautiful body, which is itself already a transcription of the *Venus victrix.* He then replicates that transcription in an artificial being: Edison has found the "formula" that will allow him to duplicate the object of man's desire and to improve on it (*L'Ève future,* 1:905).

Just after the "film" scene, in which the artificial Evelyn is taken apart, Edison proceeds to explain how he is putting together the new, perfect being as he examines the nearly completed android. It is almost as if the taking-apart of the artifice of Evelyn Habal sets the stage for the verbal dismantling of the android that Edison now "dissects" for Ewald. Edison here enumerates all the scientific wonders that go into Hadaly's manufacture: the artificial flesh, the phonograph voice, the mercury-balanced gait. In order to show her inner workings, Edison uses a crystal scalpel to open her: "[L]a table (...) reprit sa position horizontale avec l'Andréide à présent couchée sur elle comme une trépassée sur une dalle d'amphithéâtre. 'Rappelez-vous le tableau d'André Vesale! dit en souriant Edison; bien que nous soyons seuls, nous en exécutons un peu l'idée en ce moment.' Il toucha l'une des bagues de Hadaly. L'armure féminine s'entrouvrit lentement" (*L'Ève future,* 1:907). [The table (...) went back to its horizontal position with the Android now lying on it like a dead woman on a slab in an amphitheater. "Remember the picture by Andreas Vesalius!" said Edison smiling; "even though we are alone, we are in a way carrying out that idea right now." He touched one of Hadaly's rings. The feminine armor opened slowly.] In the famous Vesalius image, a woman lies on the dissecting table, her abdomen cut open to reveal the area of the womb, and she is viewed by a large group of men.[27] Both Edison and Vesalius look into the origins of "life," either natural or artificial.

If Edison's lecture on Hadaly's body follows the pattern of a kind of dissection, the images of her creation unsurprisingly portray it as a kind of gestation (we recall here from our Introduction the words of Jordanova as she specifically links the interest in the dissection of the human body not simply with the quest for knowledge but also with the desire to create life: "once you think about pulling the body apart in order to build up skeletons for study or to examine its constituent parts, you are close to the enormous transgression of Frankenstein" [Jordanova, *Sexual Visions,* 108]). Hadaly's veiled face is like that of an unborn child: "[E]lle a pris l'attitude de l'enfant qui va naître: elle se cache le front devant la vie" (*L'Ève future* 1:906). [She has taken on the aspect of the child about to be born: she hides her face before life.] Ewald witnesses the first stirring of his potential "lover," which would be undesirable in the natural world (as it would have been for Flaubert): "En vérité, si l'on pouvait voir, d'une façon rétrospective, les commencements *positifs* de celle que l'on aime et *quelle était sa forme lorsqu'elle a remué pour la première fois,* je pense que la plupart des amants sentiraient leur passion s'effondrer" (1:909). [In truth, if we could see in retrospect the *concrete* beginnings of the one we love and *what her form was when she stirred for the first time,* I think the majority of lovers would feel their passion plummet.]

Here we have, once again, the fantasy of the scientist giving birth in these metaphors of gestation. Villiers, influenced by Nerval's translation of *Faust,*[28] replays some of that text here. Edison is like Vagner, the scientist who combines just the right elements in his beaker to make a human being, as Nerval renders Goethe:

> De ce moment, la femme devient inutile; la science est maîtresse du monde [. . .]
>
> "Bon! dit Vagner: une femme et un homme, n'est-ce pas? C'était là l'ancienne méthode; mais nous avons trouvé mieux. Le point délicat d'où jaillissait la vie, la douce puissance qui s'élançait de l'intérieur des êtres confondus [. . .] tout ce système est vaincu,

27. In the seventeenth century, in fact, Vesalius "described the human organism as a 'factory'" (Rabinbach, *The Human Motor,* 51).

28. Nadine Satiat, introduction to *L'Ève future* (Paris: Garnier Flammarion, 1992), 12. Villiers himself wrote an early poem entitled "Faust," and that myth haunted him until he died (Raitt, *Villiers et le mouvement symboliste,* 196–99).

> dépassé; et si la brute s'y plonge encore avec délices, l'homme doué de plus nobles facultés doit rêver une plus noble et plus pure origine . . ."
>
> En effet, cela monte et bouillonne; la lueur devient plus vive, la fiole tinte et vibre, un petit être se dessine et se forme dans la liqueur épaisse et blanchâtre; ce qui tintait prend une voix. Homunculus, dans sa fiole, salue son père scientifique.[29]
>
> [From this moment, woman becomes unnecessary; science is the mistress of the world (. . .)
>
> "Good!" said Vagner. "A woman and a man, no? That was the old method; but we have found better. The delicate point when life bursts forth, the gentle power that springs out from the interior of beings joined together (. . .) that entire system is defeated, outmoded; and if the brute plunges into it once more with delight, the man with more noble faculties must dream of a nobler and purer origin . . ."
>
> And sure enough, it rises up and froths; the light becomes brighter, the vial rings and vibrates, a little being takes shape and forms in the thick, whitish liquid; what was ringing gets its voice. Homunculus, in his flask, salutes his scientific father.]

Like Vagner, then, Edison is a "father" who gives symbolic birth to this gestating fetus, the android; the "natural" woman is no longer necessary and will disappear, as announced in an early version of *L'Ève future* entitled *L'Andréide paradoxale d'Edison:* "Vingt hommes sérieux, travaillant dix ans, avec moi, et j'anéantis la femme! À tout jamais! Oh! non pas en tant que femme, compagne libératrice, idéal vénéré, charme de l'âme,—mais en tant que misérable, infernal, grotesque et puant l'animal."[30] [Twenty serious men, working for ten years with me, and I can annihilate woman! Forever! Oh, not woman who is the liberating companion, the venerated ideal, the soul's charm, but woman who is miserable, infernal, grotesque and stinking of the animal.] Given that creating the android seems to be, once again, the fantasy of male birth, it is also not surprising to find that the underground laboratory where Hadaly is made appears to be a kind of womb, reminiscent of the machine room in *Salammbô,* and a

29. Gérard de Nerval, *Les deux Faust de Goethe* (Paris: Librairie Gründ, 1932), 428–29.

30. "L'histoire du texte," 1:1513. Edison's dissection of Hadaly is then a kind of dissection of the fetus not yet born, a bit like Pascal's dissection of the pregnant women in Zola.

contemporary of the mechanical wombs of Zola. In order to gain access to her dwelling place, Edison and Ewald descend a long passage in a kind of elevator, where they find themselves "dans la plus noire obscurité, en d'opaques et humides ténèbres, aux exhalaisons terreuses" (*L'Ève future,* 1:868) [in the blackest darkness, in impenetrable and damp shadows with earthy emanations]. After this long, dark passage, they arrive in a "spacieux souterrain" (1:869)[31] [spacious underground area].

The final physical incarnation of Hadaly and replication of Alicia are completed once Edison has dissected the particulars of Alicia's body language in the same way as Evelyn's, by image and sound recording. In this way he obtains the necessary "words" that allow him to inscribe the language of Alicia's body onto the surface of Hadaly's mechanical apparatus, allow him to have simulated hair, eyes, and other body parts manufactured for her, and allow him to transfer Alicia's voice onto the cylinders of Hadaly's lungs. This final inscription is presented as a kind of "printing" when Edison says he can read, decode these inscriptions like a master printer reads print face in reverse (*L'Ève future,* 1:912).

Marey too did not limit himself to reading and writing the language of nature. Once the body's language had been properly inscribed and understood, there was no impediment to reproducing that language, to creating a new animal machine by, in effect, "rewriting" it. As a scientist, he constructed an artificial heart and circulation system, and an artificial insect. He studied the way bird wings worked and made important contributions to the understanding of flight, so that man could "imitate" that movement. These contributions directly inspired Tatin, who around 1879 built a model "automobile" of the sky that flew for a short time (Dagognet, *Étienne-Jules Marey,* 121–22). What Marey did, then, was make machines that could imitate the language of nature once one had learned its laws: "We will thus try to analyze those very rapid actions that are produced in the flight of insects and birds; we will then try to imitate nature [. . .] Already we can affirm that, in the mechanical acts of terrestrial, aquatic, and aerial locomotion, there is nothing that can escape the analytic means at our disposal. Would it be impossible to reproduce a phenomenon that we have understood? We won't push skepticism that far" (Marey, *La machine animale,* ix). "You saw me apply the laws of physics when

31. Thus the machine is the father's creation, his own child. Noiray points out an earlier Villiers text in which a machine is a child; the locomotive is man's first child of industry in the poem "Chemins de fer," which appeared in 1860 (*Le romancier et la machine,* 2:265 n. 7).

I operated those rudimentary apparatuses that help us imitate certain phenomena that appear in living beings" (Marey, *Du mouvement,* 67).

Thus, if one could inscribe the body and understand this inscription, one might be able to replicate it—clearly an idea that is evident in Villiers. As a child, Marey built a robot, "Mr. Punch," with a friend (Dagognet, *Étienne-Jules Marey,* 7). Dagognet even speculates that Marey might have been "pushing toward robotization. It was less a man-machine or even a human machine that Marey wanted than a machine capable of replacing man, who was considered to be a machine of low productivity. It was enough to record and calculate the results of this machine to replace it with something better" (170).[32]

In sum, human imperfection and the prosthetic improvement afforded by the mechanical is a fundamental theme in *L'Ève future.* Marey studied the language of life, movement, in order to understand it and then to translate it for artificial reproduction and improvement:[33] Villiers envisioned the success of such an enterprise. The superior machines become the real, a better real, and one could open a "manufacture d'idéals" (*L'Ève future* 1:930) [factory of ideals]. Thus the beautiful, artificial orchid manufactured by Edison plays back the song of a dead nightingale and is better than what the reality once was (1:872–74) (the nightingale reminds one of Marey's work on bird flight).

32. Marey also devoted some of his time to the science of gymnastics and its possibilities for the improvement of the human body; if one could understand the proper movements to perform in exercise, one could succeed in improving performance. This push for perfecting humans (particularly soldiers) was likely in part the result of anxieties about the 1870 defeat of the French (Dagognet, *Étienne-Jules Marey,* 165, 168–70). It is interesting that Villiers was an excellent boxer and made some money giving instruction in boxing.

33. It should be emphasized that Marey was not just copying nature but inscribing life, movement, which involved time, and in his reconstructions, exact imitation was not the main principle. What was important was to imitate the formal information that the inscription made visible (Dagognet, *Étienne-Jules Marey,* 137). For instance, he dressed a man completely in black before a black background, placed white lines on the side of his body, and had the man run as Marey took a rapid series of photographs on one photographic plate. The resulting image is a formal sequence of lines and dots moving across the image (Marey, *Le mouvement* [Paris: G. Masson, 1894], 61). (This "chronophotograph" can be seen on the website of the Bibliothèque Interuniversitaire de Médecine: http://194.254.96.21/livanc/?cote=extacad32516&p=67&do=page). This was an attempt not to copy the human body but to make visible the formal forces at work in movement, so that they could be understood and used. The photographs, then, are not imitations of nature but rather translations of what is already a language. The language of the body allows for replication.

The Cyborg

If Edison were to follow Marey's path at this point, Hadaly would be a pure machine replicated from the inscriptions of another body. However, Villiers goes beyond this to create a scientific fantasy in which a soul could come to dwell in this "electric" body; it would be, in our terms today, a strange kind of cyborg: part human, part machine. Indeed, as Noiray suggests, the android could be considered a prosthetic body that could lodge Sowana's spirit (Noiray, *Le romancier et la machine,* 2:310). It is magnetism (in the sense of hypnotism) in its combination with electricity that provides Villiers with the scientific metaphor that enables him to represent the bridge between the "spirit" and the physical worlds. One finds echoes of Balzac's heroes in Edison's talents as a hypnotizer: he puts Mistress Anderson and Alicia Clary under whenever he wants to. As he says, his mesmeric talents are the means to dominate and control another human being: "[J]e me sens, aujourd'hui, la faculté d'émettre, à distance, une somme d'influx nerveux suffisante pour exercer une domination presque sans limites sur certaines natures" (*L'Ève future,* 1:1004). [I feel I now have the ability to emit, at a distance, enough nervous fluid to wield an almost limitless domination over certain natures.]

Villiers's vision of hypnosis is similar to that of Mesmer: there is a current of magnetic substance that can travel from person to person and that allows one person to "magnetize" the other. Villiers's hypnotism is linked as well to many of the traditional elements of psychiatry in Charcot's time: the hypnotic trance is related to sleep and to the somnambular state, and Hadaly calls herself "Un être de rêve" (*L'Ève future,* 1:991) [A being of dream]. Charcot believed that the hypnoid state and the hysterical state were the same; Mistress Anderson/Sowana, who appears to suffer from hysteria brought on by her husband's infidelity, can be completely hypnotized by Edison. His strong control of a magnetized person enables him to give special powers to the hysteric; he claims that he can bring a closed vial containing a drug close to a hysteric and she will begin to react to the drug through the container (1:1008–9). The text in fact makes reference to one of the popular magnetizers who publicly displayed his power over women,[34] and thus hypnotism in Villiers's work is linked to the male control of woman, as it is in the texts of Balzac and Flaubert.

34. Villiers de L'Isle-Adam, *L'Ève future,* ed. Nadine Satiat (Paris: Garnier Flammarion, 1992), 300 n. 180.

Villiers adds to this type of magnetic hypnotism the idea of electricity and its relationship to a kind of corporeal magnetic current. Mesmerist currents and electricity are both "fluids": "[L]a Science, à la fois ancienne et récente, du Magnétisme humain est une science positive, indiscutable,—[. . .] la réalité de notre fluide nerveux n'est pas moins évidente que celle du fluide électrique" (*L'Ève future,* 1:1004). [The Science of human Magnetism, both that of the past and that of recent times, is a concrete and indisputable science—(. . .) the reality of our nervous fluid is no less evident than that of electric fluid.] But, more important, nervous fluid and electric fluid seem to be similar, as Noiray points out (*Le romancier et la machine,* 2:308–9). Indeed, at this time electricity was linked to life itself, "for the century of Hermann von Helmholtz, electricity, energy and life were synonymous."[35] Electricity was even believed to be able to cure the ills of the times: just as Villiers would like to cure the ills of womankind, electricity held out the promise of restitution for degeneration and fatigue (Schivelbusch, *Disenchanted Night,* 71). Thus human life fluids and inanimate electric fluids are similar if not identical, and this electric substance thus can flow between the animate and inanimate.

This idea of the flow between different entities plays an important role in the replication of the body; through the flows of different "currents," information and souls can travel. On the one hand, because the voice can be inscribed, as demonstrated by the phonograph, and because it is transportable through the flow of a current, as demonstrated by telegraph and telephone, Alicia's voice could be reinscribed in an artificial machine—significantly in Hadaly's lungs (the location of the breath of life).[36] On the other hand, in the context of Villiers's magnetism, an electric soul can travel to and inhabit different bodies just as electricity can flow through different objects. Sowana inhabits Mistress Anderson's body and can "animate" the body of the machine, just as the electrical currents flow through the machine's parts: "Sowana—comme en proie à je ne sais quelle exaltation concentrée—me demanda de lui en [de l'Andréide] expliquer les plus secrets arcanes—afin, l'ayant étudiée en totalité, de pouvoir, *à l'occasion,* S'Y INCORPORER ELLE-MÊME ET L'ANIMER DE SON ÉTAT

35. Schivelbusch, *Disenchanted Night: The Industrialization of Light in the Nineteenth Century,* trans. Angela Davies (New York: Oxford/Berg, 1988), 71. Here Schivelbusch quotes from an unpublished manuscript of Anson Rabinbach.

36. The invention of the phonograph and its importance for this new Eve is discussed by Felicia Miller-Frank, *The Mechanical Song: Women, Voice, and the Artificial in Nineteenth-Century French Narrative* (Stanford, Calif.: Stanford University Press, 1995), 143–71.

'SURNATURELE'" (*L'Ève future,* 1:1006).[37] [Sowana—as if absorbed in I know not what concentrated exaltation—asked me to explain to her its (Hadaly's) most secret mysteries—so that she, having studied it completely, would be able, *when the opportunity arose,* TO INCORPORATE HERSELF IN IT AND ANIMATE IT WITH HER "SUPERNATURAL" STATE.]

The fact that Edison has found the secret to the mixing and control of the different types of electric currents shows his ability to combine the disparate realms of the animate and the inanimate; he sees the bridge between them and can link them. Hadaly combines electric and nervous fluids, physical electricity and Sowana's electric spirit, a "synthesis of electric fluid and nervous fluid" (Noiray, *Le romancier et la machine,* 2:341). As she says, she is in a kind of "état mixte et merveilleux [. . .], toute saturée du fluide vivant accumulé en votre anneau" (*L'Ève future,* 1:774) [mixed and marvelous state (. . .), all saturated with the living fluid accumulated in your ring].

This image of the mixture of two disparate realms, such as organic and inorganic, machine and human, expands into other contexts. Two different persons can combine artificially to make a superior being in another way—for example, through composite photography (here of Edison and Gustave Doré): "Leurs deux photographies d'alors, fondues au stéréoscope, éveillent cette impression intellectuelle que certaines effigies de races supérieures ne se réalisent pleinement que sous une monnaie de figures, éparses dans l'Humanité" (1:767). [Their two photographs from that time, blended in the stereoscope, give rise to that intellectual impression that certain effigies of superior races realize themselves in their totality only in faces struck on coins, faces that are scarce in Humanity.] The technical revision of the real creates the ideal: "The artificial world no longer appears here as the reverse, the negative of the real world, but as a door opened to the beyond, closer to the ideal" (Noiray, *Le romancier et la machine,* 2:318–19). In this fantasy, Villiers embraces technology in the service of the ideal. Furthermore, instead of fighting the crisis of distinction, as our other authors do, Villiers embraces it and uses it to imagine the exciting possibilities of ideal combinations: machine with human (Hadaly), human with human (composite photographs), nature with technology, science with art.

In sum, what makes Edison's android possible is that equation among voice, electricity, spirit, and inscription. The perfect android would enable Edison and Ewald to control her absolutely (as we shall see, this does not

37. Villiers's "scientific" interest in the paranormal was partly influenced by the English chemist and physicist Sir William Crookes (*L'Ève future,* 1:1628 n. 1).

happen). Such control shows in Edison's mastery of Sowana, who has been hypnotized so well that if she puts on a certain ring, they can communicate across great distances, effecting a kind of "long-distance call" by means of which Edison makes her obey him:

> J'en vins donc à établir un courant si subtil entre cette rare dormeuse et moi, qu'ayant pénétré d'une accumulation de fluide-magnétique le métal congénère, et fondu par moi, de deux bagues de fer (n'est-ce point du magisme pur?),—il suffit à Mistress Anderson,—à Sowana, plutôt,—de passer l'une d'elles à son doigt (si j'ai l'autre bague, aussi, à mon doigt), pour, non seulement subir, à l'instant même, la transmission, vraiment occulte! de ma volonté, mais pour se trouver, mentalement, fluidiquement et véritablement, auprès de moi, jusqu'à m'entendre et m'obéir,—son corps endormi se trouvât-il à vingt lieues. Sa main tenant l'embouchure d'un téléphone, elle me répondra ici, par voie d'électricité, à ce que je me contenterai de prononcer tout bas. (*L'Ève future,* 1:1004)
>
> [I was thus able to establish a current so subtle between that exceptional sleeping woman and me, that, after I infused an accumulation of magnetic fluid into two iron rings of related metal cast by me (is this not pure magic?), it suffices that Mistress Anderson—Sowana, rather—put one of them on her finger (if I have the other ring, also, on my finger), not only to experience at that very instant the transmission—truly occult!—of my will, but also to find herself mentally, fluidly, and truly next to me, to such an extent that she could hear and obey me—even though her sleeping body might be twenty leagues away. While holding the mouthpiece of a telephone in her hand, she will respond by means of the pathway of electricity to whatever I please to say here very quietly.]

This communication is a method of control that belongs to the *volonté* [will] of Edison, who also controls Alicia Clary by means of hypnosis (*L'Ève future,* 1:965–66).

The control that comes with hypnotism represents, in fact, the ultimate condition of the perfect woman in this text. She is the creation of the man, made in his image and made to do what he desires: "Enfin, pour vous racheter l'être, je prétends pouvoir—et vous prouver d'avance, encore une fois, que positivement je le puis—faire sortir du limon de l'actuelle Science

Humaine un Être *fait à notre image,* et qui nous sera, par conséquent, CE QUE NOUS SOMMES À DIEU" (*L'Ève future,* 1:836).[38] [Finally, in order to redeem your being, I maintain that I am able (and can prove to you in advance, once more, that I can really do this) to extract from the dust of current Human Science a Being *made in our image,* and who will consequently be to us WHAT WE ARE TO GOD.] This is accomplished first of all when Edison chooses the words she will speak, which were commissioned from the best writers: "[S]es paroles [. . .] sont imaginées par les plus grands poètes, les plus subtils métaphysiciens et les romanciers les plus profonds de ce siècle, génies auxquels je me suis adressé,—et qui m'ont livré, au poids du diamant, ces merveilles à jamais inédites" (1:910). [Her words (. . .) have been devised by the greatest poets, the subtlest metaphysicians, and the most profound novelists of this century, geniuses to whom I addressed myself—and who sold me marvels that will remain forever unpublished and that cost their weight in diamonds.] And although her conversation is "pre-recorded," it is Ewald who controls the conversation by imagining first his part of the dialogue, to which she will reply in a preordained way: "Ce sera donc à vous d'en créer la profondeur et la beauté *dans votre question même*" (1:913). [It will thus be up to you to create depth and beauty *in your question itself.*] This ideal woman needs man, like Sleeping Beauty, to affirm her: "Attribue-moi l'être, affirme-toi que je suis! renforce-moi de toi-même" (1:991). [Attribute being to me, affirm to yourself that I am! Strengthen me with yourself.] The ideal woman cedes to the man's will: "'Qu'il en soit donc selon sa volonté!' dit, après un instant et après un léger salut vers Lord Ewald, Hadaly" (1:829) ["Let it thus be so according to his will!" said Hadaly, after a moment and after a slight nod to Lord Ewald]; she serves man just as Hadaly serves the two men sherry (1:883). Hadaly indeed materializes the scientific desire to create *and* to control life.

Ultimately, however, this creation escapes from Edison's control and comprehension, and we discover that, in fact, Edison has been a pawn of a higher power. First of all, it is Hadaly/Sowana who claims to have controlled Edison by influencing his thoughts: "Je m'appelais en la pensée de qui me créait, de sorte qu'en croyant seulement agir de lui-même il m'obéissait aussi obscurément" (*L'Ève future,* 1:990). [I would call myself

38. Lathers, "Hypnotic Feminine," 47, also notes the importance of hypnosis in the re-creation of Eve, which "depends on the power of hypnosis to isolate, immobilize, and transform flesh and blood women."

into the thoughts of the one who was creating me, so that while he thought he was acting on his own, he was also obscurely obeying me.] Even though he made the physical being of Hadaly (with Sowana's help as a kind of sculptress), Sowana throws a "wrench" into Edison's machine when she joins her spirit with the android to create a being that Edison did not predict and now cannot control: "L'oeuvre effrayait l'ouvrier" (1:1006). [The work frightened the worker.] It is the triumph of a kind of scientific supernatural over reason, normal science, and nature. What the scientist invents escapes from his control: "tout couteau peut devenir poignard" (1:834) [every knife can become a dagger].[39] One might view the "death" of Hadaly at the end of the novel as the destruction of this failed attempt at the control of creation. One might also view the birth of Hadaly as an artificial/natural being born both from a man (Edison) and a woman (Sowana); they create a new being, a cyborg, through the idea.

Even though science takes second place to the supernatural, it is science such as Edison's that has made this incarnation of the supernatural possible. That is because good science is an art, an art of creation. Edison is compared with various artists, such as Beethoven, and his science rivals the imaginary power of "Les mille et une nuits" (*L'Ève future,* 1:998). Just as the best artists create, "Les seuls vivants méritant le nom d'Artistes sont les créateurs" (1:810) [The only living people who merit the name of Artist are the creators], so Edison is a creator of a new kind of being.[40]

Thus science and art in *L'Ève future* are two aspects of the same creative process. Whether it is science that creates a new flesh that is a "chef d'oeuvre" (*L'Ève future,* 1:831), or art that, by scientific means, sculpts the body of Hadaly, the two have the same performative function, that of an idea that is materialized to create a new entity, an idea that becomes real, whether a statue or artificial flesh. And the new creation is made possible because of the language of nature, which can be recorded and replicated. Thus a kind of equivalence is set up in the text between art and science, and among sculpture, engineering, and writing.

The idea that identity is constructed, that humans are made of a mixture of previous codes and rules, are all ideas that we have seen from Balzac on. But Villiers takes this one step further to a deeper fantasy about writing

39. Anzalone, "Golden Cylinders," 42, notes similarly that Edison's devices "can transcribe words and images, but they cannot control the way the recordings will be received."

40. Jennifer Forrest also observes the link between scientist and artist in "The Lord of Hadaly's Rings: Regulating the Female Body in Villiers de L'Isle-Adam's *L'Ève future,*" *South Central Review* 13, no. 4 (Winter 1996), 18–37.

and about his own novel. In *L'Ève future,* everything is a kind of writing that can be scientifically inscribed: speech, gestures, the way one carries oneself, facial expressions. It is by means of "writing" Hadaly that she exists—in a sense, one "writes" her into existence. The deep fantasy here is that a writer could be like Edison, could give birth by scripting a new Eve. What better person than Villiers de l'Isle-*Adam.* (It is notable that many names of important characters in the novel begin either with E [Ewald, Edison, Edward] or with A [Anderson, Any, Alicia], for Eve and Adam; in a sense, these names are in various ways the creators of the new being.)[41]

Accompanying this fantasy of writing are many related ideas about language that we have seen in some of the other authors. Language acts and creates reality for us in Villiers as it does in Balzac and Flaubert.[42] In one instance in Villiers, a word used over and over makes a person become that thing: "Nos maniaques s'imaginent, et souvent avec raison, que la seule vertu de ces syllabes confère, à qui les articule, même distraitement, un brevet de capacité. De sorte qu'ils ont pris la lucrative et machinale habitude de prononcer, constamment, ces vocables,—ce qui, à la longue, pénètre ces hommes de l'hystérie abrutissante dont ces mêmes vocables sont imbus" (*L'Ève future,* 1:809). [Our maniacs imagine, and often correctly, that the mere virtue of these syllables confers a certificate of competence on anyone who articulates them even distractedly. Thus they have acquired the lucrative and mechanical habit of constantly uttering these terms—this repetition eventually penetrates these men with the mind-dulling hysteria with which the words are filled.] And there are references to the biblical performative, "Fiat lux" (1:770, 792); "Et que l'*Ombre* soit!" [And let there be *Shadow* (or Darkness)] (1:969). As Raitt, through Anatole France, points out, Villiers believed in the incantatory power of words (Raitt, *Life of Villiers,* 225). In this light, the word "evoke" takes on a stronger meaning when used in relation to Hadaly: "Arrivée au seuil, elle se retourna; puis, élevant ses deux mains vers le voile noir de son visage, elle envoya, d'un geste tout baigné d'une grâce d'adolescente, un lointain baiser à ceux qui l'avaient évoquée" (*L'Ève future,* 1:829). [Having reached the threshold, she turned; then, raising

41. Carol de Dobay Rifelj notes that all the female names have similarities that link them together and that the male names link male characters in her "*La machine humaine:* Villiers's *L'Ève future* and the Problem of Personal Identity," *Nineteenth-Century French Studies* 20, nos. 3–4 (Spring–Summer 1992), 430–51, 437.

42. Villiers, writing about the purpose of the publication he wanted to establish, stated its goal as "to change, through deep study and new analysis, the minds of those people whose views are formed in good faith and are befogged only by too strong prejudices, too exclusive beliefs" (Villiers quoted by Raitt, *Life of Villiers,* 211).

her hands toward the black veil on her face, she sent a distant kiss with a gesture bathed in adolescent grace to those who had evoked her.]

This performative function of language thus makes this very book the inscription of words that will change humankind, create a new humanity, because we are "written." Indeed, there is a clear equivalence between this very text and Hadaly, an equivalence noted by several critics. First, Gasché notes, Hadaly is a kind of "book" that Edison opens for Ewald and the reader: "When Edison sets out to explain her machinery, he opens the android's chest like a volume and makes Lord Ewald read the numerous inscriptions of her potentialities, those, in particular, of her intelligence which are imprinted on the golden leaves of her lungs" (Gasché, "The Stelliferous Fold," 321). Schefer notes that "the woman Lord Ewald cannot love is declined in all her aspects (form, gait, voice . . .); this declension *constitutes* the simulacrum. Declension here is the *order* and chronology of what is recited; it opens up a structure at the same time" and "the body parts of the Android are in fact parts of the story, each section constituting a chapter (there is thus an episode about the dermis, about hair, about teeth)."[43] Kai Mikkonen observes that "narrative development is metaphorized in Villiers's novel as an electric current" and that "woman's body and its partitioning functions as an allegory for the metonymic development of the plot."[44] This book itself is thus the inscription of Hadaly's body that will be written, encoded on the reader, and will write the new Eve. If, as we saw, Villiers felt the "besoin vraiment inouï d'une restitution de la Femme" [the truly unprecedented need for a restitution of Woman], Léon Bloy's next words ring especially true: "Il s'agit de retrouver ce fameux Jardin de Volupté, symbole et *accomplissement* de la Femme, que tout homme cherche à tâtons depuis le commencement des siècles [. . .] Il en avait un besoin si furieux qu'après l'avoir cherchée, vingt ans, parmi les fantômes de ses rêves, il essaya résolument de la créer, comme eût fait un Dieu, avec de la boue et de la salive" (Bloy, "La résurrection de Villiers de l'Isle-Adam," 11–12). [It involves finding that famous Garden of Pleasure, the symbol and *completion* of Woman, which every man has been blindly seeking since the beginning of time (. . .) He had such a furious need for her that, after having looked for her for twenty years among the phantoms of his dreams, he tried resolutely to create her, as a God would have done, with dust and saliva.] In the fantasy of this metaphor, Villiers would radically regenerate woman via this text itself.

43. Jean-Louis Schefer, "Du simulacre à la parole," *Tel Quel* 31 (Autumn 1967), 86, 88.

44. Kai Mikkonen, *The Plot Machine: The French Novel and the Bachelor Machines in the Electric Years, 1880–1914* (New York: Rodopi, 2001), 151.

CONCLUSION: THE POWER OF LANGUAGE

Who shall tell what may be the effect of writing?

—GEORGE ELIOT, MIDDLEMARCH

Why dream of creating an artificial woman? Beyond the common mythic image of Pygmalion or of the literary trope that equates writing with giving birth, what underpins this fantasy shared by these four authors? In our literary texts we have found certain anxieties caused by a crisis in the understanding of human identity, what we have analyzed as a crisis of distinction. It is in part the problem of the distinction of the human species, which, because of theories of transformism and evolution, appeared to be losing hold of its place of privilege. It is also, as Prendergast, Chambers, and Schor have shown, the crisis of class and gender distinctions brought about by political and social changes in the nineteenth century.

To be more specific, for Balzac the crisis involves the distinction between the body and what lies outside it in his understanding of the influence of the milieu, as represented in the noxious, typhoid-like influence of the *pension* Vauquer on its owner. It can be as well the crisis between man and machine, between man and animal. But the crisis emerges most forcefully in the dangers facing Balzac's six mesmerist heroes as it grows to include that between man and woman, sanity and insanity, and most important, language and reality.

For Flaubert, it is once again the crisis of man the animal machine that manifests itself in scenarios in which humans are puppets in processes beyond their control. In his works, the crisis plays itself out in the mechanical substitutability not only of things but also of humans. It is a substitutability that is an essential part of language in Flaubert's world, where man is a kind of talking machine, formed by culture and language, that rehashes over and over the same empty clichés.

For Zola, the crisis between man and animal continues, but in his works it blends together more fully with the crisis that links man with his own technological products, his machines. Man in Zola's world *is* a natural, animal machine. Finally, for Villiers, man is always already artificial, and therefore a kind of machine, and he is in the process of reaching the lowest common denominator: the bourgeois hordes of Alicia Clary rule the world. There is little distinction left, reserved only for the likes of Edison and Ewald, who seek to create a distinctive female creature worthy of them.

The attitude these authors take toward this crisis is ambivalent. On the one hand, it appears as an anxiety-producing threat or malady; on the other hand, the fact that individuals can be changed, shaped by their environment and by culture, promises the exciting possibility of re-creating or curing humankind itself. The authors negotiate these two contradictory effects of the crisis by locating the malady of their times in woman and by imagining a cure for woman's imperfections in their re-creation of woman. This therapy would replace the imperfect, real woman with an artificial re-creation.

In Balzac, when the dissatisfaction with the world as it is turns to the desire to improve on it, we find our mesmerist artists/scientists who turn away from deficient reality and for whom artificial musings and creations supplant the woman in their lives and/or replace the real worlds around them. Louis Lambert withdraws from the world to the realm of his mind (in his insanity) on the day before he is to be married to the real Pauline; Claës turns away from his beloved wife and turns to his desire to create; for Sarrasine, the only perfect woman is the artificial one; Frenhofer believes that his artificial creation of a woman has become real and is perfect; Raphaël, who admits to loving the fetishistic trappings of femininity more than woman herself, finds that Pauline has become the woman he worked to form. Vautrin manages to transform Esther and Lucien, only to lose them. For Balzac, these dreamers, however, themselves succumb to the crisis: they die literally or symbolically, or become mad in some way.

In the texts we have read by Flaubert, whose dissatisfaction with the crass leveling of the society of his time is itself a commonplace, certain metaphoric representations situate the flaw of humankind in natural reproduction and birth from the woman's body. The disgust associated with natural procreation and crass reality is countered by the attraction to an artificial world of dreams and to an ideal woman; Frédéric, who was repulsed by the idea of being the natural father of Rosanette's child, prefers his artificial dreams of Madame Arnoux.

In Zola, human defects originate in part in the contaminations found in the modern world and society: "[I]l y a eu dans notre société un détraquement général, et la machine, mal remise de la terrible secousse, crie et grince."[1] [There was a general breakdown in our society, and the machine, poorly recovered from the terrible jolt, squeaks and grates.] These and other flaws can be passed on by mechanical processes of heredity, specifically through the woman's body. Healing would take place by avoiding procreation as it exists in the modern world and perhaps, as envisioned in the more idyllic, post *Rougon-Macquart* world, by finding a new, postnaturalist means of reproduction (naturalism being a representation of the contaminated world represented in the *Rougon-Macquart*). *Fécondité* could be seen to envision a utopian, natural process of reproduction far from the contaminating, abortive influence of the modern city. And *Travail* represents the perfect regulation of the machine.[2] This late work enacts what Noiray (*Le romancier et la machine,* 1:467) describes as both "mechanical perfection and feminine perfection."

Echoing Flaubert's dissatisfaction with bourgeois values, Villiers specifically embodies the illness of crass bourgeois society in woman. The entire text of *L'Ève future* enacts the desire to cure woman's ills by re-creating her in artificial perfection, as we saw in Bloy's description (*Histoires désobligeantes,* 10), in which Bloy says that Villiers expresses an "unexampled need for the restitution of woman." Thus in all four authors the maladies of society are linked to the real woman and, in Flaubert, Zola, and Villiers, to natural reproduction.

In his rich study of the naturalist novel, Mark Seltzer provides an explanation of this anxiety about woman and reproduction by showing that it belongs to a set of "anxieties about production and reproduction, technological and biological" encountered during the period of naturalism. For Seltzer, this becomes a rivalry in the naturalist text between the artificial, technological production of industry and natural, biological reproduction (Seltzer, *Bodies and Machines,* 4, 157).[3] As we have seen,

1. Zola, "Seconde lettre d'un curieux," *Oeuvres complètes* 13 (Paris: Cercle du Livre Précieux, 1966), 46.

2. See Noiray for a brief discussion of two images of the machine giving birth in *Lourdes* and *Travail* (1:461).

3. Most important, Seltzer, *Bodies and Machines,* 32, sees the naturalist novel as attempting to negotiate these conflicting modes of production with the following result, which is similar to what we find in our French novelists: "what unites these stories is the desire to project an alternative to biological reproduction, to displace the threat posed by the 'women people' (the reduction of men to 'mere animalcules' in the process of procreation) and to devise a counter-mode of reproduction (the naturalist machine)." As we saw in the Zola chapter, Seltzer, quoting in part Barker-Benfield, points to an interesting offshoot of this preference in certain American medical literature of the second part of the nineteenth century, where the purpose is to replace natural reproduction with male medicine.

however, these anxieties reach back before the naturalist novel and out from it, from Balzac to Villiers, in the confrontation in the texts of all four of our authors between the machine, the ideal artificial woman, and the real woman and/or natural reproduction.

What our authors show in the preference for the artificial woman is a kind of triumph (whether good or ill) of the artificial, the technological, over the natural. And this leads us to an important conclusion about the reasons that this rivalry between the natural and the artificial is figured by the creation of a woman. On the one hand, it is simply the fantasy of male procreation, that man could have the ability to create new human beings. On the other hand, Villiers's creation reveals something different about this process. The creature he would invent is an artificial "future Eve": she does not originate in normal, natural reproduction but rather is a machine created by man, and she represents the production of a new "species" of future generations of artificial humans (even though this reproduction is halted in the text). Future android generations would represent once again not simply the metaphor of the man-machine but rather that this is a new human who is in part artificial and who was created by human technological processes. This creation has two significations: more literally, man is physically changed, reshaped by his own technology (the human soul of Sowana reembodied); metaphorically, man is a fabricated product of his own artificial culture and, specifically, in our authors, of language.

In the literary texts, we have indeed seen that man can at times appear to be the product of the machines he creates, or even that he himself becomes the machine he creates. As early as Balzac, the artificial Zambinella of *Sarrasine,* a creation of man's surgical "art," seems to materialize by means of a machine: this "homme artificiel" (*Sarrasine*, 6:1047) [artificial man], "création artificielle" (6:1052) [artificial creation], "semblait être sorti de dessous terre, poussé par quelque mécanisme de théâtre" (6:1050) [he seemed to have emerged from underground, pushed by some theatrical mechanism]. Raphaël, in response to the dangers of the *peau,* makes himself into a "machine à vapeur" (*La peau de chagrin,* 10:217) [steam engine]. In Flaubert's *Madame Bovary,* the influence of machines on man becomes more literal; Charles's medical "moteur mécanique" destroys the old Hippolyte with, as a result, the creation of a new, hybrid man, part organic, part "mécanique compliquée." In Zola, mechanical wombs seem to give birth to real children. And in Villiers's *L'Ève future,* the new Eve, symbolic origin of a new humankind, is a man-made machine with a human soul.

Clearly, in the nineteenth century's increased industrialization, technological creations were having more and more influence on various aspects of everyday life. It is Schivelbusch who best analyzes concrete ways in which machines at this time actually created new realities for people. As he describes it, a ride in a train changed the way people envisioned time and space: it fundamentally changed human perception. As a passenger looked out a train window, the landscape viewed was in fact "filtered through the machine ensemble" (Schivelbusch, *Railway Journey,* 24); the passenger observed the rapidly moving landscape produced by the train's movement, a landscape punctuated by the telegraph poles along the tracks. When the traveler arrived, the point of destination seemed to be the product of the railway itself, and thus this new place appeared to be the product of a machine (39). Both Schivelbusch[4] and Noiray conclude that the machine at this time created a new kind of unnatural reality, as Noiray states: "Powered by thermal energy, granted its own excessive and brutal life by steam, these new machines superimposed a different, radically strange form of existence on the natural realm" (Noiray, *Le romancier et la machine,* 1:16). Not only do these machines create new realities, they also seem to transform people. A passenger riding in a train is "conditioned by the unit in which he functions"; he becomes a "parcel," and thus a kind of "object of an industrial project" (Schivelbusch, *Railway Journey,* 160, 73). As Noiray points out, this is not just that machines change perception but, more generally, that they give rise to a kind of new, mechanistic vision of the world: "The human body, language itself, history, the government, the entire universe will soon seem, because of the complexity of their functioning, like real machines" (Noiray, *Le romancier et la machine,* 1:15–16). This transformation of everyday life is profound; machines change the lives of people and perhaps make visible that strange kind of circularity: man's creations in turn re-create him.

However, what is really most important in this concept of the way in which machines make people is, for our authors, the way in which the modern *social* world creates persons. Here it is the category of the artificial, the man-made aspect of culture that links it with the technological product and opposes it to nature. For Balzac, Chabert's life is not his biological, natural body but rather the social definition of his identity. For Flaubert, Emma is "written" by the texts she has read. For Zola, the miners are tragic products of the man-made world of the mine. And in Villiers, human

4. See Schivelbusch, *Railway Journey,* 64.

identity is quite simply artificial, social, linguistic. It is a product of social construction, a product "made" by humans themselves. As Schivelbusch states, and as our authors illustrate, machines shape lives in a way that is similar to the way social codes and rules do: "Social rules and technologically produced stimuli structure the individual in a similar manner, regularizing, regulating, shaping him according to their inherent laws" (Schivelbusch, *Railway Journey,* 168). And, as we saw in Chapter 1, Bourdieu also links social coding (habitus) and mechanical functioning in the context of the social creation of human identity. The social constructs gender in bodies and in minds, and it does so in those invisible, mechanical ways, by means of "deep-rooted mechanisms" (Bourdieu, *Masculine Domination,* 9).

For Bourdieu, it is the example of what he calls symbolic violence that best shows how much gender is inscribed in mentalities, as when, for example, doors are opened to women who refuse to go through them (Bourdieu, *Masculine Domination,* 39). It is interesting that Bourdieu calls the construction of female gender a "negative Pygmalion effect," by which he means that reduced expectations of girls shape their desires, what they want to do: "Thus, by virtue of the universal law of the adjustment of expectations to chances, aspirations to possibilities, prolonged and invisibly diminished experience that is sexually characterized through and through tends, by discouraging it, to undermine even the inclination to perform acts that are not expected of women—without them even being denied to them" (61).[5] What Bourdieu describes here in our contemporary language is what the nineteenth century was understanding more and more. Michelet understood in a certain way that women were formed by men in their married lives. And Yvonne Knibiehler and Catherine Fouquet have identified the fact that there was an awareness in the medical community of this construction of gender identity near end of the nineteenth century (Knibiehler and Fouquet, *La femme et les médecins,* 209–10), which can be seen specifically in the 1877 article "Femme" with which this book begins: "But civilization, in its tendency to divide labor, has always led to creation of an artificial woman, that is to say, to development of certain abilities that guarantee the superiority of a particular function, to the detriment of the quality of the whole."[6]

5. In a curious way, this makes Emma Bovary's refusal to accept her female destiny all the more radical and surprising.

6. Knibiehler and Fouquet, *La femme et les médecins,* 209–20. E. Dally, "Femmes," in *Dictionnaire encyclopédique des sciences médicales,* ed. M. A. Dechambre, ser. 4, vol. 1 (Paris: G. Masson, P. Asselin, 1877), 438. Gallica: http://gallica.bnf.fr/ark:/12148/CadresFenetre?O=NUMM-31288&M=imageseule.

We have seen in our four literary authors that the fascination with formative mechanical processes shows their insight into this social programming. Certainly Balzac is coming to an awareness of it, as we saw in his understanding of "habit," particularly in the crucial distinction between natural aristocracy nature (passed on by the blood) and learned aristocracy (social coding, here elegance): "Or, l'élégance, n'étant que la perfection des objets sensibles, doit être accessible à tous par l'habitude" (Balzac, *Le traité de la vie élégante,* 12:231-32).[7] [Thus elegance, being only the perfection of perceptible objects, must be accessible to all by means of habit.] Flaubert represented and discussed specifically the ways in which women are made by society, and his curiosity about automatisms, along with his exploration of cliché, links the mechanical with the social (linguistic). Zola's much more physical understanding of identity gives great importance to the way in which the contamination of modern, man-made, and often mechanical milieus determine human life, including human social identity, which can be seen in the example of the mine's production of a population of passive, colorless people (and spiders). For Villiers, man functions as a machine by automatically enacting previously existing codes and rules, whether social, linguistic, or physical.

Bourdieu's analysis of gender construction continues in the path of many previous studies by showing in the sociological context how "femininity" and "masculinity," social constructs, come to appear to be natural, anatomical. The social definitions of gender are propped onto anatomical differences: a "naturalized social construction ('genders' as sexually characterized habitus) appear[s] as the grounding in nature of the arbitrary division which underlies both reality and the representation of reality" (Bourdieu, *Masculine Domination,* 3). This, in a sense, deconstructs the illusion of natural gender identity. Balzac, for instance, could also be seen to deconstruct the innate, "natural" idea of identity when he confronts the biological, "natural," and innate understanding of identity (Chabert's body) with a socially determined one (he has been declared dead). For Chabert, the artificial is the more powerful and thus puts into question the possibility of natural identity. And, as we saw in Chapter 1, Balzac did indeed state that woman is already artificial: "L'une des gloires de la Société, c'est d'avoir créé *la femme* là où la Nature a fait une femelle" (Balzac, *Les secrets de la princesse de Cadignan,* 6:964). [One of Society's

7. Bourdieu, *Masculine Domination,* 60, in fact, links male gender coding to codes of aristocracy.

glories is to have created *woman* where nature made a female.] This confrontation between natural and artificial identity is expressed in our literary texts by the rivalry between artificial and natural reproduction.

Bourdieu in fact shows how, in Kabyle culture and elsewhere, the obvious, "natural" fact that women are the ones who give birth to children is devalued by culture and how her role gets relegated to a subordinate place, somewhat surprisingly taking a back seat to the less evident and less lengthy male work in reproduction:

> The decisive weight of the economy of symbolic goods, which, through the fundamental principle of division, organizes all perception of the social world, weighs on the whole social universe, that is, not only on the economy of economic production, but also on the economy of *biological reproduction*. This explains why it is that, in Kabylia and also in many other traditions, the specifically female work of gestation and childbearing is effaced in favour of the specifically male work of impregnation [. . .] The constraints of the economy of symbolic goods [. . .] require biological reproduction to be subordinated to the necessities of the reproduction of symbolic capital. (Bourdieu, *Masculine Domination,* 46)

Could we perhaps see the rewriting of reproduction by our authors as an enactment or reinforcement, in the culture in crisis we have described, of this kind of symbolic assignment of reproductive value to the masculine? This certainly would fit with the progressive takeover of the midwife profession by the male medical establishment that can be seen in nineteenth-century France (Knibiehler and Fouquet, *La femme et les médecins,* 181–84).

In any case, our authors represent the "machine" of culture as an instrument that writes bodies and identities, and language is an important component of this social writing. Thus their very texts, composed of language, can be viewed as part of the social apparatus that can write people. Their novels are artificial, man-made machines, powered, in a sense, by science, as Noiray describes the realist and naturalist novel: "Originating in science, like the machine, and like it destined to produce a specific effect, the realist and naturalist novel thus seems, in both its form and its function, like a real technical object, a machine that reproduces and expresses the real" (Noiray, *Le romancier et la machine,* 1:40). Serres states it bluntly when he says that *Le docteur Pascal* functions "like a motor, subjected to the regulations of motors" (Serres, *Feux et signaux de brume,* 68). Thus, like a machine, the novel takes a piece of reality and shapes it into another form. Seltzer also notes that the multiplicities and instabilities of naturalist narratives "may ultimately function as a flexible and polyvalent textual mechanism of relays, conversions, and 'crisis' management—as, in fact, a thermodynamic that forms part of the textual mechanism itself" (Seltzer, *Bodies and Machines,* 31). The novel is thus a kind of machine that regulates the crisis these authors saw in their century and that aims to resolve tensions, inefficiencies, and malfunctions. And it can be seen to regulate the crisis involved in the tensions between the natural and the artificial: "The naturalist machine operates through a double discourse by which the apparently opposed registers of the body and the machine are coordinated within a single technology of regulation" (44). Their texts function as imaginary regulators of the crises they represent.[8]

But as we have seen in our analyses, these authors portray language, social codes, machines, not just as representing and managing oppositions but as actually changing the world and the people in it. It is particularly this power of language to act on the world that best embodies the possibilities that the textual machine might realize Pygmalion's dream. Balzac's performative "je veux" [I want], Flaubert's "prendre la lune avec les dents" [to take the moon by the teeth], Zola's notion of the writing on Madeleine's body, Villiers's "Et que l'*Ombre* soit!" [And let there be *Shadow/Darkness*]—all point to the suggestive, performative power of language,[9] to the importance of the role of language in defining the reality of humans.

For Bourdieu as for our novelists, this is the important "part played by words in the construction of social reality" (Bourdieu, *Language and Symbolic Power,* 105). The power of language is in part the power to name, to define, both people and their roles, to institute and to consecrate. Those who have the authority and ability to define, to name, have great power: "By structuring the perception which social agents have of the social world, the act of naming helps to establish the structure of this world, and does so all the more significantly the more widely it is recognized, i.e. authorized. There is no social agent who does not aspire, as far as his

8. See Noiray, *Le romancier et la machine,* 1:223, for an analysis of the post-*Rougon-Macquart* series and utopia in the control of the mechanical.

9. The performative here is used in the expanded sense of Austin's definition of language that performs actions in the social world, such as the sentence "I promise," which itself performs the function of promising (J. L. Austin, *How to Do Things with Words*).

circumstances permit, to have the power to name and to create the world through naming" (105). This brings to mind Balzac's "Notre nom, c'est nous-mêmes" [One's name is one's self.] Giving someone a "name," a title, can change the world, as Bourdieu states:

> The process of investiture, for example, exercises a symbolic efficacy that is quite real in that it really transforms the person consecrated: first, because it transforms the representations others have of him and above all the behaviour they adopt towards him (the most visible changes being the fact that he is given titles of respect and the respect actually associated with these enunciations); and second, because it simultaneously transforms the representation that the invested person has of himself, and the behaviour he feels obliged to adopt in order to conform to that representation. (119)

Bourdieu, in fact, discusses Balzac's role in the construction of the social category of the "bohemian"; Balzac sets out to define this category, and because the bohemian is an artist who imposes rules, Balzac "names" himself to this powerful position. Bourdieu here quotes Balzac: "'The artist [. . .] does not follow the rules. He imposes them [. . .] He is always the expression of a great thought and he dominates society'" (*Rules of Art,* 56). Bourdieu goes on: "Force of habit and complicity prevent us from seeing everything that is at stake in a text like this, that is, the work of constructing a social reality in which we participate more or less as intellectuals by affiliation or by aspiration, and which is nothing other than the social identity of the intellectual producer. The reality designated by words in ordinary usage—writer, artist, intellectual—has been made by cultural producers (Balzac's text is only one among thousands), by normative statements, or better yet, by performative ones like this one" (56). It is interesting to note that Bourdieu views this kind of construction of reality as a way to set up boundaries: "To institute, to give a social definition, an identity, is also to impose *boundaries*" (*Language and Symbolic Power,* 120). The performative utterances of these authors thus could impose boundaries that would manage the ambiguous borders they encounter in their crises. Words do indeed change the world; their books may do the same.

Thus the very words that the reader consumes would act to change the reader, and thus to change the world. These authors would like to control those changes, to push for a cure for their world, because the illness is social. For Balzac, his texts might give rise to a return to the better values of the past. Balzac would be the teacher who would shape his audience, as he says, quoting Bonald: "'Un écrivain doit avoir en morale et en politique des opinions arrêtées, il doit se regarder comme un instituteur des hommes; car les hommes n'ont pas besoin de maîtres pour douter,' a dit Bonald. J'ai pris de bonne heure pour règle ces grandes paroles" ("Avant-propos," 1:12).[10] ["A writer must have firm opinions in his morals and his politics, he must view himself as a teacher of men; for men do not need masters in order to doubt," stated Bonald. I took these great words as my rule early on.] His accomplishment would be a strengthening of "la Religion, la Monarchie, deux nécessités que les événements contemporains proclament, et vers lesquelles tout écrivain de bon sens doit essayer de ramener notre pays" ("Avant-propos," 1:13) [Religion, Monarchy, two necessities that contemporary events proclaim, and back to which every writer of good sense must try to lead our country]. The world re-created by him is represented by the new Galatea, Pauline: rich, beautiful, devoted to Raphaël, pure at heart, seemingly formed to Raphaël's own aristocratic taste by him. As seen in Pauline, it would be wealth freed of bourgeois struggle, fidelity combined with love, aristocracy of taste and behavior, a kind of realization of the fantasy of an aristocratic existence formed to Balzac's taste by him.

Flaubert's ideal, on the other hand, remains a dream; a relationship with the ideal woman is not allowed to come into being in the sordid reality of his time. He does not envision a utopian ideal for society; he merely sets up his texts as vehicles that might raise the consciousness of his readers, that would open their eyes to the crass leveling taking place. His texts would perform a kind of surgery that would open up the social body to show the maladies of his times so that perhaps, someday, that very consciousness might allow for a cure.

For Zola, it would mean purification: woman purified of the contaminations of the modern world and reproductive purity. Created by Zola himself, it would be Clotilde and Marianne. It would be the human control of the man-machine made possible by Zola himself. It would be the novel as "a technique, an instrument of the investigation of the real and the domination of the world" (Noiray, *Le romancier et la machine,* 1:41). And Noiray feels that this dream is the dream of every creator, which would include Zola: "the old dream of Doctor Pascal, the hope and salvation of every creator, of every man of thought and science:

10. Rothfield, *Vital Signs,* 78, links Benassis and his efforts to create a healthy society to Balzac's desires as an aspiring professional.

to help, like Jordan, in the perfect regulation of the cosmos" (1:500). For Serres too, Zola's project, as echoed in Pascal's, is "To say everything, thus, and understand everything. But one must also cure everything: speaking, knowing have this goal alone" (*Feux et signaux de brume,* 59). For Villiers, it would be Hadaly, women with otherworldly souls combined with bodies in the shape of man's best artistic creations. It would be a life far from bourgeois crassness, immersed in the spiritual and the ideal, wealthy without measure, lives like those of Edison and Ewald.

As one considers the scientific aspects of these writers' works, it can be both amusing and troubling to note how some of their representations have been realized. One wonders what Balzac might have thought about current-day hypnosis, about that kind of thought control. About sex-change operations far beyond that of Zambinella. About the kind of cross-species hybrids that can be created today, like those Balzac mockingly imagined in "Guide-âne." One wonders what Flaubert might have thought about artificial-limb replacements that succeed better than the one imposed on Hippolyte. About scientific reproduction without sex, about cloning (which Mary Orr sees symbolically in *Bouvard et Pécuchet*),[11] which might eliminate, at least in part, the disgust Flaubert expressed for natural reproduction. What Zola might have thought about the possibilities offered by genetic manipulation. What Villiers might have thought about artificial intelligence, robots, plastic surgery. We know at least that their texts envision these things in primitive form, but also that this dream is accompanied by the possibilities of catastrophic results: death or insanity in Balzac, Hippolyte's tragedy in Flaubert, the sacrifice of woman in Zola, the shipwreck of the *Wonderful* in Villiers. These authors create in their texts scenarios in which humans shape their own existence, and they raise our consciousness of the extent to which we are our own products. They represent this as a power that is both dangerous and promising.

11. Orr, *Flaubert: Writing the Masculine,* 201, writes: "Attempts to clear androcentric space outside female economies of reproduction is nowhere better exemplified than in Bouvard and Pécuchet's 'abortive' attempt at fostering and child-rearing. The final bid to make child-*bearing* redundant in Les Chavignolles is terrifyingly portentous of current research in IVF and the cloning of humans. Throughout the whole of Flaubert's *oeuvre,* this text gets closest to the catastrophes of genetic experimentation which are only a tiny step removed from Dolly the sheep."

BIBLIOGRAPHY

Anzalone, John. "Danse macabre, ou le pas de deux Baudelaire-Villiers: Essai sur un chapitre de *L'Ève future*." In *Jeering Dreamers: Villiers de L'Isle Adam's "L'Ève future" at Our Fin de Siècle*, edited by John Anzalone, 117–25. Atlanta, Ga.: Rodopi, 1996.

———. "Golden Cylinders: Inscription and Intertext in *L'Ève future*." *L'Esprit créateur* 26, no. 4 (Winter 1986), 38–47.

Austin, J. L. (John Langshaw). *How to Do Things with Words*. Cambridge: Harvard University Press, 1962.

Baguley, David. *Émile Zola, L'assommoir*. New York: Cambridge University Press, 1992.

———. *Naturalist Fiction: The Entropic Vision*. New York: Cambridge University Press, 1990.

Balzac, Honoré de. "Guide âne à l'usage des animaux qui veulent parvenir aux honneurs." In *Vie privée et publique des animaux, vignettes par Grandville*, edited by P. J. Stahl (pseudonym), 267–86. Paris: J. Hetzel & Paulin, 1880. Gallica: http://gallica.bnf.fr/ark:/12148/bpt6k203884z/CadresFenetre?O=NUMM-203884&M=tdm.

———. *La comédie humaine*. 12 vols. Edited by Pierre-Georges Castex with Pierre Barbéris, Thierry Bodin, Nicole Cazuran, Roland Chollet, Pierre Citron, Madeleine Fargeaud, Rose Fortassier, Henri Gauthier, René Guise, Michel Lichtlé, André Lorant, Anne-Marie Meininger, Arlette Michel, Nicole Mozet, Roger Pierrot, Maurice Regard, Guy Sagnes, Jean-Louis Tritter, and Moïse Le Yaouanc (for the volumes used in this study). Paris: Gallimard, 1976–81.

———. *Correspondance de H. de Balzac, 1819–1850*. Vol. 2. Paris: Calmann Lévy, 1876.

Barnes, Julian. *Flaubert's Parrot*. New York: McGraw-Hill, 1985.

Bart, Benjamin. *Flaubert*. Syracuse, N.Y.: Syracuse University Press, 1967.

Beizer, Janet. *Ventriloquized Bodies: Narratives of Hysteria in Nineteenth-Century France*. Ithaca: Cornell University Press, 1994.

Bell, David F. *Circumstances: Chance in the Literary Text*. Lincoln: University of Nebraska Press, 1993.

Bellos, David. "From the Bowels of the Earth: An Essay on *Germinal*." *Forum for Modern Language Studies* 15 (1979), 35–45.

Bertrand Jennings, Chantal. *L'éros et la femme chez Zola: De la chute au paradis retrouvé*. Paris: Klincksieck, 1977.

Bloy, Léon. "La résurrection de Villiers de l'Isle-Adam." In *Histoires désobligeantes*, 3–22. Paris: François Bernouard, 1947.

Borie, Jean. *Mythologies de l'hérédité au XIXe siècle*. Paris: Éditions Galilée, 1981.

Bourdieu, Pierre. *Distinction: A Social Critique of the Judgement of Taste*. Translated by Richard Nice. Cambridge: Harvard University Press, 1984.

———. *Language and Symbolic Power*. Translation of *Ce que parler veut dire*. Edited by John B. Thompson. Translated by Gino Raymond and Matthew Adamson. Cambridge: Harvard University Press, 1991.

———. *The Logic of Practice*. Translated by Richard Nice. Stanford, Calif.: Stanford University Press, 1990.

———. *Masculine Domination*. Translated by Richard Nice. Stanford, Calif.: Stanford University Press, 2001.

———. *The Rules of Art: Genesis and Structure of the Literary Field*. Translated by Susan Emanuel. Stanford, Calif.: Stanford University Press, 1996.

Braun, Marta. *Picturing Time: The Work of Étienne-Jules Marey*. Chicago: University of Chicago Press, 1992.

Bruneau, Jean. *Les débuts littéraires de Gustave Flaubert, 1831–1845*. Paris: Armand Colin, 1962.

Chambers, Ross. "Irony and Misogyny: Authority and the Homosocial in Baudelaire and Flaubert." *Australian Journal of French Studies* 26, no. 3 (1989), 272–88.

Cohen, Margaret. *The Sentimental Education of the Novel*. Princeton: Princeton University Press, 1999.

Coleman, William. *Biology in the Nineteenth Century: Problems of Form, Function, and Transformation*. New York: Wiley, 1971.

Crabtree, Adam. *From Mesmer to Freud: Magnetic Sleep and the Roots of Psychological Healing*. New Haven: Yale University Press, 1993.

Culler, Jonathan. *Flaubert: The Uses of Uncertainty*. Ithaca: Cornell University Press, 1985.

———. "The Uses of Madame Bovary." In *Flaubert and Postmodernism*, edited by Naomi Schor and Henry F. Majewski, 1–12. Lincoln: University of Nebraska Press, 1984.

Czyba, Lucette. *Mythes et idéologie de la femme dans les romans de Flaubert*. Lyon: Presses Universitaires de Lyon, 1983.

Dagognet, François. *Étienne-Jules Marey: A Passion for the Trace*. Translated by Robert Galeta with Jeanine Herman. Cambridge, Mass.: Zone Books, 1992.

Dally, E. "Femmes." In *Dictionnaire encyclopédique des sciences médicales*, edited by M. A. Dechambre, series 4, vol. 1, 427–39. Paris: G. Masson, P. Asselin, 1877. Gallica: http://gallica.bnf.fr/ark:/12148/CadresFenetre?O=NUMM-31288&M=imageseule.

Darnton, Robert. *Mesmerism and the End of the Enlightenment in France*. Cambridge: Harvard University Press, 1968.

Descharmes, René, and René Dumesnil. *Autour de Flaubert: Études historiques et documentaires, suivies d'une biographie chronologique, d'un essai bibliographique des ouvrages et articles relatifs à Flaubert et d'un index des noms cités*. Paris: Mercure de France, 1912.

Donaldson-Evans, Mary. *Medical Examinations: Dissecting the Doctor in French Narrative Prose, 1857–1894*. Lincoln: University of Nebraska Press, 2000.

Flaubert, Gustave. *Carnets de travail: Gustave Flaubert*. Edited by Pierre-Marc de Biasi. Paris: Balland, 1988.

———. *Correspondance*. Edited by Jean Bruneau. 4 vols. Paris: Gallimard, 1973–91.

———. *Oeuvres complètes*. Preface by Jean Bruneau. Edited by Bernard Masson. 2 vols. Paris: Éditions du Seuil, 1964.

———. *Plans, notes et scénarios de "Un coeur simple."* Edited by François Fleury. Rouen: Lecerf, 1977.

Forrest, Jennifer. "The Lord of Hadaly's Rings: Regulating the Female Body in Villiers de L'Isle-Adam's *L'Ève future.*" *South Central Review* 13, no. 4 (Winter 1996), 18–37.

Foucault, Michel. *The Birth of the Clinic: An Archaeology of Medical Perception.* Translated by A. M. Sheridan Smith. New York: Vintage Books, 1994.

———. *The Order of Things: An Archaeology of the Human Sciences.* New York: Vintage Books, 1973.

Garelick, Rhonda. *Rising Star: Dandyism, Gender, and Performance in the Fin-de-Siècle.* Princeton: Princeton University Press, 1998.

Gasché, Rodolphe. "The Stelliferous Fold: On Villiers de l'Isle-Adam's *L'Ève future.*" *Studies in Romanticism* 22 (Summer 1983), 293–327.

Gauld, Alan. *A History of Hypnotism.* New York: Cambridge University Press, 1992.

Goncourt, Edmond de. *Journal des Goncourt: Mémoires de la vie littéraire.* Vol. 4, 1870–71, 18 October 1871. Paris: Fasquelle Charpentier, 1911.

Haeckel, Ernst. *Histoire de la création des êtres organisés d'après les lois naturelles.* Paris: C. Reinwald, 1874.

Harris, Ruth. *Murders and Madness: Medicine, Law, and Society in the Fin de Siècle.* New York: Oxford University Press, 1989.

Haxell, Nichola Ann. "Childbirth and the Mine: A Reading of the Gaea-Myth in Zola's *Germinal* and the Poetry of Marceline Desbordes-Valmore." *Neophilologus* 73, no. 4 (1989), 522–31.

Hennessy, Susie. *The Mother Figure in Émile Zola's "Les Rougon-Macquart": Literary Realism and the Quest for the Ideal Mother.* Lewiston, N.Y.: Edwin Mellen Press, 2006.

Hiddleston, J. A. "Flaubert and *L'art industriel.*" *French Studies Bulletin,* Summer 1985, 4–5.

Huet, Marie-Hélène. *Monstrous Imagination.* Cambridge: Harvard University Press, 1993.

Huyssen, Andreas. *After the Great Divide: Modernism, Mass Culture, Postmodernism.* Bloomington: Indiana University Press, 1986.

Jacob, François. *The Logic of Life: A History of Heredity.* Translated by Betty E. Spillmann. New York: Pantheon Books, 1974.

Janson, H. W. *Apes and Ape Lore in the Middle Ages and the Renaissance.* London: Warburg Institute, University of London, 1952.

Jordanova, Ludmilla. *Lamarck.* New York: Oxford University Press, 1984.

———. *Sexual Visions: Images of Gender in Science and Medicine Between the Eighteenth and Twentieth Centuries.* Madison: University of Wisconsin Press, 1989.

Jullien, Dominique. "Le 'Ventre' de Paris: Pour une pathologie du symbolisme dans *L'oeuvre* d'Émile Zola." *French Forum* 17, no. 3 (September 1992), 281–99.

Kelly, Dorothy. "Between Bodies and Texts: A Psychoanalytic Reading of *Le père Goriot.*" In *Approaches to Teaching "Old Goriot,"* edited by Michal Ginsburg, 109–17. New York: Modern Language Association of America, 2000.

———. "Emma's Distinctive Taste." *Australian Journal of French Studies* 43, no. 2 (2006), 121–37.

———. "Experimenting on Women: Zola's Theory and Practice of the Experimental Novel." In *Spectacles of Realism: Body, Gender, Genre,* edited by Margaret Cohen and Christopher Prendergast, 231–46. Minneapolis: University of Minnesota Press, 1995.

———. *Fictional Genders: Role and Representation in Nineteenth-Century French Narrative.* Lincoln: University of Nebraska Press, 1989.

———. "Gender, Metaphor, and Machine: *La bête humaine.*" *French Literature Series* 16 (1989), 110–22.

———. "Language as Knowledge or Language as Power: Performative and Constative Language in *La peau de chagrin.*" *Linguistics in Literature* 5, no. 3 (Fall 1980), 35–58.

———. "Teaching *Madame Bovary* Through the Lens of Poststructuralism." In *Approaches to Teaching Flaubert's "Madame Bovary,"* edited by Laurence M. Porter and Eugene F. Gray, 90–97. New York: Modern Language Association of America Publications, 1995.

———. *Telling Glances: Voyeurism in the French Novel.* New Brunswick, N.J.: Rutgers University Press, 1992.

Kittler, Friedrich. *Grammaphon, Film, Typewriter.* Translated by Geoffrey Winthrop-Young and Michael Wutz. Stanford, Calif.: Stanford University Press, 1999.

Klein, Melanie. *Love, Guilt, and Reparation, and Other Works.* New York: Free Press, 1975.

Knibiehler, Yvonne, and Catherine Fouquet. *La femme et les médecins: Analyse historique.* Paris: Hachette Littérature Générale, 1983.

LaCapra, Dominick. *Madame Bovary on Trial.* Ithaca: Cornell University Press, 1982.

Lathers, Marie. "*L'Ève future* and the Hypnotic Feminine." *Romanic Review* 84, no. 1 (January 1993), 43–54.

Lesch, John E. *Science and Medicine in France: The Emergence of Experimental Physiology, 1790–1855.* Cambridge: Harvard University Press, 1984.

Malinas, Yves. *Zola et les hérédités imaginaires.* Paris: Expansion Scientifique Française, 1985.

Marcus, K. Melissa. *The Representation of Mesmerism in Honoré de Balzac's "La comédie humaine."* New York: Peter Lang, 1995.

Marey, Étienne-Jules. "Cinquante ans d'applications de la méthode graphique en physiologie." In *Cinquantenaire de la Société de biologie: Volume jubilaire,* 39–47. Paris: Masson et Compagnie, 1899. Bibliothèque Interuniversitaire de Médecine, http://web2.bium.univ-paris5.fr/livanc/?cote=21950&p=52&do=page.

———. *Du mouvement dans les fonctions de la vie: Leçons faites au Collège de France.* Paris: Germer Baillière, 1868. Bibliothèque Interuniversitaire de Médecine, http://194.254.96.21/livanc/?cote=31057&p=3&do=page.

———. *La machine animale: Locomotion terrestre et aérienne.* Paris: Librairie Germer Baillière, 1873. Bibliothèque Interuniversitaire de Médecine, http://194.254.96.21/livanc/?cote=32624&do=chapitre.

———. "Moteurs animés, Expériences de physiologie graphique." *La nature,* 28 September 1878, 273–78; 5 October 1878, 289–95.

———. *Le mouvement.* Paris: G. Masson, 1894. http://194.254.96.21/livanc/?cote=extacad32516&p=67&do=page.

Michelet, Jules. *L'amour; La femme.* Paris: Flammarion, 1985.

"Micro-tasimètre d'Edison." *La nature,* 27 July 1878, 135.

Mikkonen, Kai. *The Plot Machine: The French Novel and the Bachelor Machines in the Electric Years, 1880–1914.* New York: Rodopi, 2001.

Miller-Frank, Felicia. "Edison's Recorded Angel." In *Jeering Dreamers: Villiers de L'Isle Adam's "L'Ève future" at Our Fin de Siècle,* edited by John Anzalone, 141–66. Atlanta, Ga.: Rodopi, 1996.

———. *The Mechanical Song: Women, Voice, and the Artificial in Nineteenth-Century French Narrative.* Stanford, Calif.: Stanford University Press, 1995.

Nerval, Gérard de. *Les deux Faust de Goethe.* Paris: Librairie Gründ, 1932.

Noiray, Jacques. *Le romancier et la machine: L'image de la machine dans le roman français, 1850–1900.* 2 vols. Paris: José Corti, 1981–82.

Olds, Marshall C. *Au pays des perroquets: Féerie théâtrale et narration chez Flaubert.* Atlanta, Ga.: Rodopi, 2001.

Orr, Mary. *Flaubert: Writing the Masculine.* New York: Oxford University Press, 2000.

———. "Reading the Other: Flaubert's *L'éducation sentimentale* revisited." *French Studies: A Quarterly Review* 46, no. 4 (October 1992), 412–23.

Pauly, Philip J. *Controlling Life: Jacques Loeb and the Engineering Ideal in Biology.* New York: Oxford University Press, 1987.

Perrone-Moisés, Leyla. "*Quidquid volueris:* The Scriptural Education." In *Flaubert and Postmodernism,* edited by Naomi Schor and Henry F. Majewski, 139–59. Lincoln: University of Nebraska Press, 1984.

Petrey, Sandy. *In the Court of the Pear King: French Culture and the Rise of Realism.* Ithaca: Cornell University Press, 2005.

———. "The Reality of Representation: Between Marx and Balzac." *Critical Inquiry* 14, no. 3 (1988), 448–68.

Pouchet, F.-A. *Hétérogénie; ou, Traité de la génération spontanée, basé sur de nouvelles expériences.* Paris: J. B. Baillière & Fils, 1859.

Prendergast, Christopher. *The Order of Mimesis: Balzac, Stendhal, Nerval, Flaubert.* New York: Cambridge University Press, 1986.

Rabinbach, Anson. *The Human Motor: Energy, Fatigue, and the Origins of Modernity.* Berkeley and Los Angeles: University of California Press, 1992.

Raitt, Alan. *The Life of Villiers de l'Isle-Adam.* New York: Oxford University Press, 1981.

———. *Villiers de l'Isle-Adam et le mouvement symboliste.* Paris: José Corti, 1965.

Régnier, Henri de. *Portraits et Souvenirs: Portraits et souvenirs—pour les mois d'hiver.* Paris: Mercure de France, 1913.

Rifelj, Carol de Dobay. "*La machine humaine:* Villiers's *L'Ève future* and the Problem of Personal Identity." *Nineteenth-Century French Studies* 20, nos. 3–4 (Spring–Summer 1992), 430–51.

Rivers, Christopher. *Face Value: Physiognomical Thought and the Legible Body in Marivaux, Lavater, Balzac, Gautier, and Zola.* Madison: University of Wisconsin Press, 1994.

Robert, Marthe. *Roman des origines et origines du roman.* Paris: B. Grasset, 1972.

Rosenberg, Rachelle A. "The Slaying of the Dragon: An Archetypal Study of Zola's *Germinal.*" *Symposium,* Winter 1972, 349–62.

Rothfield, Lawrence. *Vital Signs: Medical Realism in Nineteenth-Century Fiction.* Princeton: Princeton University Press, 1992.

Sainte-Beuve, Charles-Augustin. *Causeries du lundi.* 15 vols. Paris: Garnier Frères, 18??.

Sartre, Jean-Paul. *The Family Idiot: Gustave Flaubert, 1821–1857.* Translated by Carol Cosman. Vol. 1. Chicago: University of Chicago Press, 1981.

Schefer, Jean-Louis. "Du simulacre à la parole." *Tel Quel* 31 (Autumn 1967), 85–91.

Schivelbusch, Wolfgang. *Disenchanted Night: The Industrialization of Light in the Nineteenth Century.* Translated by Angela Davies. New York: Oxford/Berg, 1988.

———. *The Railway Journey: The Industrialization and Perception of Time and Space.* Berkeley and Los Angeles: University of California Press, 1986.

Schneider, William H. *Quality and Quantity: The Quest for Biological Regeneration in Twentieth-Century France.* New York: Cambridge University Press, 1990.

Schor, Naomi. *Zola's Crowds.* Baltimore: Johns Hopkins University Press, 1978.

Schuerewegen, Franc. "'Télétechné' fin de siècle: Villiers de l'Isle-Adam et Jules Verne." *Romantisme* 20, no. 69 (1990), 79–87.

Seltzer, Mark. *Bodies and Machines*. New York: Routledge, 1992.

Serres, Michel. *Feux et signaux de brume, Zola*. Paris: B. Grasset, 1975.

Smith, Bonnie. *Ladies of the Leisure Class: The Bourgeoises of Northern France in the Nineteenth Century*. Princeton: Princeton University Press, 1981.

Sonnenfeld, Albert. "Émile Zola: Food and Ideology." *Nineteenth-Century French Studies* 19, no. 4 (1991), 600–611.

Starobinski, Jean. *La relation critique*. Paris: Gallimard, 1970.

Stebbins, Robert E. "France." In *The Comparative Reception of Darwinism*, edited by Thomas E. Glick, 115–63. Austin: University of Texas Press, 1972.

Sternberger, Dolf. *Panorama of the Nineteenth Century*. Introduction by Erich Heller. Translated by Joachim Neugroschel. New York: Urizen Books, 1977.

Tanner, Tony. *Adultery in the Novel: Contract and Transgression*. Baltimore: Johns Hopkins University Press, 1979.

Terdiman, Richard. *Discourse/Counter-Discourse: The Theory and Practice of Symbolic Resistance in Nineteenth-Century France*. Ithaca: Cornell University Press, 1985.

Thiher, Allen. *Fiction Rivals Science: The French Novel from Balzac to Proust*. Columbia: University of Missouri Press, 2001.

Toulouse, Édouard. *Émile Zola*. Vol. 1, *Enquête médico-psychologique sur les rapports de la supériorité intellectuelle avec la névropathie: Introduction générale*. Paris: Société d'Editions Scientifiques, 1896.

Villiers de l'Isle-Adam. *L'Ève future*. Edited by Nadine Satiat. Paris: Garnier Flammarion, 1992.

———. *Oeuvres complètes*. Edited by Alan Raitt, Pierre-Georges Castez, and Jean-Marie Bellefroid. 2 vols. Paris: Gallimard, 1986.

Walker, Philip. "The Ébauche of *Germinal*." *PMLA* 80, no. 5 (December 1965), 571–83.

Wall, Geoffrey. *Flaubert, A Life*. New York: Farrar, Straus & Giroux, 2002.

Weinberg, Bernard. *French Realism: The Critical Reaction, 1830–1870*. New York: Modern Language Association of America; London: Oxford University Press, 1937.

Wettlaufer, Alexandra. *Pen vs. Paintbrush: Girodet, Balzac, and the Myth of Pygmalion in Postrevolutionary France*. New York: Palgrave, 2001.

Zola, Émile. *Madeleine Férat*. Paris: C. Marpon & E. Flammarion, 18??.

———. *Le roman expérimental: Les romanciers naturalistes*. Preface by Gilbert Sigaux. Vol. 32 of *Oeuvres complètes*. Paris: Cercle du Bibliophile, 1968?.

———. *Les Rougon-Macquart, histoire naturelle et sociale d'une famille sous le Second Empire*. 5 vols. Edited by Armand Lanoux and Henri Mitterand. Paris: Gallimard, 1960–67.

———. "Seconde lettre d'un curieux." In *Oeuvres completes*, vol. 13. Paris: Cercle du Livre Précieux, 1966.

———. *Thérèse Raquin*. Paris: G. Charpentier, 1882.

INDEX